The Australian
BACKYARD

The Australian
BACKYARD

How to create your ideal backyard

Cheryl Maddocks

VIKING

Contents

3 Backyard projects 126

4 Planting 220

Your ideal backyard

AUSTRALIANS love their backyards. It doesn't matter whether it's a small inner-city courtyard or a couple of rambling country acres, a secluded suburban sanctuary or a low-maintenance entertaining area, a great backyard perfectly matches your particular lifestyle and needs. It's the ultimate expression of who we really are.

The Australian Backyard not only celebrates the great Australian icon, it gives you everything you need to create a great backyard of your very own. Once upon a time, the backyard simply meant a lawn, a shed, a Hills hoist and a vegie patch. Today it can be whatever you want. So whether you have a young family or teenagers, or your focus is on entertaining or productive gardening, *The Australian Backyard* contains inspirational ideas and expert practical information to help you turn your dream into reality. It shows you how to plan and design your backyard according to your lifestyle, how to accurately assess your needs, how to budget and how

to choose a backyard style that suits your land, climate and environment.

Then, using the step-by-step checklists and inspired by hundreds of photographs and illustrations, you'll be able to plan the backyard you want. You can select a backyard style or combination of styles from the many stunning examples throughout the book. Each one reveals how individual needs such as entertaining, play areas for the kids and even utility areas can be catered for in attractive, practical ways.

Once you've decided what you want in a backyard, you are shown how to achieve it. All the principles of garden design are presented in an easy, accessible way – drawing up the garden layout, incorporating your house into the design and using visual tricks to 'bring the outside into the house'. You'll discover which plants will look best in your design, how to borrow views from surrounding gardens and how to create eye-catching focal points.

Next, a wealth of practical projects shows you how to actually

build your ideal backyard. Simple step-by-step instructions explain everything from making a simple birdhouse through to laying pavers, making paths and walls, and building a barbecue area. Even if you decide to call in the experts, you'll have the information you need to ensure a good job is done.

Naturally, the plants you choose and how you use them will determine the ultimate look of your backyard. *The Australian Backyard* includes expert advice on selecting the right trees, shrubs, annuals, perennials, climbers and other plants to make the most of both large and small areas. The book also reveals how to use colour, shape and foliage to achieve visual effects. And there is a comprehensive planting guide with cultivation requirements for all the plants that suit your needs.

Whether you're planning a complete makeover or you have a specific project in mind, *The Australian Backyard* provides you with the ideas and information you need to create the backyard of your dreams.

Backyard styles

There are so many different and exciting backyard styles that choosing the best one may not be easy. The main considerations, however, are your particular needs and lifestyle. Whatever your requirements may be, this section shows you the styles that are suitable for a range of purposes and tastes as well as the elements that are needed to create those styles.

Modern courtyards

Courtyards have become part of modern living, and their use has become a major new lifestyle trend. Courtyards are no longer limited to cities. As urban backyards get smaller, courtyards are becoming increasingly popular as outdoor rooms for a multitude of purposes. Courtyards offer seclusion, privacy and visual strength. They are natural extensions of the house and offer areas for relaxation on weekends and after work, entertaining with barbecues, lunches, cocktail parties and long evening dinners in summer, or simply spending time with your family.

Courtyards are not a new concept. They have formed the basis of gardens from very early times. The great Islamic gardens of the Persians and Moors and the monastery gardens of Europe were set within closed courtyards. Today the courtyard thrives in a thousand forms, and individual styles depend on the requirements of the family.

The limitations imposed by courtyards are part of their appeal. After all, the walls, hedges or buildings that create the space for a courtyard also define its boundaries. A courtyard thus provides the owner with a small, distinct area in which to create a unique atmosphere.

But making the most of limited space is always a challenge. The smaller the space, the more important it is to give attention to detail. The choice and use of materials will determine the success of your courtyard design.

Courtyard design

Think carefully about what you want from your courtyard. Do you entertain a lot or do you want a place to simply relax away from the rest of the world? Does your family have regular barbecues? Do you want it to have a formal or informal style? With a formal look you can create a cutting-edge, minimalist courtyard. But perhaps you would prefer the softness, texture and colour of carefully selected plants.

The allocation of space and the type of materials used are very important parts of your design.

Design points
- The style should be dictated by the style of the house, especially if the courtyard is attached to or near the house. This prevents the courtyard from looking like an afterthought.

OPPOSITE   Sandstone pavers extend from the courtyard to a path beyond. Using the same pavers extends the sense of space.

- Hard surfaces should link the courtyard to the house and other areas of the garden. This is most important in an unwalled courtyard that is part of the garden.
- One focal point – such as a water feature or a sculpture – is more than enough in a small space.
- Don't use too many varieties of plants in small spaces. Repeat plantings give a clean, uncluttered appearance.
- A couple of large pots or planter boxes can be more effective than numerous small pots, which can have a cluttered look.
- Allocate enough space for garden furniture. A table and four chairs need an area of at least 3 square metres to accommodate people comfortably.

This courtyard design makes the most of a small space. The deck extends the living area into the garden.

Walled courtyards

The image of the typical courtyard is that of a small area enclosed on all sides by walls. Such a courtyard is usually found in cities, and its walls give it a climatic advantage. This makes it an ideal outdoor room or private sanctuary that is closely linked to the house.

Some city courtyards can be tiny, so the effective use of space is very important. Simple, clean lines are usually more effective than a busy look. Many walled courtyards lend themselves to a formal style because of the widespread use of raised beds and hard surfaces such as paving and walls. Their predominantly square or rectangular shapes also suit a formal style.

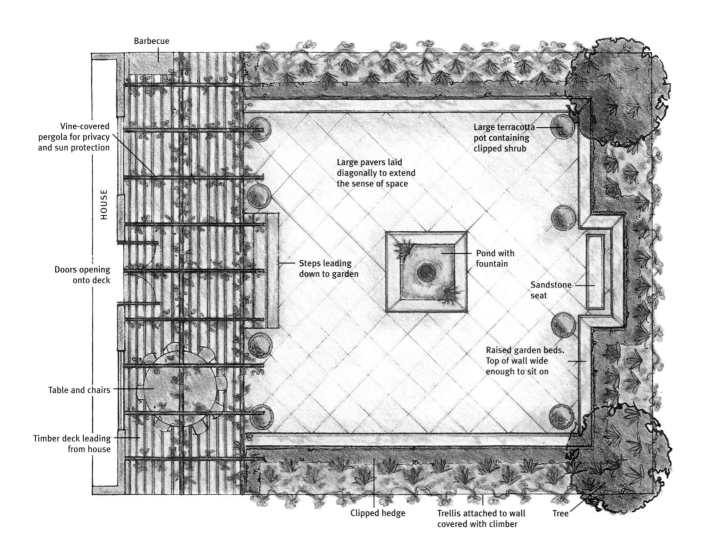

Barbecue

Vine-covered pergola for privacy and sun protection

HOUSE

Doors opening onto deck

Table and chairs

Timber deck leading from house

Large terracotta pot containing clipped shrub

Large pavers laid diagonally to extend the sense of space

Steps leading down to garden

Pond with fountain

Sandstone seat

Raised garden beds. Top of wall wide enough to sit on

Clipped hedge

Trellis attached to wall covered with climber

Tree

Making a walled courtyard look bigger

While you can't physically increase the area of a walled courtyard, you can employ a few visual tricks to produce the illusion of space.

- A change of level – even if it's only one step – can give the illusion that there are two gardens.
- Laying the paving in a geometric pattern gives the impression that the space has been lengthened and widened.
- Allocating more space for sitting and walking than for planting makes a courtyard feel more spacious.
- Light paving and wall colours create a sense of space.
- Breaking up the area with a line of contrasting paving will separate the entertaining area from the children's area.
- Strong flower colours such as yellow, red or orange stand out and advance towards you and can enclose a space. Blues, purples and greys tend to recede.
- Placing a large mirror on one of the walls will extend the sense of space.

Decorating the walls

Courtyard walls should not be too dominating or boring. They can be brought to life in many ways, and even a coat of paint will do wonders. Link the courtyard to the house by choosing a similar or matching colour.

You can attach wire to a wall in any pattern and train a climber to flesh out the design. Diagonal

LEFT A mirror placed behind the seat extends the sense of space in this small courtyard. The lighter coloured pavers add a soft contrast to the brick wall. The large, bold leaves of acanthus frame the seat and their architectural shape contrasts sharply with the clipped box.

BELOW Courtyard walls need not be boring. Decorative containers on this blue wall make a feature above the seat.

Trompe l'oeil

Trompe l'oeil is a term used about art that tries to make a picture look like it's a real part of the landscape.

Old bricks give this courtyard a rustic feel. Mondo grass and clipped box lining the pathway have a directional effect.

patterns look good, but the choice is yours. Drill holes and insert rawlplugs for galvanised roofing screws and pull the wire tight between the screws to create the pattern. You might consider accentuating your climber's flowers and foliage by painting the wall a contrasting colour. Do the painting before you plant the climber.

Trellis is another way of decorating courtyard walls. Fix a square, rectangle or arch of trellis to the wall as a feature then plant a climber at the base and train it over the trellis. Choose an evergreen climber that can be clipped to the shape of the trellis as it grows. A cunning approach is to incorporate this structure into a *trompe l'oeil*.

A piece of outdoor art from a nursery or speciality garden-art supplier and ceramic planters or plaques will also enhance a courtyard wall.

Urban courtyards

The urban courtyard has become a fashionable living area. Not necessarily confined by walls, it can be linked to a family room or it can be a private room somewhere in the garden.

Australians love a barbecue, and if you link the courtyard to the kitchen or family room you can break down the division between indoors and outdoors. You can link a courtyard to the interior of the house by having a pergola with overhead beams running from the house to provide a shaded sitting area.

Use similar paving materials to the paths in the rest of the garden. If this is not possible, you should at least make sure the materials are complementary so that the courtyard is tied into the garden.

You could have more than one courtyard – one for entertaining

linked to the kitchen or lounge room, and one outside your bedroom, for privacy.

You may like to place your courtyard further down your backyard. Perhaps you could position it under a large tree, where there is a pretty view or simply in the sunniest area of the backyard. If you live in a tropical climate you could place it in a cool spot surrounded by greenery.

You can partially enclose the area by surrounding it with a formal clipped hedge, clipped balls, a small wall, trellis or well-placed large pots. Or the courtyard area can be designated by a change of floor material from the hard surface of pavers to a soft surface such as grass.

Changes of level are also interesting. A sunken courtyard you can walk down to from your kitchen or family room is inviting.

Link the courtyard to the house by using similar pavers. Too many different materials in a small space can cause disharmony, so try to choose complementary materials for the floor and edges.

Decks are ideal for courtyards. Rather than stepping down into the courtyard, you can build a raised deck so that the courtyard is on the same level as the house. It's also popular to create the illusion of space by using a courtyard deck as the entertaining area from which you can step down into the garden.

Pergolas

Pergolas linked to the house can become a ceiling for part of your courtyard. You can cover them with climbing plants to give shade. Choose a perfumed climber and enjoy the fragrance. A plant-covered pergola can also provide privacy from neighbours over-looking the area.

Structural elements

Paving, pergolas, water features and raised beds are all elements that will help you to make the most of your courtyard.

Courtyard floors

Hard surfaces such as paving play a major role in courtyard design. Again, attention to detail is needed when making a small floor. Courtyard floors can be subtly laid stone or can be a feature in themselves with beautiful decorative tiles or pavers (see page 150 for ideas).

You can soften the look of large pavers (especially concrete ones) by leaving spaces between them and planting low-growing plants in the gaps. Pebbles of different textures and sizes can be worked into interesting courtyard floor surfaces.

Decorative paving plays a feature role in this courtyard floor. The raised pond has an edge wide enough to act as seating while simple fountains provide the sound of moving water. A bold planting of strappy-leafed aspidistra softens the wall.

ABOVE A simple water spout produces the sound of running water in this geometric courtyard.

RIGHT The clever juxtaposition of the living elements of plants and the hard element of concrete paving creates a pretty picture on this courtyard floor.

A pergola running across a long, narrow courtyard half or two-thirds of the way down can divide it into different areas without taking up space at ground level. Pergolas can also be used to introduce height into a garden where a tree may not be suitable.

Water features

Water is very desirable in a courtyard. It can be a simple water bowl, a fountain or a sunken or raised pond. Water brings life to a courtyard and makes an impression on the senses. You can enjoy its many moods and aspects – tranquil and contemplative or lively and invigorating. It may lie quietly in the shade or sparkle in the sun.

A wall-mounted fountain in a terrace will enhance both the wall and its surroundings. You can have raised ponds on one side of your courtyard with walls wide enough to sit upon. Or the pond could be placed at the end of the courtyard so that your eye is led to it.

Raised beds

Raised beds can look good, especially in walled courtyards. Use the same material as the walls or floor, or make sure all the materials are complementary. You can add extra seating to small courtyards by making the sides of raised beds wide enough to sit upon. You can also trail climbing plants down the sides of a raised bed to soften the look.

Planting

Every centimetre of space counts in a courtyard and every plant should fulfil its purpose well. Because space is limited, plants should be chosen for their year-round appeal. There is no point growing plants that flower for a couple of weeks and then look uninteresting for the rest of the year. Make use of handsome foliage plants that hold their own throughout the year. Avoid plants with sharp leaves unless they are tucked away at the rear of courtyard beds. Plants that drop a lot of fruit can also be a nuisance.

White flowers are ideal for small spaces as they are not dominating. They also shine in the night and can highlight a fountain or pond.

Correct positioning of plants according to cultivation needs is of

paramount importance, as small spaces can magnify problems. Get to know the micro-climate (specific atmospheric conditions) in your courtyard and plant accordingly.

The micro-climate of an enclosed courtyard is ideal for growing many of our native rainforest plants. Bird's-nest ferns have a strong shape and suit shaded areas.

In small courtyards a formal look is often more appropriate than an informal planting. With a formal look you should keep the plantings simple. Repeat plantings of the same species and clipped hedges give the courtyard a clean, uncluttered appearance. Box, small camellias, *Lonicera nitida*, murraya, the native shrub westringia and duranta make good hedges. They may also be grown in large pots and clipped to shape. Mondo grass makes a good edging and looks good planted between pavers.

Climbers make excellent coverings for bare walls. Make use of perfumed climbers such as Chinese star jasmine (*Trachelospermum jasminoides*), *Beaumontia grandiflora*, *Hoya australis*, *Jasminum sambac* and *Stephanotis floribunda*.

Container plants

You can make good use of containers such as pots, tubs, troughs and hanging baskets in a courtyard. Containers are ideal for annuals, which will provide seasonal colour. And the annuals bring variety to the courtyard as they can be changed throughout the year. Container plants also lend themselves to clipping – spheres, squares and triangles look good. The more adventurous among you may like to try your hand at turning them into topiary shapes.

Architectural plants such as *Agave attenuata*, cycads, cordylines, grass trees and conifers look exceptional in containers all year round.

Large tubs of citrus are both productive and attractive. And containers full of culinary herbs are always useful.

Different-coloured pavers form a border and define the pathway in this tiny courtyard. The planting is low maintenance – an architectural agave takes pride of place and is surrounded by low-water-use ornamental grasses and succulents.

The tropical look

The tropical look is becoming increasingly popular because of the large areas of Australia that have tropical, subtropical and temperate climates. You don't have to live in the tropics to create a tropical garden, but you do need warm summers and frost-free winters. Tropical gardens are especially popular in small inner-city gardens where one can create a cool sanctuary – the ideal place to relax outdoors with a book in summer. A tropical garden also makes a perfect area for spending time with family and friends.

Tropical design

Tropical gardens have a lush appearance as the look relies on luxuriant foliage rather than the temporary appeal of individual flowers. You can use palms and tree ferns to form the canopy, with epiphytes billowing from their trunks and vines to provide screening. Vines can also be allowed to simply ramble through the top growth. Ferns, large-leafed plants and colourful foliage are all part of the scene. Although the tropical look relies on foliage, arresting tropical flowers add to the effect.

This is not a high-maintenance style as its natural appearance lends itself to informality. You can take a formal approach, however. Clipped hedges, fountains and formal ponds work well with tropical plants such as colourful bromeliads and architectural cycads.

Structural elements

Natural elements look much more at home in a tropical garden than artificial ones. Logs covered in ferns, ponds and natural building materials such as rocks and river stones are in keeping with tropical gardens.

Ponds

Ponds are perfect for tropical gardens. The presence of water makes the garden feel cooler. Make sure your approach is consistent by using a formal pond design in a formal tropical garden and an informal design in an informal tropical garden. You can create a pond with a fibreglass shell (see Installing a pond on page 174) or build one using concrete. Place rocks around the edge of an informal pond to make it blend into the garden. Grow ferns among the rocks.

OPPOSITE **Brightly coloured pavers add charm to this tropical style backyard.**

Other water features

If you have a small garden or a tropical courtyard and don't have room for a pond, there are many other water features suitable for the tropical look.

Water spheres are popular in small spaces. The sphere, over which water trickles from the top, can be placed in its own dish and surrounded by pebbles. It's as much a garden sculpture as a water feature. A similar trickling effect can be created using a collection of large pebbles with water spilling gently from a spout. A good position for a water feature is the point at which paths meet or intersect. In a courtyard garden you should position it where it can become a focal point.

You can create an imitation stream bed with the use of rocks and pebbles. Soften the edges with overhanging plants.

Garden furniture

Timber furniture is particularly appropriate in tropical gardens. Benches, tables and chairs can be unpainted or brightly coloured for a more exotic look. Stone and concrete seats also fit into the style. Asian-style furniture works well, as do bamboo screens. Seats rough-hewn from wooden slabs and logs are also suitable.

Pathways

Pathways should look natural and not be too dominating. You can use combinations of railway sleepers and pebbles or river stones. A slightly raised path made from decking is ideal. Railway sleepers also look good with bark mulch. Square stone pavers suit a formal tropical look, while irregular shapes look good in informal gardens. Stepping stones or large, square stone pavers can be combined with gravel for a natural look.

Accessories

Natural stone statuary, bamboo, urns, carved wood and statues in an Asian or Pacific Island style all look at home in a tropical design. Large, deep-blue or red containers work well, especially for a formal look, as do containers with an Asian appearance.

RIGHT This natural pond is suited to a tropical garden. River rocks and pebbles line the pond and a mass planting of bromeliads creates a colourful groundcover. A simple waterfall has been used to feed the pond.

BELOW Water spheres make an attractive feature in a more formal tropical design.

Planting

The emphasis should be on architectural plants and plants that make strong statements. In this regard, colourful foliage reigns supreme. Palms and tree ferns can provide height while at ground level you can use the colourful leaves and strong shapes of cycads, bromeliads and ferns.

How to start

Tropical plants need a lot of moisture, and this is especially true of the large-leafed ones. The soil should be able to retain moisture but still have free drainage. Dig in copious amounts of well-rotted manure or compost before you start and add it regularly as a mulch during the year. Composted leaves make a natural-looking mulch but you can also use lucerne. A watering system is ideal (see Installing a lawn watering system on pages 178–9).

The upper canopy

If you already have trees in the garden you can use these as part of the upper canopy and intersperse them with tree ferns and palms. If you are starting from scratch, commence with tree ferns and palms. Both palms and tree ferns always look better when planted in groups. Bananas are also suited to the tropical look.

Palms do not need a great deal of maintenance. You may have to pick up the occasional dead frond, but they do not need pruning. Like most tropical plants, they require moist but well-drained soil and shade, especially when young.

Palms for tropical gardens

- *Archontophoenix alexandrae*
- *Chamaedorea costaricana*
- *C. elegans*
- *C. microspadix*
- *Chamaerops humilis*
- *Dypsis ambosetra*
- *Linospadix monostachya*
- *Livistonia chinensis*
- *Phoenix roebelenii*
- *Ravenea glauca*
- *Rhapis excelsa*
- *Trachycarpus fortunei*

This tropical plan is based on a large outdoor living area overlooking a water feature. There is also a timber walkway for relaxing and viewing the garden.

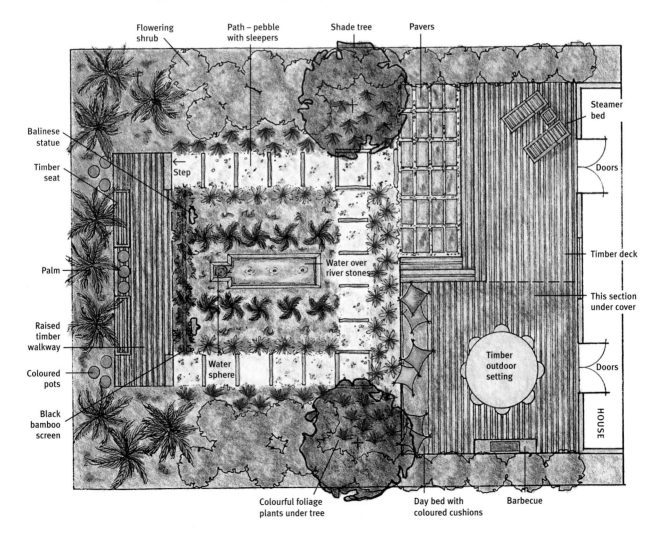

Flowering shrub · Path – pebble with sleepers · Shade tree · Pavers · Balinese statue · Timber seat · Step · Steamer bed · Doors · Palm · Water over river stones · Timber deck · Raised timber walkway · This section under cover · Coloured pots · Water sphere · Timber outdoor setting · Doors · Black bamboo screen · HOUSE · Colourful foliage plants under tree · Day bed with coloured cushions · Barbecue

Smart tip

Grow epiphytic Spanish moss *(Tillandsia usneoides)* on tree trunks where it will have a soft, billowing effect.

Bromeliads

- *Aechmea*
- *Ananas*
- *Billbergia*
- *Neoregelia*
- *Tillandsia*
- *Vriesea*

Potted palms and a large staghorn fern enhance the patio while colourful cushions complete the look.

Large leaves

Large leaves with their architectural shapes are essential to the tropical style. Plants with large leaves create an impact and can be grown under taller palms.

Heliconias range in height from 1 m to 4 m and grow well in filtered sun. Their conspicuous flowers are in shades of red, yellow, pink and orange.

Giant taro or elephant's ears (*Alocasia macrorrhiza*) and its relative *Xanthosoma sagittifolium* add a decidedly tropical touch. The edible taro (*Colocasia esculenta*) is similar in appearance and its root may be boiled or roasted.

Ornamental gingers work in tropical settings, as do some of the edible members of the ginger family. Consider red ginger (*Alpinia purpurata*) and galangal (*Alpinia galanga*), the root of which is essential in Thai cooking. Add some common ginger (*Zingiber officinale*), cardamom (*Elettaria cardamomum*) and turmeric (*Curcuma domestica*).

The strap-like leaves of cordylines and yuccas look good next to rounded leaves. And the fern-like foliage of our native cycads is quite exceptional.

Brightly coloured leaves

The brightly coloured leaves of coleus (*Solenostemon scutellarioides*) rival those of any flower. Just as colourful is beefsteak plant (*Iresine herbstii*), which has purple-red leaves. You can clip the purple leaves of *Alternanthera dentata* to make an attractive hedge. Cultivars of *Cordyline terminalis* also have colourful leaves.

Acalypha, *Aglaonema*, *Caladium*, *Croton*, Rex begonias, *Maranta* and *Calathea* all have species or cultivars with large or colourful leaves that will hold their own in any tropical setting.

Bromeliads

The bold, colourful and architectural foliage of many of the bromeliads make aesthetically pleasing arrangements of shapes and patterns and create evocative images in tropical-style gardens. Bromeliads always look better

planted in groups rather than separately.

Most of the bromeliads like dappled sunlight or positions in an easterly part of the garden where they receive the morning sun. Midday and hot afternoon sun can damage the leaves, as can cold winds.

Because they like good drainage, bromeliads can be grown in containers and positioned anywhere in the garden. An advantage of this approach is that containers may be moved if they are not doing well in a particular situation. Container growing also allows you to change the look. You can disguise the containers by screening them behind rocks or logs.

Ferns

Ferns offer leaf contrast and texture to the tropical garden. Tree ferns such as cyathea and dicksonia give a sense of height. The feathery fronds of *Asplenium bulbiferum* add texture and the leathery fronds of the bird's-nest fern (*Asplenium nidus*) make an eye-catching

statement. Maidenhair fern (*Adiantum aethiopicum*) makes a delicate groundcover. The epiphytic elkhorn fern (*Platycerium bifurcatum*) and staghorn fern (*Platycerium superbum*) can be grown on tree trunks. Other suitable ferns include *Pteris, Polypodium, Todea, Doodia, Blechnum, Polystichum* and *Nephrolepis*.

Maintaining the look

Many tropical and subtropical plants have surface roots. To avoid damaging them, you should pull out weeds by hand rather than by digging or hoeing.

Most tropical plants are heavy feeders so it is necessary to apply fertiliser in early spring even if you regularly add compost and old manure. Foliage spraying with a diluted solution of fish manure or a commercial seaweed preparation can also be used. It's best to spray in the evening as spraying in full sun can damage the leaves.

Smart tip

When it comes to tropical blooms, hibiscus have it all. There are some fabulous flower shapes in a variety of colours. Hibiscus like a sunny position, and a trim after flowering will maintain shape and encourage more flowers.

Fruits for a tropical garden

Delicious fruits can be grown in your tropical garden. Consider feijoas, babaco, guavas, passionfruit, pawpaw, pepino, naranjilla, tamarillo or avocado.

Large rocks on the side of the swimming pool create a natural tone in this tropical garden.

Cottage gardens

Cottage gardens derive from traditions that go back centuries, traditions that balance the beautiful and the practical. Cottage garden beds overflow with a seemingly chaotic mixture of perennials, annuals, roses, bulbs, herbs and vegetables. Climbing plants weave through trees and drape over arches. Self-seeded flowers appear spontaneously in unusual places. Cottage gardens combine a sense of mystery with charm and grace, which makes them a delight to be in. The overall effect on the senses is both relaxing and soothing.

Cottage garden design

While the magic of a cottage garden derives from its informality and almost chaotic charm, an overall plan is a good idea (see Designing your backyard on pages 82–125). It has been said that a cottage garden is not made from a plan, but from a feeling heart. Although these words are true there is no reason why you can't use both.

Cottage gardening in Australia is as old as the first European settlement. The first cottage gardens were planted as soon as houses were built and fences erected. Early records show that soon after the First Fleet arrived in 1788 food crops were planted around cottages. While poorer settlers used most of their land for food, the larger estates reserved areas for flowers.

A cottage garden can have a relatively formal design featuring straight paths edged with box or lavender, but it's the easy-going, informal planting style that gives the cottage garden its air of informality.

Design points

- Build wandering paths to lead you through the garden or to a quiet sitting spot.
- Allocate lawn areas for children or create a special 'room' for them that can be tucked away in the garden.
- Grow old-fashioned flowers and group them informally.
- Make use of climbers billowing out of trees and over arches.
- Space annuals and perennials so that their leaves touch when each plant is mature. This prevents weeds growing in bare spots and keeps roots cool.
- Place a free-standing pergola on a flat site. It adds height to the garden and invites you to look beyond it.

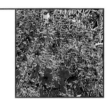

OPPOSITE **A profusion of cottage flowers surrounds this cottage. Dahlias provide vivid colour and purple-pink verbena adds height to the bed.**

Along the way

Plants tumbling onto the sides of a path are part of the cottage garden effect. A straight path is softened and will even appear to curve if plants are left to grow over the sides. Choose plants that have a creeping or bushy habit. Suitable plants include thyme, snow-in-summer (*Cerastium tomentosum*), Swan River daisy (*Brachyscome iberidifolia*), catnip (*Nepeta* species), *Arenaria montana*, *Convolvulus cneorum*, yellow alyssum, lavender, everlasting daisies, *Dampiera linearis* and *Kennedia prostrata*.

The rustic pergola adds a sense of height to this cottage garden. While neatly clipped hedges add a formal touch, their effect is offset by an informal planting scheme.

Structural elements

Wandering paths, rose-covered archways, arbours and quiet sitting spots are all part of the cottage garden charm. An arbour can make a feature out of a shelter or seat and arches may be used to lead you from one area of the garden to another.

Paths

Cottage garden paths are not merely practical but should produce pleasure. They are based on the principle that what you experience along the way is as important as your destination. A path doesn't simply have to follow the shortest distance between two points, so cottage garden paths are allowed to wander. You are enticed from one delightful spot to another. And curving paths create the impression that the garden is larger than it actually is.

Make paths from materials that have a mellow quality. Irregular pavers, old house bricks, paving bricks, sandstone and gravel are ideal. Construct all the paths and steps in the garden from the same material to create harmony.

Seats

A seat positioned beside a path tempts you to stop and sit, providing you with the opportunity to enjoy a whole area of the garden. Place perfumed plants such as lavender, rosemary and roses near the seat.

Brightly painted or natural wooden seats are well suited to cottage gardens. Sandstone also looks good.

Arbours and arches

An arbour can enhance a shady sitting spot. Arches may be used to lead you from one part of the garden to another. Always make sure that arches are wide enough – at least 1.2 m. There is nothing more uncomfortable than trying to squeeze through a narrow arch covered in a prickly rose.

Accessories

Accessories are an intrinsic part of the overall cottage garden setting. Statues, sundials and birdbaths all contribute to the garden's charm.

Terracotta or stone pots billowing with old-fashioned plants can appear unexpectedly throughout the garden. Pots placed on either side of a pathway entrance provide interesting points of emphasis.

Planting

Planting a cottage garden depends very much on trusting your instincts, and it gives you an opportunity to exercise your artistic skills. While rules that embody the knowledge and experience of others can be helpful in some circumstances, you should keep in mind the fact that each cottage garden is unique.

Cottage gardens are about abundance, sensuality and perfumed plants. The plants most favoured by cottage gardeners are the old-fashioned types that have not been heavily hybridised. These have an intrinsic charm that lends itself naturally to informality. If you choose the right plants you can have something blossoming continually.

Wandering pathways, quiet sitting areas and outdoor living spaces feature in this cottage garden plan.

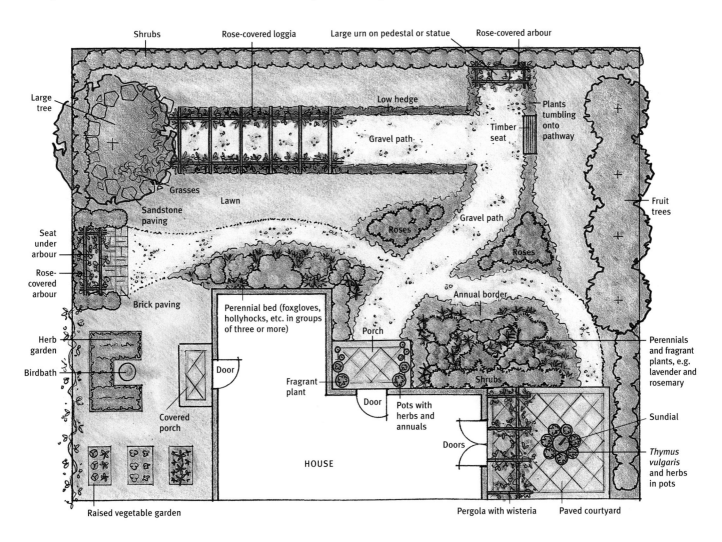

A dry-stone wall has been used to divide this cottage garden. Strawberries, lamb's ears, catmint and erigeron soften the appearance of the brick path.

This garden has an attractive combination of flowers and foliage. The arch and climber add height and structure.

How to start

Many plants used to create the cottage look have been favourites for centuries. They include hollyhocks, Canterbury bells, nasturtiums, convolvulus, polyanthus, sweet William, heartsease, sunflowers, larkspur, calendula, stock, aster and primroses. These annuals and perennials fill the spaces under trees and between shrubs. Plant annuals and perennials informally in groups of three or more and drift the groups into each other (see Your planting guide, pages 252–61).

The modern cottage garden is not restricted to exotic plants: it can be purely native or a mix of natives and exotics. Many Australian native plants are suitable for cottage gardens.

Annuals and perennials

The ground between the shrubs should be densely planted with annuals and perennials. Annuals and perennials will act as a groundcover on bare soil and help suppress weed growth. The density of the planting also leads to mutual support and forms a micro-climate that prevents plants drooping on hot days.

Choosing annuals and perennials that will grow to different heights is most important if you want to avoid a flat and uninteresting appearance.

Ornamental grasses

Ornamental grasses are suited to the cottage garden look. They are features in themselves and their swaying leaves are fascinating to watch. Plant ornamental grasses among other foliage and flowering plants.

Lofty grasses act as finely textured screens and short ornamental grasses can be grown *en masse* as interesting ground-covers.

Romantic climbers

No cottage garden is complete without a few climbers weaving through it. A clematis or a rose entwined in the branches of an old apple tree looks delightful. And these climbers won't damage the host tree.

Climbers are ideal for small cottage gardens because they take little ground space but provide an abundance of foliage and flowers. Grow a couple of climbers over an arch or arbour or train them over fences and along verandah railings. Careful choice of plant combinations can provide long flowering periods.

Vegetables

Productivity has always been part of the cottage garden tradition. The aim is to have an attractive garden that provides food. Growing food is one of the most satisfying aspects of gardening and it doesn't take any more time than growing flowers.

You can create a permanent vegetable plot in your cottage garden or simply grow vegetables among your flowers. Tomatoes look good when planted at the back of a flowerbed. The lace-like foliage of carrots and the attractive leaves of silver beet outdo the foliage of some ornamental plants. And the pretty leaves of lettuce and parsley make excellent garden borders.

Herbs

Herbs have an important role to play in cottage gardens. Grow them among flowers or in pots, or create a special 'herb room'. The leaves of many herbs are scented and the flowers of most will attract bees and butterflies to the garden. Fragrant herbs include basil, bergamot, hyssop, lavender, lemon balm, lemon verbena, mint, rosemary, sage, scented geraniums, southernwood, sweet woodruff and thyme.

Ornamental grasses

- Blue fescue (*Festuca glauca*)
- *Calamagrostis* × *acutiflora* 'Karl Foerster'
- *Carex* species
- Common tussock grass (*Poa labillardieri*)
- *Helictotrichon sempervirens*
- Kangaroo grass (*Themeda triandra*)
- *Miscanthus sinensis* 'Zebrinus'
- Snowgrass (*Poa* species)
- Swamp foxtail (*Pennisetum alopecuroides*)
- Wallaby grass (*Danthonia* spp.)

Smart tip

Callistemons are available in various heights and flowers come in shades of pink, red, violet and lemon. Some have a pretty, weeping habit. They are suited to cottage gardens and their pollen-filled flowers attract honeyeaters.

Flowers and vegetables mingle in this attractive and productive garden.

The Mediterranean style

The Mediterranean garden is one for relaxing in, whether it be by the swimming pool or under a vine-clad pergola. Because the Mediterranean style is suited to the climate in large areas of Australia, it's increasing in popularity. The tone is sociable and friendly, so it's natural to enjoy eating and drinking there. Although the effect of a Mediterranean garden is relaxed, a great deal of consideration must be given to the planning and planting. Large terracotta pots overflow with brightly coloured flowers, and colourful tiles blend with pebbles or gravel.

Mediterranean design

The Mediterranean style is particularly suited to climates that have hot, dry summers and those in which winters are mild and frost-free. Plants traditionally used in the Mediterranean region are suited to these conditions, and the garden is low maintenance. Naturally you don't have to grow these plants if your climate is not suitable – you can substitute plants of similar appearance that do well for you.

The Mediterranean look is suited to small or large gardens. An entertaining area is a prominent aspect of Mediterranean gardens as such gardens are to be lived in. They are ideal for long lunches and evening meals outdoors in a relaxed and easy-care backyard. Because of this, Mediterranean gardens have been rapidly accepted as part of our easy-going lifestyle.

Structural elements

The structural elements give the Mediterranean style its look. Bright colours and terracotta pots and pavers create the tone.

Paths
Stone slabs, terracotta pavers, gravel and pebbles set in concrete are perfect for pathways and entertaining areas. Large, square pavers with each one set in a border of pebbles look effective.

Raised beds
Raised beds made from old stone or painted render suit the style. Sandstone squares can also be used for this purpose. Umber, deep pinks, reds, oranges and blues are classic Mediterranean colours. Maintenance need not be a problem as old, flaky paint is part of the look. Trailing plants flowing over the edges of beds will soften the appearance.

OPPOSITE   Box hedging used to edge garden beds directs you towards the water feature. Sage, roses and daylilies are the dominant plantings.

The focus of this Mediterranean plan is on entertainment. A water feature contributes to the style.

Containers

Terracotta and stone pots are popular in Mediterranean backyards and a patina of old age makes them look more beautiful than when they were new. You can speed up the weathering process by painting the outside of the pot with a coat of live yoghurt. In a shady position the pot is soon covered in moss, while in the sun it develops grey-white patches. Another method of ageing old pots is to paint on a thin solution of cornflour and water.

Because of their porous nature, it's an idea to line the inner sides of terracotta pots with black plastic. But don't cover the bottom or drainage will be impeded. Water-retaining granules can be added to the potting mixture.

Large planter boxes filled with citrus, bougainvillea or olive trees work well.

Simplicity and uniformity can be most effective. Groups of pots planted alike may not sound horticulturally challenging, but the effect can be stunning. Try a row of terracotta pots containing lavender, cotton lavender, rosemary, pelargoniums, petunias, citrus or clipped box.

Be bold and paint concrete pots in deep blues, reds or ochres. Use a water-based paint. A more subtle appearance can be achieved by lime-washing terracotta pots, and a little raw umber tint added to the lime-wash produces a stone-like colour.

Accessories

Brightly painted tables and chairs or those made from wrought iron or wirework suit the Mediterranean style. Decorative wall tiles in a variety of vibrant colours can be used to cover courtyard walls.

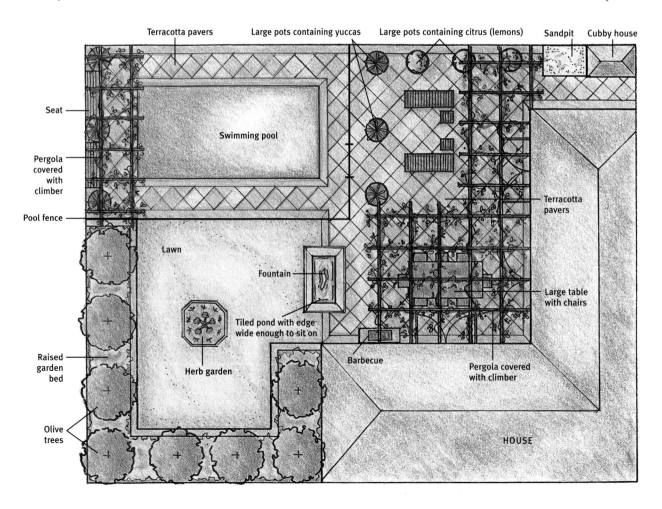

Water

A water feature provides a cooling influence in a Mediterranean backyard. A formal, raised pond with wide edges that you can sit on adds extra seating when you are entertaining. The walls of a raised pond can be tiled for extra effect. Add a fountain such as an elegant statue or just a simple water spout. In courtyards a simple wall fountain can be just as effective.

Folly

A stone wall built with an aged and slightly crumbling appearance makes an eye-catching folly in a Mediterranean backyard. A grotto will also suit the look.

Planting

What you choose to grow in your Mediterranean garden is crucial to an authentic look.

Trees

Citrus grown in containers or in a garden bed are popular plants. You can grow olives, with their attractive grey-green leaves, in large containers or as a grove if you have the space. You can also grow the pomegranate to provide fruit.

Our native wattles fit the look, and you should choose them with care so that they suit your climate. If you want a columnar effect, consider the Port Jackson pine (*Callitris rhomboidea*), a native conifer. It can be clipped to shape if it grows too wide.

Leyland cypress (× *Cupressocyparis leylandii*) can be clipped to shape to form tall hedging. The cultivar 'Naylor's Blue' is more columnar in habit. *Cupressus sempervirens* 'Stricta' also has a columnar habit. The cultivar 'Gracilis' has a narrower habit and bright-green foliage.

Palms such as *Phoenix canariensis* and *Chamaerops humilis* are also suitable.

Shrubs

Clipped balls of box, bay trees and small conifers look good in containers or raised garden beds. The silvery grey foliage of artemisias looks fabulous. Oleanders are suitable for clipping into standards. You can also clip rosemary, tree germander (*Teucrium fruticans*), or our native westringia. Even box works well in this style. The architectural shape of yuccas makes good sculptural plants.

Rock roses (*Cistus* species) are hardy plants for garden beds. Other shrubs include *Myrtus communis*, Jerusalem sage (*Phlomis fruticosa*), lavender, roses, *Phlomis italica*, santolina, flax (*Phormium*) and cordyline.

Climbers

Climbers growing over simple pergolas are desirable in Mediterranean gardens. Wisteria, edible and ornamental grapes and bougainvillea are the widely grown climbers. Edible and ornamental passionfruit suit the style, as does *Trachelospermum jasminoides*.

The Mediterranean style is about outdoor living. Bright-blue shutters and furniture set against light-coloured tiles and walls have an inviting, relaxing appearance.

Japanese gardens

Japanese gardens are very appealing to modern gardeners because they do not require a lot of space. Except in their large public gardens, the Japanese design small gardens that emphasise natural elements. While European gardeners use the notion of formality as a starting point, Japanese gardeners attempt to create a human element in completely natural surroundings. The natural tone of a Japanese garden is especially suited to modern inner-city and suburban gardens that are designed to provide an escape from the harshness of city landscapes.

Japanese design

In Japanese gardening there is a true acceptance of nature, and the result can appear to be too casual and unplanned to a Western eye. But in fact the opposite is true, as the Japanese regard garden design as a fine-art form. The casual appearance that results actually takes meticulous planning.

You can create a Japanese garden in a courtyard or a small or large garden. Even a very tiny space could contain some of the traditional elements such as several potted bonsai and a water bowl.

Structural elements

The main structural elements in a Japanese garden are water, rocks and timber. These natural elements are used with deliberate intention and a restrained approach to produce an immaculate outcome. The aim is to create a garden that looks as if it has not been touched by people, despite the tremendous amount of time and energy that has gone into developing it.

Water
Water is regarded as essential in creating a feeling of tranquillity. Water is the essence of life, and can be used in a number of ways in Japanese gardens.

Water bowls were originally used to supply water for washing hands or for use in the tea ceremony. Water was ladled from the bowl and poured over the hands as the Japanese never washed directly in the water bowl. Modern Japanese gardens in Australia use water bowls mainly for decoration.

On a larger scale, a pond will mirror the sky and reflect whatever

OPPOSITE Careful placement of rocks, a pond and different textures on the garden floor feature in this Japanese garden.

Smart tip

A water bowl in the form of a shallow, scooped-out rock is perhaps the simplest way of introducing water to the garden. These bowls attract birds, which drink and bathe in them. A water bowl can be placed among other rocks or at the base of a tree among mosses and groundcovers.

Smart tip

If you don't want to have water in your Japanese garden you can use dry stones to imitate a flowing stream.

RIGHT A stone lantern is framed by camellias and Japanese iris flank the bridge.

BELOW Water spills gracefully from bamboo pipes into the pond.

is around it. But a pond must have a natural appearance in accordance with Japanese design principles. A pond should always be an object of serene contemplation. You should ensure that any pond will reflect the form and scale of the garden as a whole.

The edges of the pond should be covered with rocks. The surface area of the pond must be large enough to ensure that the water does not appear to be overpowered by the rocks selected.

Running water adds a sense of vitality as well as an auditory dimension. The splash of running water or the sound of water moving over pebbles can be very calming, providing relief from urban busyness. But unless you are fortunate enough to have a stream, you will have to use plumbing and pumps to create this effect.

Rocks

Rocks have many more uses than in the construction of waterfalls. The Japanese use three main types: round, low and vertical.

Round rocks represent a hill or low mountain. These rocks produce a tranquil effect. They are often placed close to the border of a garden bed to define it.

Low rocks have a strong relationship with the earth and create the sense of hugging the ground. They also produce stability in the landscape and should be used carefully so that they are not overpowered. When used on their own, low rocks can make an impressive single feature. They also look good in combination with lanterns or water bowls, or beside ponds.

Vertical rocks are used in Japanese gardens to produce

a feeling of height. It's very important that the stone itself has a naturally vertical shape, and large, flat rocks on their edges should not be considered. Vertical rocks make effective statements on their own, or they can be used with low rocks for a more subtle look. A combination of vertical and low rocks will relieve monotony in a flat area.

The floor

Gravel makes a good floor for a Japanese garden. And if you have the time you can rake it into shapes. Square paving stones make a simple path or you can combine square pavers with oblong pavers to add interest. Square paving stones combined on a path with irregularly shaped stones create an interesting effect. Or a stone path of irregular shapes with gravel between the pavers will work well.

Stepping stones through a lawn or surrounded by pebbles suit the Japanese style. In a shady area, moss between the stones looks superb.

Containers

Stone containers are the first choice for Japanese gardens. Place them in strategic spots and plant them with ornamental grasses, palms, Japanese maples or ferns. Pots of bonsai also look good.

Garden structures

The rule for the creation of garden structures is quite simple: use restraint. When used inappropriately, structures can ruin the natural tone of a Japanese garden. A bridge that is too big for the pond or stream will destroy the balance of the garden.

If you decide to construct a tea house, arbour, pavilion or gazebo,

A sculptured pine, a water bowl and a stone path are all typical of Japanese design.

The Japanese style relies on the simple use of natural elements.

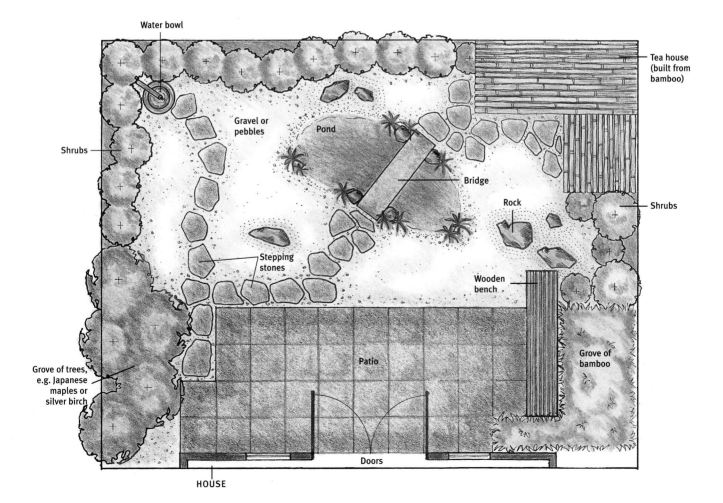

Water bowl

Tea house (built from bamboo)

Shrubs

Gravel or pebbles

Pond

Bridge

Rock

Shrubs

Stepping stones

Wooden bench

Grove of bamboo

Grove of trees, e.g. Japanese maples or silver birch

Patio

Doors

HOUSE

RIGHT   There are many stone accessories suited to Japanese gardens.

BELOW   A figurine holding a lamp is highlighted by the dwarf variegated bamboo.

it's essential to make sure that it is in proportion to everything else in the garden. Harmony and simplicity are the keys here. Natural building materials such as unpainted wood, straw and bamboo should be used. A shingle roof for a tea house is ideal.

Accessories

Accessories should not be placed too close to each other or the effect of their use will be weakened. Spirit houses and lanterns look good and are usually made from stone. Place them where they will attract the eye to a particular perspective or to balance a composition.

Lanterns are more decorative than functional these days. While stone lanterns were originally used for lighting near shrines and on paths leading to tea houses, they are now often used to add a human touch to the natural elements of the garden. If a stone lantern is not available, an arrangement of rocks imitating the shape of a lantern can also be used as an attractive garden ornament.

Planting

Once you have established the permanent framework of rocks, paving and water, you should think about living elements for the garden. Evergreen trees provide a sense of stability and continuity, but if you use any deciduous varieties, remember to think about their winter form as well.

Because Japanese gardens attempt to imitate nature by including natural elements, almost any type of plant can be used. Most of the plants mentioned below are grown extensively in Japan but it would be futile to plant the same species if they are not suited to your climate. It's not so much which plants you use as the manner in which you use them that is important.

Trees

Trees symbolise the cycle of nature to the Japanese. They are usually planted as a backdrop to the garden but they also look good when planted in groves or as a feature.

Japanese maples (*Acer palmatum*) and the full-moon maple (*Acer*

japonicum) are synonymous with the Japanese style. The many different cultivars of Japanese maples allow for a variety of heights. The Japanese admire the light and shadows maples produce.

Flowering cherries are also valued for the light that filters through their branches and their beautiful hanging flowers, which leave a magical carpet on the ground when they fall.

Other popular trees include the maidenhair tree (*Ginkgo biloba*), *Lagerstroemia* species, persimmon and conifers, the last-named of which are rigorously pruned to shape. Popular conifers are cryptomerias, thujas, junipers, cedars and the Scots pine (*Pinus sylvestris*).

Pruning trees

Trees in Japanese gardens are pruned to promote their artistic qualities. Pruning is carried out to reveal the shape of the trunk and branches. Branches are removed all the way up the trunk except for a few at the top, which are pruned to have a horizontal appearance. This exploits their height and enhances the outline of the tree. Large shrubs such as camellias, arbutus,

box and photinias are given the same treatment.

Cloud topiary is another popular pruning method. All growth is stripped from selected side branches except for that at the ends of the branches, which is clipped to resemble floating clouds.

Shrubs

Shrubs that lend themselves to pruning into regular spheres, balls or as a mass are suited to the style. Balls can be irregular in size and texture, can act as a counterbalance to rocky outcrops or can be used to accentuate pool or stream edges. Similar shapes should be used together so that there is overall harmony in the garden.

Shrubs suitable for this sort of pruning include box, *Lonicera nitida*, myrtle, *Pittosporum* species and azaleas, as well as our native westringia. Rosemary can also be clipped for a fragrant touch.

Other plants

Other plants that are commonly found in Japanese gardens include bamboo, grasses, mondo grass, Japanese iris and ferns.

LEFT Harmony and simplicity are exhibited in clipped rounds of azaleas, strappy mondo grass and rocks. The red earth path adds an Australian touch.

BELOW A path made from natural paving stones combined with gravel leads onto a bridge constructed from irregular pavers. The bamboo rail also suits the look.

Australian native gardens

Many of our Australian native plants are strikingly unusual, colourful and beautiful. More gardeners are turning to these plants as they recognise their beauty, hardiness and suitability for our climate. In most cases native plants have the advantage of attracting native birds, bees and butterflies. And gardeners are becoming far more aware of the native plants that live or once lived locally and are therefore particularly suited to their own areas. The use of such plants helps to create corridors and habitats for wildlife.

Native design

The growing of Australian plants in gardens has changed a great deal in the past thirty years. In the 1970s natives were regarded as the answer to the creation of a low-maintenance garden. The idea was to plant and forget because native plants 'managed on their own'. The result after a few years was often straggly, untidy shrubs that eventually died. The fact that they were native did not mean they did not need any care. An Australian plant has to be pruned and fed in the same way as any exotic plant once it has been taken out of its natural habitat. The failure of native gardens actually turned many gardeners away from the use of natives and towards creating gardens that were predominantly exotic.

But the wheel has now turned as gardeners realise that native plants have much to contribute to garden form, colour and visual effect. There are now more native plants and cultivars of Australian native plants available than ever before. And whatever job an exotic will do in your garden you can find a suitable native to do the same.

While most native gardens have a natural design with wandering paths and informal plantings, you can design your backyard in a formal way and use Australian plants exclusively. You can also have a mixture of natives and exotics.

Gardening with natives

- Native gardens are not necessarily low maintenance. As in any garden, the plants need pruning, feeding, watering and checking for pests and diseases.
- There is a difference between native and local indigenous plants.

OPPOSITE   The purple pea-like flower of *Hovea lanceolata* creates a pretty picture in early spring.

Just any Australian plant will not necessarily grow in your part of the country. For example, some plants from Western Australia may not be suitable for the east coast. Try to choose some natives that are indigenous to your area to keep corridors open for local birds and wildlife.

• Some natives don't grow well with exotics. Proteaceae family members – which include grevilleas, banksias, hakeas and waratahs – should be cultivated separately and grouped together in beds of their own or with other natives. This is because they don't like fertilisers that are high in phosphorus. Feed them with blood and bone, cow manure or a fertiliser that is specific to natives.

• Choose the right plant for the right place.

Structural elements

Natural elements are frequently used in native backyards. Rustic seats, bush rocks in walls and on garden edges, and packed-earth paths suit the look. Hardwood used in the construction of pergolas or arches suits the native approach, and treated pine can also be used.

If you are lucky enough to have natural bush rock on your property, then make the most of it. You can build your garden around large rocks to make them a feature, and you can use smaller outcrops as garden edging.

Paths and steps

Sandstone, bush rock, gravel, bark mulch, river stones, packed earth and concrete stepping stones suit the native garden. Square stepping stones can be used in a courtyard to provide an interesting contrast with a surrounding informal planting. And old bricks will lend a rustic tone when used in both courtyards and paths.

Meandering paths with slight curves look best in gardens that have a natural style. Steps can be made from rocks or railway sleepers. Raised wooden walkways also work well in native rainforest gardens.

Native and exotic plants have been combined skilfully in this delightful backyard.

Raised beds

Raised beds are good for growing Australian natives in, especially if drainage is a problem. Railway sleepers, treated pine logs or rock can retain the soil.

Accessories

Rustic furniture made from eucalypt hardwood is popular in native backyards. If the furniture is made from unseasoned timber it will weather and gain character. Children's play equipment made from pine is also acceptable, and looks best when stained in natural tones.

Timber outdoor tables and chairs blend well with timber courtyards and patios.

Pergolas

Wooden pergolas over courtyards made from rustic timber or treated pine can be covered with native climbers. Decorate them with hanging baskets full of ferns. Staghorn ferns mounted on bark or wood can be attached to uprights and palms can be grown in terracotta or stone pots.

Containers

Terracotta, stone and wooden containers suit the native style. Containers of different heights can be filled with natives and placed in courtyards. Palms look interesting when grown in terracotta or stone pots.

Ponds

A pond with a natural appearance will suit the native style. You can construct it using a pond liner or make it more permanent by using concrete. Surround it with bush rocks and plant ferns such as those of the *Asplenium* species to soften the edges. Make use of the upright stems of tassel cord rush (*Restio tetraphyllus*) to make an arresting visual impression around the pond.

Plants placed around the pond will also create places for frogs to hide from predators.

A few old logs around the edges will contribute to the natural appearance.

Planting

There is an Australian plant for any position in the garden. Whether you want a neatly clipped hedge or an informal cluster of shrubs, you will be able to find suitable native plants for the purpose. By their very nature, native plants attract a multitude of birds and wildlife to the garden.

A large outdoor timber deck enables you to enjoy the wide variety of native plants in this well-planned backyard.

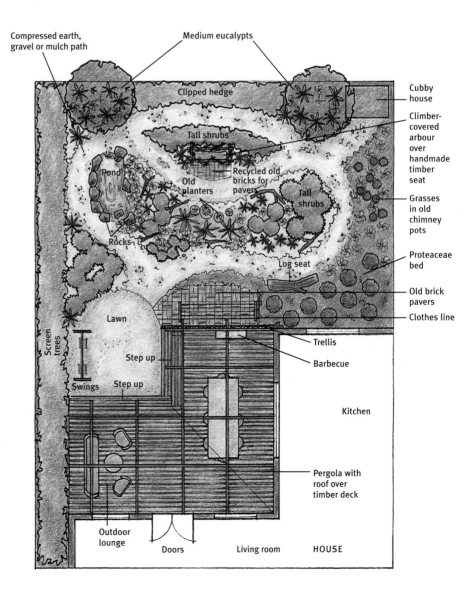

ABOVE Banksia 'Birthday Candles' makes a stunning native groundcover.

RIGHT Banksias and kangaroo paws create a colourful combination.

Tree ferns create a lace-like overstorey that provides shade for lower growing ferns. Terracotta birdbaths have been included to entice local birds.

Trees – the overstorey

There are many native trees that are suited to the average-sized backyard (see Your planting guide, pages 279–83, and Wildlife-friendly habitats, page 63). Choose types that suit your climate. The most popular include dwarf apple (*Angophora hispida*), lemon ironwood (*Backhousia citriodora*), blueberry ash (*Elaeocarpus reticulatus*), *Eucalyptus caesia, E. cinerea, E. haemostoma, E. lehmannii, E. leucoxylon* subsp. *megalocarpa, E. torquata*, bottlebrush (*Callistemon* species), *Melaleuca* species and native frangipani (*Hymenosporum flavum*).

Shrubs – the understorey

Australian shrubs are available in a wide variety of heights and shapes. Hakeas, grevilleas, wattles and banksias are popular because birds love their nectar.

Native plectranthus (*Plectranthus argentatus*), which has beautiful, large silver leaves, makes an eye-catching statement.

Many native shrubs can be clipped and used as hedges.

These can also be used to screen off a children's area or to border a garden bed.

Natives for clipping

Cultivars of the coast rosemary (*Westringia*) are ideal for formal gardens, hedges and clipped garden shapes. There is a wide range of these cultivars, and they revel in sunny positions, well-drained soil and, of course, coastal conditions.

The attractive silver bush *Leucophyta brownii* likes similar conditions to those appreciated by coast rosemary. The more compact form 'Nana' requires no trimming at all.

Syzygium cultivars make good substitutes for box hedges in frost-free climates. You can choose from 'Tiny Trev', 'Lilliput', 'Blaze' and 'Bush Christmas'. *Austromyrtus acmenioides* 'Afterglow' has glossy foliage and shiny red new growth that is encouraged by pruning to shape. *Grevillea rosmarinifolia* is also suitable, and *Acacia howittii* can be kept low or used as a tall hedge.

Groundcovers

There are some pretty groundcovering natives suitable for rockeries. You can have groundcovers spilling over retaining walls or use them as a living mulch. *Scaevola aemula* 'Purple Fanfare' makes a fabulous show with its purple flowers on bronze stems. 'Mauve Clusters' produces masses of vivid mauve flowers from spring to summer. Dampieras are frost-hardy and will bloom in your garden for months. They grow well near the coast. There are also groundcovering grevilleas, banksias and leptospermums.

Climbing plants

There are some fabulous Australian climbing plants that are useful for screening, decorating, and growing over pergolas. False sarsaparilla (*Hardenbergia violacea*) makes a good trailing groundcover or climber. It bears mauve-purple or white-flowers in late winter and spring.

Pandoreas also produce exquisite flowers. Consider the white-flowering *Pandorea jasminoides* 'Lady Di' or 'Charisma', which has variegated foliage and pink flowers. Just as beautiful are cultivars of the wonga vine, *Pandorea pandorana*. Cultivars include 'Claret and Cream', 'Golden Showers' and 'Snow Bells'.

You could also consider *Clematis aristata* and *Kennedia rubicunda*.

Perennials and annuals

Perennials and annuals can be used to underplant trees and shrubs or you can plant them in beds to create an alluring natural effect. Place annuals and perennials with different leaf shapes next to each other for the best effect. And also consider using a variety of leaf and flower colours.

Biennial and annual daisies should be sown direct in autumn.

Among the hardiest are the *Rhodanthe* species. *R. manglesii* and *R. chlorocephalum* subsp. *rosea* have pink flowers.

Grasses

Many native grasses have fine swaying leaves and attractive seed heads. They vary in height from short to tall. You don't have to cut or water these native grasses and they rarely need fertilising. There is a native grass suited to all soil types, conditions and climates.

While native grasses have been used extensively in broad-acre landscaping, many home gardeners have been unaware of their beauty and ease of cultivation. They make ideal soil stabilisers for embankments and can be used as an understorey in native gardens. These grasses come into their own as features when grown in clumps and with careful selection you can create subtle designs using a variety of grasses.

Native rock orchids (*Dendrobium speciosum*) create a pretty picture alongside the path.

The formal style

Although formal gardens have a long history that can be traced to the Egyptians and Persians, they are very suitable for modern times. The geometrical lines, sense of proportion and balance that are featured in formal designs adapt well to the straight lines of most suburban and inner-city building blocks. The formal style is also useful for creating individual rooms within the garden. In addition to providing visual interest, these rooms are extensions of the house that can be used for a variety of purposes.

Background

Geometrical and symmetrical designs have been used in gardens from the earliest times. The Egyptians, Persians and Moors all used formal designs, as did the Italians during the Renaissance. Formal designs have also been used throughout Europe to build huge gardens of impressive grandeur.

Many of these gardens were created to showcase design features that were attractions in themselves. Their hard lines and angles were mathematically precise, and were designed so that one side of the garden mirrored the other exactly.

Because many of these gardens were on large estates, they relied on cheap and plentiful labour to make them viable. Nevertheless, the principles of the formal style can be used on a small scale very effectively in modern gardens.

Formal design

Apart from the use of geometric patterns, the formal garden has a number of design features. It should provide a strong link between the house and the garden. This link should be apparent from the inside of the house as well as the outside.

The formal style is characterised by linear hedges, stone or gravel paths, formal pools or ponds and the use of framed views. Paths are often used to form axes, and balustraded terraces, classical statuary and topiary feature.

The symmetrical design of formal gardens often relies on a 'mirror' effect, in which one side of an evenly divided garden reflects the other side exactly. This is especially true of the parterre garden.

The parterre garden, which was popular in the 17th century, is

OPPOSITE **Simple but beautiful – gravel paths and a parterre edged with box.**

returning to favour today. A separate area of the garden, usually delineated by high hedges or walls, features curving or straight geometric patterns outlined in low hedging, often of box. The spaces are filled with plants ranging from bulbs to herbs, depending on the desired effect. There is often a statue, urn or fountain at the centre of the pattern to provide a focal point.

You may wish to have a formal design for the whole backyard, but you can also have formal areas that form garden 'rooms'. Formal designs can be used in even the smallest gardens. The organised, neat tone of a formal garden is suited to city environments in which there are often high walls and adjoining buildings to create a private space. The sense of order found in a formal garden produces a calming effect that can provide a welcome contrast to urban noise and bustle.

Structural elements

Any materials used in a formal garden should be sympathetic to those used in the construction of the house. The overall setting of the garden should also be considered. Consistency of materials is very important, particularly in such elements as paving and hedging.

Paving and paths
Paving should be simple and elegant. Repeated geometrical patterns are common in formal paving. Rectangles, squares and circles are used to define paved areas.

As paths are so important to the formal look, pathway paving should be laid out using classic patterns. Straight paths are used to form axes or divide mirrored sections of the garden.

Gravel can be used on paths and as a substitute for stone in large paved areas. It's traditional and has

Square pavers set in the grass lead you to a pond that has an olive tree on either side.

the advantage of being cheaper than the alternatives.

Lawns

Open areas of lawn are often found in formal gardens. They should be shaped to complement the shapes of garden beds and paved areas, but not be cluttered with permanent furniture.

Water features

Make your pool or pond rectangular, square or round. A raised pond containing a fountain can be an interesting feature. Ensure that any stone work around the pond is of regular shape.

A small wall fountain of traditional design is an ideal feature for a formal courtyard.

Pergolas and arches

Pergolas and arches are commonly used in formal gardens. Before building an arch or pergola, you should consider other shapes in the garden to make sure your structure will complement them.

A series of arches placed at regular intervals on a main path can look effective. Grow shade-forming climbers over them.

Avoid using bright colours on pergolas and arches and take the colour of buildings into account.

Walls and fences

Walls made from stone or brick are suitable for formal gardens. Stones used should be regular in shape. Bricks or stones should match or complement paving used in the garden.

This formal garden plan features different areas for a variety of purposes.

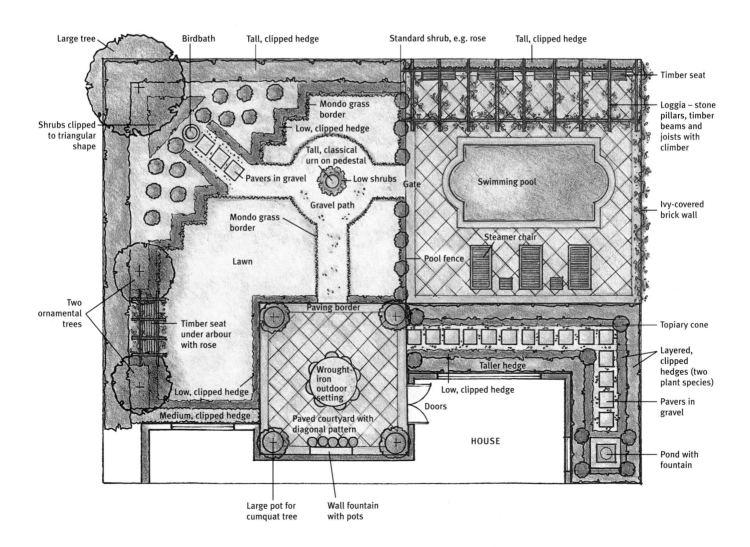

ABOVE   Standard cumquat trees and clipped box hedges make this a stylish entertaining area.

RIGHT   The sense of order found in this formal garden produces a calming effect.

Timber fences should be of uniform height. Consider using substantial fence posts with decorative shapes. Timber capping on a fence can also provide a formal finishing touch.

Garden furniture

Wrought-iron tables and chairs are suited to formal gardens. Timber garden furniture in traditional designs is also appropriate. Dark or subdued timber tones and paint finishes should be used. Stone seats also look good.

Accessories

The type of pots or urns used is also important to the formal style. Simple, classical lines are preferred, and pots should be placed to emphasise a sense of symmetry.

Pots of the same design, for example, containing clipped standards placed on either side of a gateway or entrance, will enhance the formal look.

Planting

Given the strictly architectural style of formal gardens, hedging is one of the main elements. Hedging is often used on the perimeters of the garden as screening and is also used to define the edges of beds. The two varieties most commonly used are box (*Buxus* species) and yew (*Taxus baccata*), but there are alternatives.

If you don't want to go with the fashion flow for box, try other

clipping choices such as *Syzygium* 'Blaze' and 'Bush Christmas', or cultivars of *Hebe*. 'Lemon and Lime', which has lemon stems and lime leaves, is worth seeking out. The distinctive black-red foliage of *Coprosma* 'Karo Red' is another desirable clipping alternative. It can be grown near the coast and will withstand dry soil.

Make sure that you select structural trees and shrubs that have similar shapes and habitats. Place them at regular intervals throughout the garden.

The architectural tone can be enhanced by creating garden beds that mirror each other in design exactly. These beds should contain the same types of plants. Choose plants with a regular and consistent habit.

Clipping plants

It's much cheaper to buy a large, unclipped box and shape it yourself than to buy one that has already been shaped. But keep in mind that it does take several years to obtain a good shape, which accounts for the relatively high cost of clipped box.

Clipping plants into different shapes does take some skill, so if you want the fantasy and whimsy of topiary without the hard work, you can cheat by buying a topiary frame from a nursery. Wire frames are available in a wide variety of interesting shapes, including spherical, oblong and circular.

While the frame provides the basic shape, you add character and detail in the planting and training stages.

Clipped hedges create a formal outline in this predominantly green garden.

By the sea

Australia has some of the best coastline in the world. The seemingly endless white beaches and blue ocean lure many people to adopt a seaside lifestyle. Activities such as surfing and fishing are irresistible to many, and it's not surprising that the bulk of our population is on the seaboard. Seaside gardens also focus on enjoying the outdoors in a relaxed manner. After all, there are few more pleasant activities than sitting on a timber deck with ocean views enjoying a barbecue with friends and family.

Seaside design

Straight lines and regularly shaped garden beds do not look at home by the sea. Think instead of plants in drifts set among pebbles and swathes of grass swaying in the breeze. Obviously plants indigenous to your area will grow better than introduced species. And the use of indigenous plants allows you to blend your seaside garden into the surrounding landscape. Indigenous plants also create corridors for local birdlife.

It cannot be stressed too strongly that coastal areas are very fragile and that minimal impact should be made upon the natural heritage of the area. You don't want to spoil the very reason you enjoy living by the sea. Check with local nurseries or your council that plants chosen for your garden will not become weeds in the surrounding landscape.

Structural elements

Natural elements work in seaside gardens. Timber, stone, gravel, pebbles, driftwood and rocks are all part of the seaside style.

Paths and decks

Paths and decks in seaside gardens look wonderful when made from timber. Living by the sea is all about outdoor recreation and decks or courtyards are essential. Timber blends with the surrounding environment and decks make wonderful outdoor living spaces.

Create walkways of timber to harmonise with timber decks and use timber steps to create changes of level.

Stone or a mixture of stone and timber is also effective for courtyards or for paths. The subtle colour of sandstone also blends in well.

OPPOSITE **A hedge under tall banksias provides a windbreak in this pretty seaside garden, while the summerhouse allows you to enjoy the view.**

Accessories

You could make a feature of a garden shed by painting it bright blue or blue with white stripes so that it looks like a beach hut. Timber tables, chairs and seats suit the seaside style. They can be brightly painted or left with a natural finish.

Large pebbles look good in garden beds and can be used as a mulch in the same way as smaller pebbles. You can also clump them as features around the garden.

Flotsam and jetsam found on beaches make interesting accessories. So do old fishing nets and shells.

Containers

Wooden planter boxes and stone containers work well in seaside gardens. Native grasses are suitable subjects for seaside containers. Pots covered in seashells suit the look and succulents make low-water-use container plants.

Planting

While living by the sea has many pleasures, it's not always a paradise for gardeners. Salt, sand and wind often combine to make growing conditions difficult. But there are many plants that cope well near the ocean.

Protection and successful soil management are essential for seaside gardens. If you want to protect your garden from the elements, you need to create its

The large patio and deck areas have been designed for maximum outdoor use in this seaside setting.

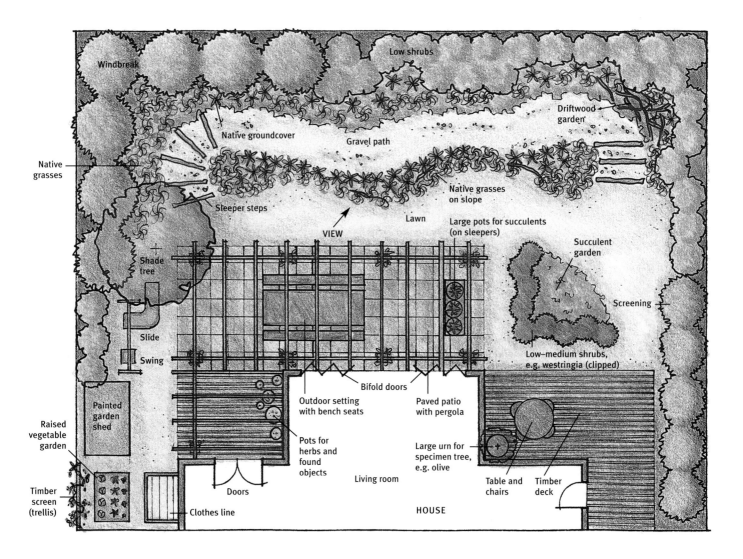

own micro-climate. Start with a windbreak of salt-tolerant trees and sheltering shrubs. This line of defence will protect the garden from onshore winds and allow you to establish some tender plants.

Groundcovers

In seaside gardens it's important to keep the soil covered to reduce its surface temperature and prevent moisture being lost through evaporation. You can use organic mulches, or inorganic ones such as gravel or pebbles, but many groundcover plants make ideal 'living mulches'.

Climbing plants

Climbing plants take up little horizontal space and can provide privacy from neighbours. They are also valuable where space is limited. Drape them over deck railings or on a dividing trellis fence.

Grasses

A very natural way to plant a seaside garden is to use native grasses in sweeping swathes. Vary them in height from small to tall and lofty. You can mulch around them with gravel or pebbles.

Looking after the soil

You must manage the soil carefully in a seaside garden. You will most likely have poor, sandy soil. The garden will definitely not succeed until the soil is in reasonable condition. A critical factor for new seaside gardens is the importation of organic matter, which should be dug into the existing soil as evenly as possible.

Continual replenishment of organic matter is a must for sandy soils as it helps to retain water in the soil and encourages earthworms. Apply organic matter in the form of compost, poultry or cow manure at the beginning of each season. In fact, a compost heap is an absolute necessity for seaside gardens to ensure that there is a continuous supply of organic matter.

Both new and established seaside gardens should be mulched continuously. Use organic mulches such as grass clippings, lucerne, leaf mould or whatever is freely available in your area.

Watering

As with all gardens, one deep watering is more beneficial than frequent light waterings. Very windy areas always need to be watered more frequently than other areas. It's worth considering the installation of an irrigation system, as this is undoubtedly the most efficient way to water sandy soils. Gardens that are close to the sea may be washed down in the late afternoon on very windy days to remove the day's salt deposits from the leaves.

Try to use natural elements where possible. Echeveria and aeonium encircled by seashells make an attractive garden bed.

A wooden deck allows you to enjoy the view and a hedge of westringia forms a border to the garden.

The natural approach

Sweeps, clusters and colonies are three words closely associated with the 'new naturalism'

planting style becoming a favourite with many garden designers. This style uses plant groupings

that are true to nature, and relies heavily on wild and unrestrained displays of flowers and foliage.

The free-flowing tone is intended to help you imagine that you are away from artificial environments.

The new naturalism style is quite relaxing, and many sections of gardens designed in this style are

secluded and tranquil.

History

The natural garden desired by so many today is actually a development that originated with some influential late 19th century English landscape designers. William Robinson, for example, was a great advocate of informality and naturalness and his ideas influenced designers such as Gertrude Jekyll. Robinson favoured mixed borders of native and exotic plants and used colour and plant associations in a soft and subtle way. He planted bulbs throughout grassed areas – a design move that was disliked by the lovers of neatly clipped, green English lawns.

Closer to home, the work of Robinson and Jekyll had a great influence on Edna Walling (1895–1973), one of Australia's best known landscape designers and gardening writers. Walling frequently quoted Jekyll in her writings and, like Robinson, favoured using hardy plants in natural plantings. But she was also happy to use an informal planting inside a rigid, geometric garden bed. The distinctive features of Walling's work so appropriate to the natural look of today were her love of native plant materials and her ecological approach to garden design.

Natural design

This backyard style is reliant on a relaxed but carefully planted look comprised of selectively placed compositions designed to achieve a natural appearance. The style works with nature rather than against it by encouraging you to observe the types of plants growing in your climate and soil and to exploit what occurs naturally.

OPPOSITE   Blue convolvulus, cream Californian poppies and silver-leafed lychnis, euphorbia and day lilies line the stepping-stone pathway in this natural garden.

A natural garden isn't subject to fixed rules because it should not appear to be contrived or artificial. Individual plants are less important than the overall scheme. The contrast of flower shape and foliage texture adds interest to a natural design, while a range of leaf shapes and colours carries the garden through when flowers are scarce.

Both native and non-native plant materials are planted in bold swathes to harmonise with the landscape.

Structural elements

Natural elements obviously work well in a natural garden. Wandering paths and rustic wooden fences and furniture enhance the look. Stone can be used in retaining walls and as stepping stones, while rocks can be used as garden borders and to create natural ponds.

Paths

Stepping stones, gravel, brick pavers, hard packed earth and bark are suited to natural gardens. Paths edged with bush rock or river stones also suit the style. Meandering paths that invite you to wander through the garden suit the style more than straight lines, which are appropriate for formal designs.

Accessories

Stone and rustic timber seats are suited to the natural style, as are timber outdoor table settings. Stone or terracotta containers work well.

Natural elements and materials predominate in this natural garden design.

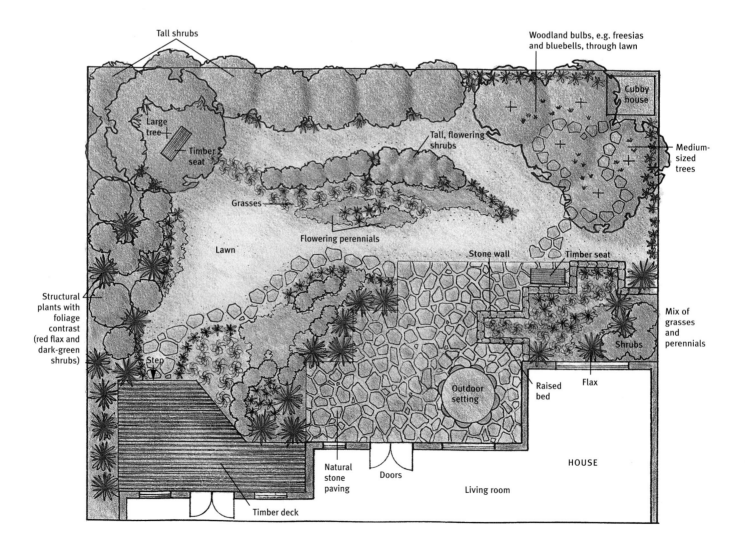

Planting

A natural garden relies on a meadow-like look, which is achieved mainly with perennials, grasses and annuals as fillers. The key is to choose hardy exotic and native perennials. The finished look depends on the way plants are utilised in garden beds.

As with any planting scheme, the emphasis is on plant associations. Interesting leaf and flower combinations as well as bold or soft colour schemes set the overall tone. The same plant can be seen weaving in and out to unify the effect, or you can allow one plant to dominate the planting.

Choose plants that are appropriate to your area so that the garden will be low-maintenance. If the area is hot and dry, for example, use only plants suited to those conditions.

Shrubs can be background features for privacy and low-growing types can be interspersed among the perennials, grasses and annuals for structure.

Perennials

Perennials in a natural garden should be planted in drifts with each drift being a different shape and size. The size of the drift depends on the size of your garden beds and the width of the perennial. Consider using at least three to a drift for small gardens and start with seven in large gardens. Tall grasses can be added singly and smaller ones can be planted in drifts.

You can repeat certain plants throughout the bed to pull the scheme together.

Think of the process as grouping plants to make pictures. Position the plants to create harmonies and contrasts. Plant spires of flowers next to rounded shapes or mounds of different heights. The way in which you associate the plants will produce an impact and affect the mood of the garden.

As with most perennials, there is an opportunity to transplant and divide to increase the show. You can make unobtrusive paths through garden beds by using rocks as stepping stones.

Perennials suitable for natural gardens

Achillea species, Swan River daisy (*Brachyscome multifida*) and its cultivars 'Lemon Drops', 'Pink Haze' and 'Alba', *Dianthus* species, daylilies, angel's fishing rod (*Dierama pulcherrimum*), South African wild iris, *Dietes grandiflora*, *Gaura lindheimeri*, *Sisyrinchium striatum*, *Salvia* species, bergamot (*Monarda didyma*), agapanthus, African daisy (*Arctotis × hybrida*), aster (*Aster novi-belgii*), *Echium* species, gazania, echinops, lavender, Marguerite daisy, native pelargonium (*Pelargonium rodneyanum*), perennial phlox (*Phlox paniculata*), seaside daisy (*Erigeron karvinskianus*), paper daisy (*Rhodanthe* 'Rosy Everlasting'), paper daisy (*Rhodanthe manglesii* 'Mangles Everlasting'), penstemon, *Lychni coronaria*, lamb's ears (*Stachys byzantina*), sedum, shasta daisy, golden rod (*Solidago* species) and statice. Herbs such as lemon balm, oregano and thyme could also be included.

LEFT   A lattice pergola provides shade for this sitting area.

BELOW   A packed-earth path fits in well with a natural design.

A natural planting scheme of annuals creates a pretty garden picture in this backyard.

Grasses for a natural garden

Blue fescue (*Festuca glauca*)
Features beautiful powder-blue foliage.

***Calamagrostis × acutiflora* 'Karl Foerster'**
A tall grass whose mauve-brown flowers age to creamy beige. The cultivar 'Overdam' has white-striped leaves.

Carex petriei
Has arching bronze-mahogany leaves.

Common tussock grass
(*Poa labillardiera*)
Forms a dense clump and has greyish green leaves and slender purplish or green flowering stems. The cultivar 'Eskdale' has grey leaves.

Helictotrichon sempervirens
Has fabulous blue-grey foliage.

Japanese blood grass
(*Imperata cylindrica* 'Rubra')
Has beautiful red leaves.

Kangaroo grass (*Themeda triandra*)
Native to all states of Australia.

Lemon grass (*Cymbopogon citratus*)
Attractive arching green leaves.

Lomandra longifolia
An extremely hardy grass whose strappy green leaves look good throughout the year. The cultivar 'Cassica' has wider leaves and 'Katrinus' has a weeping habit.

***Miscanthus sinensis* 'Zebrinus'**
The tall green leaves are white along the mid-rib and slowly develop creamy-yellow markings. Beautiful cultivars include 'Graziella', 'Silber Feder' and 'Variegatus'.

Snowgrass (*Poa* spp. *australis*)
A small tussock grass with fine grey foliage.

Swamp foxtail (*Pennisetum alopecuroides*)
Has beautiful purple to brown plumes. The dwarf cultivar 'Woodside' is also attractive.

Wallaby grass (*Danthonia* spp.)
Will grow in sun or semi-shade.

Annuals

Annuals are essentially used as infills. While perennials and foliage are the garden's mainstays, annuals produce colour and interest at particular times of the year. Annuals provide a sense of change throughout the seasons. You can choose different-coloured annuals each season and those that have different heights, flower shapes and sizes. To achieve a continuity of annuals, purchase them throughout the year or sow seed during each season for the next one.

Allow self-seeding annuals such as cornflower, cosmos, Chinese forget-me-not, Californian poppy, alyssum, honesty, heartsease and Flanders poppy to set seed and you will be surprised where they turn up in the garden the following year.

Ornamental grasses

Ornamental grasses are suited to informal gardens. Their swaying leaves make strong statements when planted among perennials. Lofty grasses act as finely textured screens and short ornamental grasses can be grown *en masse* as interesting groundcovers.

Lawns

Many gardeners who like a natural style wish to exclude lawns from their gardens. But lawns are often necessary as play areas for children, or you may simply wish to have one to lounge around on. Bulbs planted in drifts throughout a lawn to produce a meadow-like effect suit this style, or you can be even bolder and use a low-growing ornamental or native grass as a lawn substitute.

Woodland

If there are large numbers of trees in your garden, you can beautify the areas beneath them by using a naturalised planting style. There are some appropriate and hardy plants that will happily grow in full or semi-shade.

You could include ajuga, *Aspidistra elatior*, bergenia, bluebells, cineraria, columbine, crinum, *Cyclamen* species, snow poppy (*Eomecon chionanthum*), English daisy, *Euphorbia amygdaloides* subsp. *robbiae*, foxgloves, *Geranium maderense*, *Geranium phaeum*, false spirea (*Astilbe* species), heartsease, hellebores, honesty, hostas, impatiens, Jacob's ladder (*Polemonium caeruleum*), lamium, lily-of-the-valley, mondo grass, *Plectranthus* species, polyanthus,

primroses, Solomon's seal (*Polygonatum* species), snowflakes, torenia and violets.

Maintenance

Plants co-exist happily in this style with relatively little need for the intervention of the gardener. You may need to stop one plant swamping another in some situations, but the essential aim is to create an artificial version of a natural ecosystem.

Thoughtful mulching will reduce the amount of water used in the early stages. Once established, an annual feeding and a selective cutting back of perennials will be all that is needed.

Clumps of daffodils and bluebells give the lawn a meadow-like appearance.

Smart tip

In addition to the appealing low-maintenance aspect of natural planting schemes, they have the advantage of being environmentally friendly. This type of design advocates the use of plants indigenous to your area. This in turn encourages butterflies, birds and friendly predators to the garden and creates corridors for wildlife. Because this approach involves very close planting, the need for weeding is reduced considerably.

Kitchen gardens

You can let your imagination run wild in a kitchen garden as there are so many approaches and designs. Lovers of formal gardens plant everything in neat rows, while those who prefer a more relaxed appearance use a delightfully informal style. You can make your kitchen garden the major focus, or it can blend with the rest of the garden. The kitchen garden has recently enjoyed a revival as many gardeners rediscover the productive and decorative advantages to be gained from growing flowers, herbs and vegetables in the one bed.

Kitchen garden design

For centuries people have grown their own vegetables, fruit and herbs. The Romans grew fruit, vines, and medicinal and culinary herbs. Later many of these plants were also found in enclosed monasteries. In Tudor times the gardens became more formal and the Elizabethans perfected the art of formal kitchen and herb gardens in beautifully designed 'knot' or parterre gardens.

Many of today's most striking kitchen gardens have kept the shape of the 'knot' as it provides a practical solution to the use of space. Even a small kitchen garden can be decorative and productive. You can give your kitchen garden pride of place in your backyard or you can give it its own 'room' if you have the space.

For convenience, a kitchen garden should be placed as close to the kitchen as possible. But this may not always be practical if that position doesn't receive sufficient sun. Choose the sunniest position, even if it is away from the house.

The formal kitchen garden

If you prefer an orderly vegetable garden with neat rows, then a formal style may suit you. You can make a simple parterre or knot garden. Hedges traditionally border the edges of such gardens, and you could use santolina, box, germander (*Teucrium fruticans*), lavender or rosemary for this purpose. While they look fantastic, keep in mind that hedging plants take up valuable planting space. Chives and parsley make an interesting border alternative.

You can plant vegetables ornamentally in the parterre in rows or groups. You can also border the garden with a low fence and espalier fruit trees along it.

OPPOSITE **Garden beds edged in box form the design in a courtyard kitchen garden. Coloured-stemmed silver beet makes a striking foliage feature.**

Designing a simple knot or parterre

Creating a geometric kitchen garden is an interesting gardening challenge. The original designs were either elaborate or based on simple geometric shapes with interconnecting systems of paths. Choose a design that suits the dimensions and shape of your garden.

If you decide to make a simple knot or parterre garden, you will need a good supply of strong string and wooden pegs. Mark out the outer edge of the design, followed by the centre point, which can be located by crossing the diagonal lines. To mark out the basic geometrical inner design, scratch the design into the ground or use sand or lime trickled out of a bottle.

The informal kitchen garden

An informally designed kitchen garden looks wonderful in cottage and natural gardens. It can even be separated from the main garden by a picket fence or another kind of wooden fence. It can be any shape and size and the boundaries and paths may disappear seasonally beneath foliage, flowers and fruit. Make the garden a rich mixture of perennials, vegetables, edible flowers and fruit.

In small spaces

You can create a kitchen garden in a cartwheel form with triangles of herbs and salad leaves. Use gravel or brick pavers in the spokes as paths. Place a sundial or large container in the centre of the wheel as a feature.

A well-designed kitchen garden is both practical and attractive.

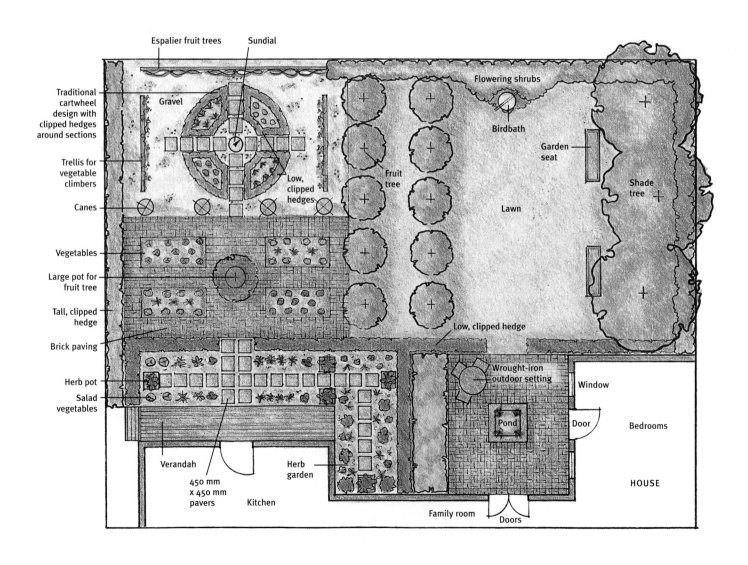

Structural elements

Paths, containers filled with edible plants and colourful tripods all work well in the kitchen garden.

Paths

Paths in a formal kitchen garden may be made of brick, gravel, pavers, stone or even mown grass. Gravel, mown grass and woodchips suit an informal style. Large pavers interplanted with chamomile or thyme add a fragrant touch.

Accessories

Large containers filled with citrus or bay trees make magnificent kitchen garden features. Plant a row of them as a divider if you wish to separate the kitchen garden from the rest of the garden. Tall terracotta pots filled with chives, parsley or marjoram also work well.

Climbing peas or beans can be grown on tripods. Try painting the tripods bright colours for an arresting effect. Sundials also look good in kitchen gardens.

Fences

If you have dogs, you can enclose the kitchen garden with a wooden or wire fence. Drape the wire fence with climbing vegetables and fruit. An arch or pergola leading into the garden can be covered with edible climbers.

Planting

You can plant a kitchen garden in the same way that you would any other type of flowerbed. Many vegetables and herbs have extremely pretty leaves or flowers. The sight of tomatoes ripening among their green leaves or brussels sprouts forming on stems can be fabulous. Eggplant and capsicum look good before the fruit starts to form and even more attractive as they grow and start to colour. Grow the tall stems of corn with their strap-like leaves at the back of a garden bed. Plant vegetables in clumps or in rows to create visual impact.

Choose and grow vegetables and herbs that you enjoy eating and not just those that have aesthetic appeal. They should be able to grow well in your climate (see The vegetable garden on pages 243–6).

Perennial vegetables

Perennial vegetables include asparagus, cardoon, globe artichoke, horseradish, rhubarb and sorrel. These versatile vegetables should be planted in permanent positions in your kitchen garden so that you will be able to harvest them year after year.

Herbs

Grow herbs among your vegetables. The flowers of many herbs, and especially those of lavender and thyme, attract bees to the garden. You can create a knot or parterre in which to grow herbs exclusively.

Parsley, celery, mustard and lettuce mingle with flowers in this attractive garden bed.

Wildlife-friendly habitats

There is far more to gardening than cultivating plants. The trees, shrubs and other plants in your garden create a microcosm of the larger environment. This microcosm can be an attractive habitat for birds, butterflies, insects and a variety of animals. By establishing the correct conditions for these creatures, you can make your garden a wildlife refuge and help restore the number of habitats lost through urbanisation, farming and the overuse of chemicals. When you relax in your wildlife-friendly backyard, you will feel in harmony with nature.

Wildlife-friendly design

Wildlife backyards are generally informal. Wandering paths, old logs, large stones and water are all part of the style. The garden should have a casual, comfortable feel. By their very nature, native gardens are wildlife refuges, but a mix of natives and exotics is just as attractive to wildlife.

If you want a formal look, use raised beds and plant your shrubbery in the beds. A formal pond will complete the look.

If your children need a lawn, you can surround it with shrubbery or have wildlife beds in one particular area of the backyard.

Position a birdbath so that it can be seen from indoors. After all, if you have gone to the trouble of cultivating plants that will attract a variety of birds, it's good to be able to see them.

Attracting birds

To attract birds successfully you need to provide them with food, shelter and water. Foods include nectar, pollen, seeds, fruit, insects and other small creatures. By planting a selection of nectar-rich trees and shrubs, for example, you can attract both honeyeaters and the small insects that are their supplementary food.

Structural elements

Materials including wood, stone and mellow-coloured bricks suit the friendly habitat style. Birdbaths, ponds for frogs and birds, and old logs for lizards will entice fauna.

Paths

Construct paths in a wildlife backyard from gravel, bark or old

OPPOSITE Butterflies and bees are attracted to lavender. The birdbath provides a drinking spot for local birds.

Nesting spots

Most species of *Eucalyptus* are visited by parrots regularly and hollow branches often provide nesting spots. You can emulate these natural nesting spots by very firmly fixing sections of hollow log or nesting boxes within large trees. The fibrous bark of trees and shrubs such as melaleucas, eucalypts and leptospermum provides good nesting material. The beautiful but vigorous native wonga wonga vine (*Pandorea pandorana*) is a climber that forms a dense nesting habitat. Grow it over an arbour or a mesh fence.

A natural design and the correct combination of plants will attract birds, butterflies and native animals to your backyard.

bricks. Position logs along the edges to provide hiding places for lizards and other creatures.

Entertaining areas can have floors of gravel or mellow pavers. Separate them from the rest of the backyard with grevillea hedges – birds love them.

Ponds

Ponds will attract frogs to the garden and provide water for birds to drink and bathe in. Place rocks around the edge of your pond and plant sedges or other bog plants between them to provide shelter for the frogs. (See Installing a pond on page 174.)

Birdbaths

A regular source of water is essential for attracting birds. Ponds are ideal, but even a shallow bowl or birdbath will do. Birdbaths should not be placed completely in

the open, because most birds feel safer when there is some protective shrubbery around. Tuck birdbaths into corners or locate them among shrubs. Better still, place them near a window of the house from where the birds' activities can be watched. And keep in mind that cats will be a menace to birds.

Accessories

Natural wooden furniture works well in a wildlife backyard.

Planting

A bird- and butterfly-attracting garden does not have to be purely native, but at least a third of plants should be native and if possible indigenous to your area. Having said that, many exotic plants will provide food for birds.

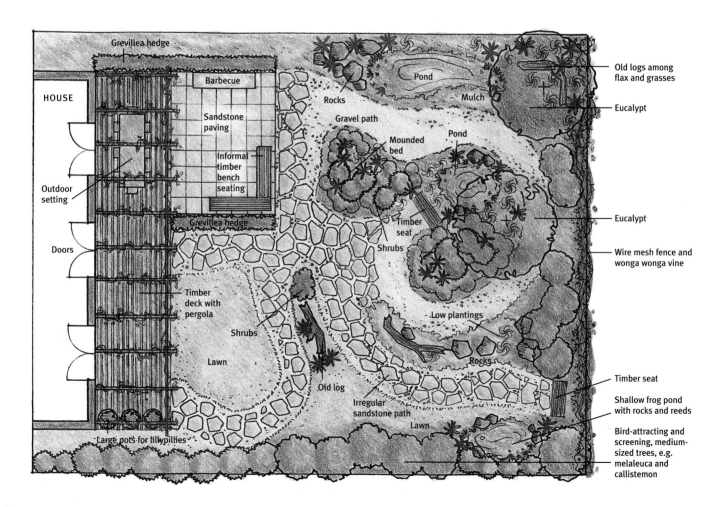

Trees and shrubs

Trees and shrubs provide ideal positions from which birds can survey the garden. Tall trees become vantage points that enable them to check that there are no dangers awaiting them when they seek out food in the garden. Trees provide the overstorey, but lower growing shrubs are required for an understorey. Providing a wide variety of plants will ensure that you attract a wide variety of birds.

Have some *Callistemon* and *Melaleuca* species in the garden as they are widely known for their bird-attracting qualities and are just as enticing to butterflies. Try to include at least one eucalypt. Consider *Eucalyptus leucoxylon* subsp. *megalocarpa*, *E. lehmannii*, *E. torquata*, *E. caesia*, *E. erythrocorys*, or *E. macrocarpa*. You can find a wattle (*Acacia*) or leptospermum for any climate. Consider also *Stenocarpus sinuatus*, *Angophora*, *Banksia*, *Pittosporum*, *Hakea* and *Tristania*.

Bird-attracting shrubs

Densely foliaged shrubs such as hakeas and grevilleas, which often have spines or sharp-pointed leaves, provide a refuge for birds. But plant them where you won't be scratched as you walk past. These shrubs often make good nesting spots. The advantage of some species of hakeas and grevilleas is that they flower in winter when other flowers are scarce.

Grevilleas (especially those with red or pink flowers) attract hordes of honeyeaters. Your local nursery will offer plants that suit your climate.

All the species of *Banksia* will attract honey-eating birds as the nectar is replenished daily to ensure a continual supply.

Surprisingly enough, it's not necessarily the flower of the wattle (*Acacia* species) that attracts birds. It's a nectar-producing gland at the junction of the leaf and stem. Choose a species indigenous to your area if possible.

LEFT   Grevillea flowers will attract a variety of native birds to the garden.

BELOW   The attractive flowers of *Asclepias curaseavica* will lure the wanderer butterfly to your backyard.

Plants that lure specific types of butterflies

Cootamundra wattle (*Acacia baileyana*) – attracts the tailed emperor (*Polyura pyrrhus*).

Citrus trees – attract the orchard butterfly (*Papilio aegeus*) and the dingy swallowtail (*P. anactus*).

Hardenbergia violacea – attracts the chequered swallowtail (*Papilio demoleus*).

Queensland wattle (*A. podalyriifolia*) – attracts the tailed emperor (*Polyura pyrrhus*).

Smart tip

When it comes to attracting butterflies, being an untidy gardener has advantages, as many butterflies depend on weeds for their existence. Reconsider before removing that dandelion and leave those small, soft grasses unmown in order to attract the common brown butterfly. Milkweed attracts the monarch or wanderer butterfly. And the flowerheads of clover provide nectar for smaller butterflies.

Attracting butterflies

Think twice before you squash that caterpillar in the garden, because it's likely that you are crushing what could have become a beautiful native butterfly. Many gardeners who prevent this metamorphosis on a regular basis do so under the mistaken impression that they are saving their precious plants from destruction. The truth is that the caterpillars of moths are usually the enemy, and not the caterpillars of butterflies. The only really harmful butterfly is the cabbage white butterfly (see pages 304–5).

Butterfly-attracting plants

Underplant the bird-attracting trees and shrubs with daisies that belong to the Asteraceae family. These will lure the Australian painted lady butterfly (*Vanessa kershawi*) as well as a variety of beneficial insects including parasitic wasps, hoverflies, lacewings and ladybirds.

Members of the Asteraceae family include cosmos, marigolds, sunflowers, China asters and dahlias. Coneflower (*Echinacea purpurea*), with its large daisy-like, crimson-mauve summer flowerheads is a most tempting butterfly plant, as is the blue flowering perennial *Stokesia laevis*. The yellow flowers of the native everlasting daisy (*Bracteantha bracteata*) are also irresistible to butterflies.

You could also include the butterfly bush (*Buddleia davidii*), common heliotrope (*Heliotropium arborescens*), cultivars of *Lantana camara*, bergamot (*Monarda* species) and *Aster novae-angliae* cultivars. A bed of cornflowers will provide a feast for butterflies, as will nasturtiums, borage, catnip, stock, alyssum and marigolds.

Attracting bees

Insecticides do not go hand in hand with wildlife gardens. They kill beneficial insects such as bees and butterflies as well as pests, so a reduction in their use is a positive step if you want a wildlife backyard. Urban development involving land clearing and landscaping can destroy bee

ABOVE A butterfly perched on a bottlebrush bloom.

RIGHT The delicate beauty of a butterfly on a coleus leaf brings life to this garden.

colonies by removing nest sites and food supplies. Planting bee-attracting plants can help to offset the effects of such development.

Bee-attracting plants

While some native bees will only visit native plants, others live happily among exotics. The top ten exotic bee-attracting plants are lavender, *Abelia grandiflora*, eucalyptus, baeckea, brachyscome, buddleia, grevillea, *Hardenbergia violacea*, leptospermum and westringia.

Bees are also attracted to plants in the Myrtaceae family and daisy family (*Asteraceae*), especially brachyscome and our native everlasting daisy (*Bracteantha bracteata*). They also like the flowers of culinary herbs such as basil, mint, thyme, sage, hyssop, lemon balm and savory and the blossoms of citrus, boronia, correa, eriostemon and murraya.

Attracting frogs

One of the great advantages of having a pond in the garden is that it will attract frogs. Frog numbers are dropping worldwide, so providing them with a habitat is one way of making a very worthwhile environmental contribution. But a pond bordered by neatly clipped lawn is not frog-inducing. Frogs need to be surrounded by lots of vegetation. This provides them with places to hide from predators such as cats and enables them to catch many of the insects they eat. Frogs love shade, luxuriant shrubbery, reedy grasses, damp, mossy crevices, flat stones and bits of bark to hide under. They will move away from ponds if it's too hard to find food there.

Because frogs absorb contaminates through their skin, they are particularly susceptible to pesticides, so do not use them in the garden.

A pond with numerous places to hide will attract frogs to your backyard.

Backyards for kids

If your household includes kids, the needs of both children and adults must be considered when you are planning your backyard. You should take the age and interests of your children into account. Very young children have very different requirements from those of teenagers, and you will have to adapt the backyard to meet the changing needs of your children as they grow. Providing areas for play and leisure activities can help develop interests that will enrich the lives of your children. You may choose to include an edible garden to stimulate your children's interest in vegetable gardening.

Take age into account

If your children are very young, you may wish to place their play area where you can see it from the kitchen window. When they are teenagers, however, you may want their territory to be as far away from the house as possible! A little planning can ensure that both will happen.

For example, the sandpit can be portable and structures such as slides and cubby houses can be taken down when the children outgrow them. Even if the sandpit is a permanent structure, it can be dismantled later if bolts are used in its construction.

This area can then be turned into flowerbeds, a vegetable garden or lawn when the children no longer play there. Similarly, a paved area used by teenagers for their skateboards and rollerblades can be used as a permanent entertaining space by adding a pergola. Or perhaps you could install that water feature you've always wanted.

Young children

Play areas for young children should be partially shaded to prevent skin damage and located on soft surfaces. Soft surfaces such as lawn or leaf mould are essential if you plan to build play equipment.

Shade can be obtained by planting trees and large shrubs. Deciduous trees have the advantage of allowing warm winter sun to enter the area. A tree with low branches is ideal for climbing. Swings and cubby houses can be placed under trees where it is difficult for lawn to grow.

It's worth keeping in mind that a children's play area will not always be neat and tidy. Creativity is often a messy process, and you

OPPOSITE This small cubby house and slide is surrounded by its own garden containing catmint and salvia.

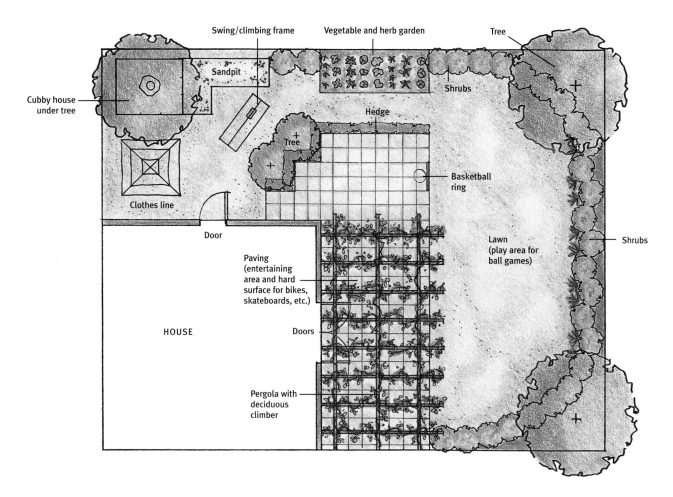

Cubby house under tree

Swing/climbing frame

Sandpit

Clothes line

Door

Tree

Vegetable and herb garden

Hedge

Basketball ring

Paving (entertaining area and hard surface for bikes, skateboards, etc.)

HOUSE

Doors

Pergola with deciduous climber

Tree

Shrubs

Lawn (play area for ball games)

Shrubs

The needs of both children and adults have been considered in this backyard plan.

will have to learn to overlook the cardboard boxes and plastic ice-cream containers strewn over the lawn.

You should consider placing the sandpit in a position that is clearly visible from the house, even if you don't like its untidy aspect. This will allow you to keep young children in view and to monitor their activities. You can also place some low screening plants or a hedge around the play area to reduce the visual impact.

Structural elements

Sandpits, swings, seesaws, slides, cubby houses and areas for skateboarding and playing basketball are among the structural elements associated with an active backyard designed with young children and teenagers in mind.

Sandpits

Of all these items, sandpits are among the easiest to build and the most popular. (See Building a sandpit on pages 188–9.) They provide endless hours of fun for very little cost. Young children love to use their imagination, and sand play is an excellent way of doing it.

Sandpits can be permanent or temporary. Permanent sandpits are either sunken or built above ground. If you decide to dig a pit, make sure that it's at least 2 square metres in area and 30 cm deep. Line the pit with black builder's plastic and pierce it here and there for drainage before adding the sand.

Above-ground sandpits can be constructed from timber (including railway sleepers) bolted together.

Swings and things

Young children love movement, and swings, seesaws and slides are perennial favourites for active play.

You can install a swing very easily by simply attaching it to a strong tree branch. Swings are also commercially available in timber- or steel-framed kit form. You may need to attach the legs of the frame to concrete footings for the sake of stability.

Remember to position the swing on a soft surface such as grass, sand or leaf mould. If you decide to hang a swing from the branch of a tree, you should do it properly by drilling holes to insert strong steel eye-bolts. This will cause less damage to the tree than rope or chain tied straight to the branch, which will wear it away as the swing moves.

Slides and seesaws also provide hours of pleasure for children. Unless you are a very skilled handyperson, you should consider purchasing these pieces of play equipment from a reputable retailer. Check carefully that they comply with safety standards, and that their design is suitable for the available space. Both slides and seesaws should be positioned to allow plenty of room for access.

The cubby house

Cubby houses are ideal for young children. Children love to have private places to which they can retreat and become involved in many types of imaginative play.

Children love to hide from each other and will use anything that is to hand for this purpose. Old cardboard packing boxes are favourites for improvisation. But there comes a time when these will not be enough, and you will have to build or buy a cubby house.

Uncomplicated cubby houses can easily be built by the home handyperson. (See Building a cubby house on pages 185–6.) The good thing about building it yourself is that you are in control

Even small, formal courtyards can contain a sandpit for children.

of the design. You can make the cubby house sympathetic to the house and other structures in style and materials.

You can also design it according to your children's needs and interests. Simple structures are always the best, and unless you live in a cold climate, you can dispense with the need for doors and windows.

Using second-hand recycled materials is a cheap option. Make sure the timber has been carefully denailed, and smooth off any rough edges. You should also ensure that the timber has not been previously painted with lead-based paint.

The cubby house should be big enough to allow three children inside it in comfort. It should also be big enough for an adult to enter for cleaning and to check for insect pests.

If you decide to purchase a cubby house, you will find that there is a wide variety on the market. Many are constructed from durable treated pine. Check that the cubby house is weatherproof and big enough to allow for your children's growth over the period of time they are likely to use it.

Some commercially available cubby houses have the advantage of combining a number of pieces of play equipment. They may have a slide or rope ladder attached, and this makes for a more compact play area.

Teenagers' areas

Older children and teenagers like to use scooters, skateboards and rollerblades. They may also like to play a variety of ball games, from basketball to handball.

A concrete or paved area situated away from the house is

Give children their own area. Here the cubby and play set are positioned at the bottom of the garden.

ideal for these activities. If the idea of light-grey concrete is unappealing, consider using some of the fashionable dark tints used in concreting these days.

Because the paved or concrete area will have few, if any, permanent structures, you will be able to convert it easily into an entertaining area. The addition of a gazebo, summerhouse or pergola will immediately change the tone of the area.

Alternatively, you can make your entertaining area larger so that children can use the hard surfaces as well.

Planting

Gardening is a great family activity and a good way to lure children outdoors away from television and video games. And gardening skills acquired at an early age will last a lifetime.

A good approach to developing a child's interest in gardening is to start with a potted plant. Annuals such as marigolds, petunias and sweet peas are ideal. Once the interest in plants has been established, you can give your children responsibility for growing a plant in the garden. Choose hardy, colourful plants for this purpose.

The edible garden

The key to promoting children's interest in vegetable gardening is to grow vegetables they like to eat. Good examples are cherry tomatoes, sweet corn and snow peas. Fruit such as strawberries and raspberries is also ideal. And why not give your child his or her very own citrus tree to look after?

Smart tip

Children love fragrant plants, so get them to grow some lavender. They can then dry the flowers and make lavender bags.

Smart tip

Buy your children packets of mixed seeds that are labelled especially for children so that they will feel fully involved.

LEFT   Children will spend hours playing in the most simple structures erected in your backyard.

BELOW   It's best to locate play areas for younger children on soft surfaces such as grass.

Perfumed gardens

Fragrance adds another dimension to your backyard. You can design the garden so that you will enjoy perfumes throughout the year. You can position perfumed plants throughout your backyard or have scented 'rooms'. Place perfumed plants near windows, doors, outdoor eating areas, seats, courtyards and alongside paths. Allow perfumed climbing plants to ramble over walls, trees and fences. Once you have developed an interest in fragrant plants, you will always be searching for another spot in the backyard where you can reap the reward of a new fragrance.

Perfumed garden design

There are different ways to design a perfumed garden. You may wish to set your perfumed plants far apart from one another to prevent the scents from mingling. Or you may wish to mingle similar aromas together in a 'scent pocket' in a particular part of the garden. This pocket will then be like a perfumed room. You can drape a perfumed climber over a pergola in your entertaining area.

Perfumed plants in raised beds will lift the fragrances towards you. Scented foliage plants may be placed alongside a pathway where your hands can brush against them as you pass by.

You may simply wish to place perfumed plants around your favourite garden seat so that you can appreciate the aromas at your leisure.

Structural elements

Archways and pergolas are ideal for perfumed climbers. Raised beds also feature in many fragrant gardens.

Perfumed pathways

Pathways can become ribbons of perfume-packed plants that create scent and colour both at ground level and around one's head. Pathways can have perfumed plants on the floor or in raised beds beside them. A pergola covering the pathway will exude perfume from fragrant climbing plants. Terracotta pots of perfumed plants can be placed alongside the edges of paths to create interest.

On the path

Perfumed groundcovers planted in between stones or bricks on paths reward you with underfoot fragrance and have a softening

OPPOSITE   The sweetly scented rose 'Leverkusen' has been grown over an arch to lure you into another area of the garden.

Smart tip

Don't limit perfumed groundcovers to paths. You can also place them in between pavers in courtyards and around garden seats.

A wisteria-covered pergola creates an evocative walkway.

effect. Thyme is one of the prettiest of all groundcovers and exudes a lovely fragrance when trodden upon. Wild or lawn thyme (*Thymus serpyllum*) forms an attractive moss-green carpet of tiny leaves and has bright, rosy lilac flowers. You could also use woolly or mountain thyme (*T. pseudolanuginosus*), which has minute grey woolly leaves and lilac-pink flowers.

The heat of pavers seems to increase the fragrance of Sweet Alice or alyssum (*Lobularia maritima*). This pretty little groundcover flowers for long periods and has white or violet flowers depending on the cultivar.

Lawn chamomile, especially the cultivar 'Treneague', can also be planted on paths. Its scent has a relaxing effect. Pennyroyal is ideal for shady paths.

Raised beds

Raised beds on each side of a path bring the perfume closer to nose level. They are not difficult to construct and are ideal for many annuals and perennials and for smaller shrubs such as santolina, gardenias, lavender, rosemary and sage. It's easy to build a raised bed if it's less than a metre high. This can be done with stone, bricks or porcupine blocks. Porcupine blocks actually fit into each other and do not need to be placed on a foundation. (See Building a brick wall on pages 139–40.)

Make the width of the bed proportional to the size of your garden. If you have the space, make the top of the wall wide enough to sit on. Alternatively, you can make a seat in the wall.

A chamomile seat

A herbal seat is one of life's absolute luxuries. The chamomile seat at Sissinghurst Castle in England is undoubtedly the most famous perfumed seat seen today, but many paintings of medieval gardens show women sitting on herbal seats surrounded by perfumed flowers.

You can make an attractive herbal seat by using sandstone blocks, porcupine blocks, or flat rocks of approximately equal size.

Planting the seat

When the walls of the seat have been built, fill two-thirds of the inside with a hard core of small broken rocks or coarse gravel. Top this with a good compost mix. A little gravel added to the compost mix will facilitate drainage.

You can plant directly into the compost so that you sit on the chamomile, or place a couple of large flat rocks on top of the compost mix and fill the spaces in between with chamomile.

You don't have to limit yourself to chamomile. You could use thyme, for example, instead of chamomile. And if your seat is in a shady part of the garden, consider using pennyroyal. You could also make the seat wider and grow lavender or rosemary at the back of it.

Planting

The living elements are central to a fragrant garden. Plants in raised beds, climbing plants and plants placed on paths and walking areas

Seasonal fragrance

Most gardeners aim to have flowers in their garden throughout the seasons. And, of course, this should be the aim with perfume. It's more difficult to achieve it in winter, but you can rely on perfumed foliage plants (placed where we brush against them) instead of flowers.

Consider the flowering period when choosing perfumed plants for your garden. With careful selection you can extend your fragrances across the seasons.

The fragrances of this garden can be enjoyed from the entertaining area or while walking on the gravel paths.

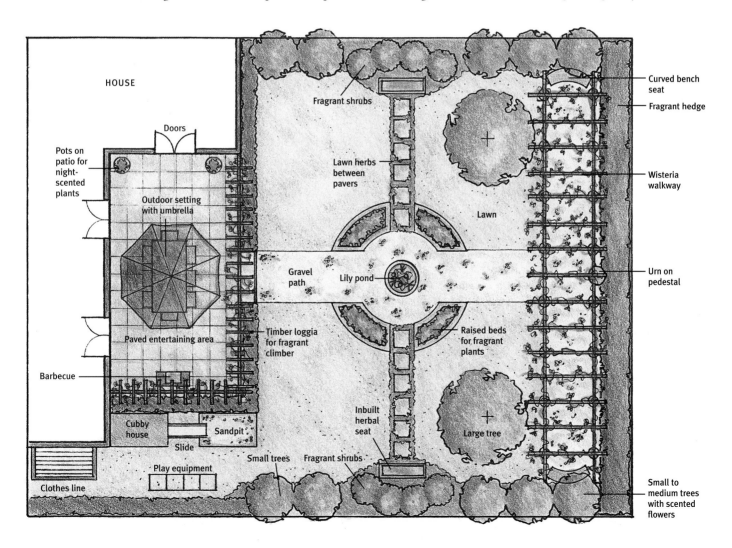

HOUSE

Pots on patio for night-scented plants

Doors

Outdoor setting with umbrella

Paved entertaining area

Barbecue

Cubby house

Slide

Sandpit

Play equipment

Clothes line

Fragrant shrubs

Lawn herbs between pavers

Gravel path

Lily pond

Timber loggia for fragrant climber

Inbuilt herbal seat

Small trees

Fragrant shrubs

Lawn

Raised beds for fragrant plants

Large tree

Curved bench seat

Fragrant hedge

Wisteria walkway

Urn on pedestal

Small to medium trees with scented flowers

Smart tip

Thyme, chamomile or pennyroyal can be placed in front of seats to create a fragrant atmosphere.

RIGHT These white liliums growing beside the path have an evocative perfume.

BELOW A perfumed sitting area is always delightful. Thyme has been planted between the pavers and lavender on each side of the seat.

should all be featured. You can enjoy these living elements day and night and, with careful planning, all year round.

Night-scented plants

The perfume of many plants is stronger during the evening than it is during the day. The night-scented stock is a good example. The flowers are rather drab but come into their own at night when their perfume is overpowering.

Night-scented plants should be placed near windows or verandahs or in courtyards where their smells are pervasive.

Moonflower (*Ipomoea alba*) is a beautiful scented perennial climbing plant suitable for use on pergolas. Its huge (15 cm), pure-white flowers unfold at dusk with a delicious fragrance that fills the air. This perennial climber reaches a height of 6 m and requires a warm, sunny position. Keep its roots cool with a mulch.

One of the most pervasive night perfumes is that of night-scented

jessamine (*Cestrum nocturnum*). It's a must for planting near a window or door or in a courtyard.

The four o'clock plant (*Mirabilis jalapa*) opens its flowers at just that time. The flowers remain open at night and fade the following morning. Flowering tobacco (*Nicotiana alata*) is also worthwhile, as is common mignonette (*Reseda odorata*). Mignonette is particularly suited to pot culture and can be brought indoors when in full flower.

Scented leaves

The attractive leaves of scented geraniums (*Pelargonium* species) release a strong fragrance when touched, which makes them popular in gardens for the visually impaired. Plant them in containers and beside paths, steps, doorways and entrances. They blend particularly well with lavender, rosemary and artemisia in sunny, dry garden beds. Fragrances include coconut (*P. grossularoides*), nutmeg (*P. fragrans*), citron ('Mabel Grey', *P. crispum*), apple

(*P. odoratissimum*), peppermint (*P. tomentosum*), almond (*P. quercifolium*) and rose ('Lemon Rose', 'Lara Starshine', 'Lady Plymouth' and 'Rober's Lemon Rose').

Fragrant lawns

Fragrant lawns are ideal for areas of the garden that are not heavily used. Imagine sitting on the apple-scented, feathery leaves of chamomile or a sweetly scented thyme lawn.

Before starting any type of lawn alternative it's essential that you remove all the weeds, especially the perennial ones. This may be done the hard way by digging and removing or simply by using a non-residual weedkiller. Dig compost, mushroom compost or well-rotted manure into the area and level it well, removing any stones or old roots.

For small lawns chamomile is an ideal alternative to grass. Use lawn chamomile (*Chamaemelum nobile* 'Treneague'). It prefers a sunny,

well-drained position. Weed the lawn thoroughly until it is established and keep it well watered, especially during the hot summer months.

Thyme is another groundcover that makes a wonderfully fragrant lawn, but watch out for bees when it's in flower. Thyme must be planted in full sun and well-drained soil. It does not like to be trodden on excessively, so to be on the safe side you should make a path through the lawn using flat stepping stones. You can use one variety of thyme or a mixture of different types.

A violet lawn can look beautiful beneath deciduous trees and has a magnificent appearance when the violets are in flower. A violet lawn is not suitable for heavy traffic, so use stepping stones where necessary.

Pennyroyal (*Mentha pulegium*) is ideal for damp, shady areas or under trees. It exudes a wonderful peppermint-like scent, particularly when its leaves are crushed.

Smart tip

Create a diffused pattern in the lawn using different varieties of thyme with different leaf and flower colours.

A variety of roses produce different scents on this perfumed pathway.

Contemporary living

The contemporary living style is characterised by simplicity, a clever use of space and a bold approach to planting. Contemporary styles encompass shapes that are geometric and those that flow with a sense of freedom. It's difficult to categorise contemporary style in a simple, straightforward definition, but there are common elements and approaches that can be discussed. Contemporary designs lend themselves to the use of hardscaped living areas featuring state-of-the-art outdoor furniture and equipment that make entertaining an exciting prospect.

Contemporary design

Contemporary design is simple and uncluttered, featuring hardscaping and an architectural use of plant material. While all gardens should be sympathetic to the architecture of the house and other buildings, gardens in the contemporary style are most suited to buildings designed in the late 20th century.

Garden floors are featured in contemporary design. Geometric paving patterns, concrete and gravel are often used. You can create innovative combinations from coloured concrete and mosaic, gravel and grass and pavers and pebbles.

Plants are used in the contemporary style in a similar way to the formal garden in that they are part of an overall effect. Many plants are selected for their sculptural value, colour and form and are arranged in the garden as

an art form. Large-leafed plants with a strong vertical element can be used to make statements. Grasses and various types of succulents are popular. Potted standards and topiary can be featured also.

Cultural fusion is found in the new designs, and it's not unusual to find Asian influences combined with traditional English styles.

Structural elements

Concrete is often used in contemporary design for court-yards, patios and paths. It's popular because it can be coloured and moulded in a variety of ways. It can also be used on walls and to make individualised containers that suit the house design.

Pavers and tiles are equally popular because they offer

OPPOSITE Pavers laid diagonally in gravel bring your attention to floor level. Purple-leafed cordylines and low-growing ornamental grasses complete the picture.

Hard surfaces, colourful walls, tiles and water features epitomise the contemporary look.

This contemporary plan features strong lines and geometric shapes.

numerous design possibilities. Steel is widely used to create garden features or for railings, stairs and arches. Timber is used in decks, walls and special features. Sand, gravel, pebbles and slate are very popular and we are even seeing the return of 'crazy paving'.

Some designers are experimenting with industrial materials such as plastics, polyester and various alloys. Glass and translucent materials are appearing in walls and garden features.

Colour

Contemporary design in this country favours the Australian tones of ochre, blue, orange, yellow and red. It's easy to see why. These colours, and various combinations of them, are found throughout Australia and reflect aspects of our natural landscape. In addition to flowers and foliage, colour is reflected in walls and garden features.

Water

Water is valued because it creates tranquillity and a sense of spirituality. The importance of water as a resource in this country has not been lost on the new breed of designers. We can no longer afford to waste water if there are viable and attractive approaches to landscaping that will reduce its use. Today, the trend is to use waterwise plants, and water-devouring lawns are being replaced by decks and paved areas.

Water features are widely used in contemporary design because they can introduce movement and sound. On the other hand, still water provides reflection and serenity. Fountains, pools and ponds are all popular. Unusual water features can be constructed from a wide range of materials, including combinations of concrete, steel and glass.

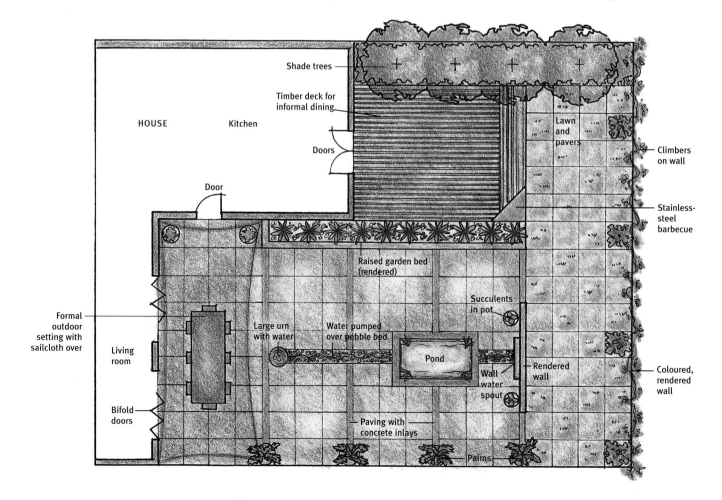

Lighting

Lighting technology and techniques have advanced enormously in recent years. Lighting can be used to greatly extend the time that can be spent in the garden. This is important to contemporary designs that extend living areas of the house outside into garden rooms. Lighting is also used to highlight aspects of design and bring garden features to life.

Furniture

Steel and aluminium furniture is often used in contemporary backyards to complement surfaces of concrete, paving and stone used in hardscaping. Laminated timber, plastic and nylon are also employed.

Accessories

Accessories suitable for the contemporary look range from stainless steel barbecues to steel garbage bins used as containers. Tinted concrete and terracotta pots can also be used. Be careful not to clutter outdoor living areas with accessories or you will lose the restraint that characterises the contemporary look.

Planting

Environmental considerations are important in contemporary design. Waterwise plants and those requiring low maintenance and few, if any, chemicals to sustain them are favoured. The garden's position in the landscape as a whole should also be considered when a backyard is designed.

Because plants are often employed to create sculptural effects, individual plants can take precedence over the garden as a whole. Plants can be used in the same way as works of art in a gallery. The choice of plants thus becomes an important issue.

What to plant

Plants with architectural features work well in contemporary gardens. Large succulents such as *Agave attenuata* make sculptural statements. And clipped topiary plants in containers or beds suit this look. Containers planted with *Echeveria* cultivars, cycads, palms, banksias, camellias, yuccas, bromeliads, lavenders or rosemary are also popular.

Topiary shapes work well in contemporary garden design.

LEFT   Simplicity is the key to success in this contemporary garden.

BELOW   *Agave attenuata* in a container make a stunning contribution to the overall design.

Designing your backyard

Do you have a picture of a dream garden in your head? Have you selected a style you like? If you have, you'll be tempted to rush out and create an instant backyard. But don't, as the most important step towards having a successful backyard is the initial design.

Before you start

The process of drawing up a backyard design is important because it allows you to get to know your backyard. All backyards are governed by permanent factors such as shape and aspect, but your backyard and its ultimate character will be determined by your needs and those of your family. Everyone has different uses for their backyard – space for children to play, a swimming pool, or simply a tranquil, low-maintenance retreat in which to spend time relaxing. Aim to have a clear idea of what you want from your backyard and what you hope to achieve.

The design process

Following the design process will answer all the questions most commonly asked about making the best use of your backyard. Designing your own backyard and making a plan are not difficult tasks. By undertaking the design process thoughtfully in the first instance, you will avoid spending hours fixing mistakes at a later date.

Your backyard should be designed as an entity from the outset, as it will eventually be a single design. This approach is far better than dividing the backyard into a couple of sections and designing each section as you go. If you have an overall plan, you do not have to build the whole garden immediately. If you can't afford to build that pond or cubby house at the moment, you can add it later on.

The big picture

The discipline of the design process encourages you to consider the backyard as a whole. It also allows you to see the logical order in which its development should be approached. Perhaps your backyard is new, or it may have an existing design that is not to your taste. If your backyard is new, it will have few features, so you can start your design with a clean slate. If it has been designed already, a plan will help you to note all the existing features and defects.

The design process has the great advantage of encouraging you to look carefully at your backyard and understand its characteristics, such as its shape and slope. It also enables you to identify which features you can work with and which aspects you want to change completely. It helps you to understand such things as the

OPPOSITE **The materials used in this low-maintenance design integrate the house and the garden.**

backyard's micro-climates, its strengths and weaknesses and areas in which problems such as poor drainage could arise. A plan will help you to maximise space, sun and shade and take into account the effect of the different seasons.

What style?

It's important to spend time deciding the particular style you want for your backyard. The style you choose should suit your lifestyle. It's as personal to you as the style of your house. Indoors we go to great lengths to decide on colour plans, where to place our furniture, objects and pictures; it's no different when it comes to the garden. Choosing your garden style is not simply about fashion – to be successful, it should fit in with your location and your needs. The style of your house will also influence the design of your backyard.

When choosing a style, you also need to consider whether you want to spend the weekend pottering in a cottage garden, or relaxing in a low-maintenance garden. Do you want a profusion of flowers, or do you want a contemporary minimalist look? Do you need to include areas for children, and how can you fit them into the style? If you live near the sea or bushland, you may wish to integrate the garden sympathetically into the landscape.

Take into consideration what already exists in your backyard, such as trees, fences, garden buildings and pathways, in order to determine how or if they can be fitted into your style.

INSET   A water feature is the centre of attention and has a cooling effect in this hot-climate garden.

BELOW   This courtyard is ideal for entertaining because there is easy access from the house.

Your climate will also affect the style of your garden. For instance, if you live in a tropical climate, you may want a tranquil retreat with an informal jungle mix of exotic plants. On the other hand, you may favour a shady, formal area. In hot, dry climates you may prefer a Mediterranean style with a cooling water feature and waterwise plants.

Much entertaining is done in Australian backyards, so thought should be given to how barbecue and entertaining areas will combine with the style you choose. If you select a Mediterranean style, for instance, you could add a water feature and surround your entertaining area with potted citrus and lavender.

Mixing styles

There is no reason why you can't mix your styles. A mixture of styles is often what gives a backyard its originality. You might decide, for example, to have a formal design with neatly clipped hedges but plant the garden beds behind the hedges informally. A formal design does not always suit the needs of children, so you can compromise by having a formal area around the house with a clipped hedge separating the children's play area. Another approach is to have a formal look near the house, which becomes progressively less formal as you move away from the building. The main point is to have a balance between the styles.

Staying realistic

It's important that the style suits your lifestyle. There is no point choosing a formal style with neat edges, expanses of lawn and clipped hedges if you do not have the time or inclination to maintain it.

A formal style can, however, look good with a period house, as it can reinforce the architectural style. A formal style is perfect for backyards that can be viewed from an upstairs window or a deck, as the outlines are clean, uncluttered and calm.

Don't be fooled into thinking that an informal style means no maintenance. Even informal gardens need to be looked after to achieve their natural look or they can degenerate into an untidy mess. If you are an avid gardener and love collecting plants, an informal style might suit you best, as it will accommodate a wide range of plants.

Outdoor living

Your backyard is your sanctuary, your space and your quiet escape from the pressures of urban existence. After all, gardens are for people as well as plants. No matter whether it's a small courtyard or a typical suburban block, you should see it as an extension of your house that provides an important visual link with nature.

If you think of your backyard as a room, it makes the concept of planning more approachable. We plan each room of a house separately, so it is logical to have a plan for your outdoor room too.

The first question you should ask yourself is: 'What do I want from this room?' Do you want a place where you can eat, read, potter, admire a view or simply watch your children play? Or do you have the space to make a variety of different rooms? Once you have identified your objectives, it's much easier to start making the backyard a pleasant place to live in.

Any time you spend initially planning your backyard will save you time and money at a later date.

A lawn provides space for children's games.

Planning your backyard

Planning is the most exciting part of designing a backyard. A plan enables you to really study your backyard and become well acquainted with its particular characteristics, so that you can use them to their best advantage. You can examine what you have, what you need or what you may improve upon. It encourages you to assess how you and your family want to spend time in it. Planning will ensure that you avoid making mistakes that may prove costly and that you get the most out of your backyard in future years.

What do you have?

Whether you are starting your backyard from scratch or redesigning an existing garden, it's important to look at what you have already. Consider the existing layout carefully before you remove anything, as you may be able to include some things in your design. With a plan, you can integrate the garden into the landscape so that it's sympathetic with its surroundings and with your needs.

Make a list of existing trees, shrubs and perennials and note their health. Trees and large shrubs form the backbone of the backyard and give it a head start, so don't remove any unnecessarily – often careful pruning, feeding and watering can restore a sick-looking plant to good health. If you have any native plants in the garden, try to leave them to encourage wildlife corridors for indigenous species.

After all, there is nothing better than a garden that attracts birds, butterflies and beneficial insects.

If your house is in a new subdivision with no trees, you will have to start from scratch. But this is not all bad, as you can choose trees to suit your particular purposes and style.

Add to the list all the hard elements such as walls, paving, paths, pool, pergolas and sheds. You can then decide what you want to keep and what needs repositioning or extending.

Include natural site features such as rock outcrops, slopes, banks and changes of level in your design. They can offer scope for retaining walls, decking and terraces. Natural damp areas can be turned into bog gardens rather than paying for expensive drainage. There are some beautiful moisture-loving plants for such conditions.

OPPOSITE **Choosing your garden style is not simply about fashion – to be successful the style should fit in with your needs.**

Planning considerations

☐ Ring the Telstra 'Dial before you dig' phone number (1100 throughout Australia) to establish the position of water, sewerage, electricity and gas services, and the location of your underground telephone cable.

☐ Check your title deed for easements. In some states an easement can be planted over but not built upon.

☐ Check with your local council for permission before removing any trees. Many trees are protected because of their size, species or historical value and hefty fines can be incurred if they are removed illegally.

What do you want to achieve?

Now you have had a look at what your backyard has to offer, you have to start thinking about what you want to achieve and what you want to introduce into the backyard. It's also time to start compiling your design and planning checklist (see page 91). There are certain considerations that need to be taken into account at this stage.

Whether your garden is brand new or old and overgrown, don't rush in too quickly. You and your family should get the feel of it and formulate ideas. You should also take into account any circumstances and needs that might change. For example, there may be further additions to the family that will require a larger play area. Later, as your children grow up, you might replace the sandpit with a hard surface and a basketball ring or extend the area for rollerblading and skateboarding. Finally, once the children have left home, new plans to integrate this area into the garden – budget permitting – could be made.

Remember that the money you have available for projects may vary over time, so if you don't have funds for your desired summerhouse now, perhaps you will in a few years' time. You may also be able to add a swimming pool at a later date.

Your backyard should work the way you want it to, look good and involve you in no more work than you are prepared to put in. Once you have decided on the key features, you have to consider what you need to do to make the changes possible.

RIGHT A low-maintenance backyard will enable you to spend more time relaxing or entertaining.

BELOW This garden features a vegetable and herb garden surrounded by paving instead of lawn.

Lifestyle

Your backyard should be designed around your lifestyle and how much time you want to spend maintaining your garden. If you are a keen gardener and plan to spend a lot of time in it, then more time-consuming plans for such things as vegetables and herbs are feasible. If, however, you are a busy family, and you wish to spend your time relaxing or entertaining, a low-maintenance garden is more appropriate. Consider how much lawn you require and how long it will take to maintain it. Perhaps paved areas, which require little maintenance, would be more suitable.

You must also consider how much space you have. For example, do you have space for a swimming pool or to divide the garden into both an adults' and a children's area?

Design and planning checklist

What you need to consider for your plan:

- [ ] Boundary fences for privacy or enclosure
- [ ] Level changes
- [ ] Easements
- [ ] Services (overhead and underground) – electricity, gas, water, telephone
- [ ] Soil type – pH, structure, texture and fertility (see The soil on pages 223–7)
- [ ] Drainage (boggy or badly drained areas?)
- [ ] Micro-climates/prevailing winds
- [ ] Privacy/views – blocking unsightly views or overlooking neighbours; taking advantage of good borrowed views
- [ ] Easy access from backyard to house
- [ ] Utility areas – clothes line, compost heap/bin, storage shed, car access, space for caravan/boat, rubbish/recycling bins, dog run/kennel
- [ ] Courtyard or other sitting area in the sun/shade
- [ ] Barbecue
- [ ] Lighting
- [ ] Children's play area
- [ ] Lawns
- [ ] Paths (wide enough for mower/wheelbarrow) and steps
- [ ] Vegetable/herb garden
- [ ] Irrigation – watering system
- [ ] Arch, pergola or arbour
- [ ] Summerhouse or gazebo
- [ ] Garden furniture
- [ ] Swimming pool/tennis court
- [ ] Water feature
- [ ] Summer shade, winter sun
- [ ] Access to the backyard during and after construction
- [ ] Future house extension plans – impact on garden design?
- [ ] Whether to build the backyard immediately or in stages

Entertaining areas

Most Australians spend time socialising outdoors, so it's important to choose the right spot for entertaining. This should be close to the house and, if you have young children to keep an eye on, overlooking the play area. Perhaps you already have an existing entertaining area but it needs extending because it is not large enough. Or do you want to lounge on a sunny deck overlooking the garden? A deck is a good solution for an outdoor entertaining area, as it links well to most house styles.

If you have or are planning a swimming pool, why not combine your entertaining area with the swimming pool? You should also consider whether your entertaining area will need to be screened from neighbouring properties in order to ensure privacy.

Children's areas

For a backyard to work successfully, both children's and adults' areas need to be taken into consideration. Play areas should be partially shaded to prevent damage to children's skin. A tree can offer shade for children's areas and provide branches for climbing. You can site the cubby house and swing under trees where it is difficult for lawn to grow. You could even divide the area with a hedge or trellis so that older children can have a 'secret garden' all to themselves.

If you plan to build play equipment, then a soft surface is needed. Bark chips, leaf mould or grass are all suitable. Keep in mind that children's needs change as they grow up – so think about how you can use that play area at a later date.

Paved paths can offer areas of hard surfaces for tricycles, scooters,

Skilful use of paving and hedging integrates the layout of the entertaining area and the swimming pool.

rollerblades and skateboards. A basketball ring can be installed for additional entertainment.

Family circumstances change over time, of course. For example, the large lawn area needed by children when they are young might not be used as frequently when they are older. With some foresight, you can design your backyard so that eventually part of the lawn could become a pond when the children have grown up.

Privacy

Privacy needs depend on your temperament. Some people don't care at all about privacy, while others dislike anyone seeing into their backyard. New gardens will often be dominated by fences and other houses and there may not be a tree in sight. You can always add height to the fence for greater privacy by planting tall shrubs in front of it or by using climber-covered trellis.

An important consideration is the degree to which neighbours' houses look into your backyard. Often a well-placed evergreen tree or large shrub will mask these houses from your view. A climber-covered pergola over an entertaining area can provide privacy from people looking down on you. This approach is especially suitable for small city gardens.

Utility areas

Most gardens need space for a clothes line, sometimes a compost heap or bin, storage shed, vehicles, rubbish and recycling bins, and a dog kennel or run; areas to accommodate these should be given consideration at this stage. If you have the space, you can design a special utility area to contain all or some of these things. The area can be concealed with a climber-covered trellis or hedge.

Clothes line

There is no need to place your clothes line in the middle of the backyard, so try to conceal it in a sunny corner. If space is limited and it's impossible to hide your clothes line, consider buying one that can be taken out when needed and tucked away at other times.

Lattice can be used to provide privacy and will also act as a host for climbing plants.

Compost

Ideally every household should try to recycle vegetable matter and, while well-made compost doesn't smell or attract flies, there is no getting away from the fact that a compost heap is unattractive. Position your compost heap in a warm, shaded position beside your garage, tucked away in the corner of a vegetable garden or behind a trellis screen covered with climbing peas or beans. Keep in mind that there has to be enough room to be able to 'work' and turn the heap. Alternatively, you can buy plastic bins that take up less space (see also Compost on pages 288–90).

Storage

Gardeners require space to store lawnmowers, wheelbarrows, garden tools, seeds and potting mixtures. You can either build your own shed or buy one of the many kit sheds available. Position it where there is easy access for removal of tools. You can always screen it with trellis and climbers or tall shrubs.

You can also buy outdoor cupboards with adequate storage space that can be built onto a wall of your house or garage.

This shed has been screened from the garden by a clipped hedge.

Vehicles

Most householders drive cars and some may also have to find room for bicycles, a trailer, a caravan and even a boat. If you have all or some of these vehicles, you will need to assess the area required to park or store them before finalising your plans for the driveway and garage.

If you park your trailer, caravan or car in the backyard, you can cleverly disguise the area with trellis or shrubs. Carports can be covered in climbers to integrate them into the garden.

In small city gardens you can make your car space double as an entertaining area by removing the car to the street during the weekends. If you park at the rear of your property, you can screen off an area to hide the car and other necessary utilities.

Pets

Pets are much loved members of the household and their spaces should be included in your design. Does your dog need a kennel, or would you like it to have its own run? If you have the space for ducks or chickens, you will have to check with your local council so that a

structure can be built to meet their requirements. If you have guinea-pigs and rabbits, remember to add space in your plan for their hutches.

Swimming pools

A swimming pool can become the focus of your outdoor living area. Take time to think about where you will place it in your design. It needs to be sited in a sunny area, unless you live in a very hot climate where sun is not as important. Prevailing winds and shade from buildings and trees must be considered also. Try to site your swimming pool away from large trees that will shed leaves into it.

There should be adequate space (at least 1.5 m) around the pool and visibility from the kitchen or living room may be desirable. Pumps and filter equipment are noisy and unattractive, so place them where they are not visible or heard by you or your neighbours. They can be screened easily with a low hedge, trellis or mixed planting.

Designing for your aspect

The aspect of your house determines the amount of sun the backyard receives. While south-facing backyards receive little sun, backyards to the north enjoy sun for the best part of the day. East-facing backyards receive morning sun, while those facing west receive the full heat of the afternoon sun. Understanding the aspect helps you decide the type of backyard you can make and the appropriate choice of plants. In hot climates shade is desirable, but in cold or temperate climates trees blocking the sun's path can cast shadows that restrict plant growth and give the garden a cold feeling.

ABOVE   This swimming pool can be viewed from the entertaining area.

LEFT   Brick arches divide the spa from the pool. The formal look suits the contemporary style of the garden.

Types of shade

Shade cast from a building or wall is permanent and the most difficult to come to terms with because it is dense and solid. It's usually found in south-facing backyards and passageways that have tall walls and fences. There are fewer plants suitable for this type of shade.

Dense shade caused by tree foliage is easy to change by altering or thinning the heads of the offending trees. Thus deep shade can become light, medium or dappled shade.

Dappled shade is the lightest shade category and is also the type of shade that provides the widest range of gardening possibilities.

There are two varieties of shade determined by location – damp shade and dry shade. Different micro-climates can exist side by side. Damp shade, which generally receives no sun and always has moist soil, can co-exist with dry shade, which is found under eaves and close to buildings.

The ideal aspect for outdoor living is one facing north or north-east. You will receive winter and summer sun but can provide summer shade with a deciduous tree, umbrella or awning. Or why not have a pergola running across your outdoor living area covered with a deciduous climber? Trees and vines let in breezes and cool the air through their constant transpiration.

Micro-climates

The many climatic variations that occur in a garden are called micro-climates. Factors creating these micro-climates include exposure to sun, proximity to ponds and pools, prevailing winds, building structures, plants, slopes and other topographical variations.

Consider the example of a house built on a block of land running north–south – a warm, sunny area facing north will be created, contrasting with a shaded area on the south side of the house. Trees, walls or fences also influence the distribution of sunlight and shade and the force of prevailing winds. The ground surface can absorb or reflect heat. Water in a pool reflects light and stabilises the temperature of the air around it. The degree to which this occurs varies according to the size of the pool.

Understanding the various micro-climates in your garden gives you the option of altering them and using them to your advantage. Following are four basic micro-climate factors that should be considered if you are to make the most of your site.

Shade

Shade occurs in every garden where there is a large plant or structure and always deserves special consideration. Shade alters the air and soil temperature, especially in dry areas, and often results in a humidity increase. Shade also dictates the use of particular plants.

Reflected heat from the pavers and house wall make this an ideal warm spot to grow herbs and vegetables.

Although shade is a general word for any darkening effect, the discriminating gardener should become aware of different types of shade (see box on page 96). One should understand differences in the quality of light, the reasons for such differences and the effect they have on the soil.

Sun

Once you have determined where sunlight falls on your property, you will have a much more accurate idea of how to design your backyard. Distribution of sunlight is equally important for people and plants. For outdoor living you may want full sun in the early morning, but you may also require shade in the same spot for lunch. When siting a swimming pool, the angle of the sun has to be given full consideration.

There is nothing better than deciduous vines or trees for providing summer shade and winter sun. This is worth considering when siting entertainment areas.

Temperature

Materials such as bitumen, concrete, stone and brick absorb a great deal of heat during the day and release it at night.

The darker the surface, the more heat that will be absorbed. In cold climates brick walls facing the sun have been used for centuries to espalier semi-tropical fruit that otherwise would be impossible to grow.

Sun and shade during the year

The sun is much lower in the sky in winter than in summer, and you may find that a south-facing spot with some sun in January is totally shaded in July. The amount of sun or shade available all year round is particularly important when it comes to deciding what to plant.

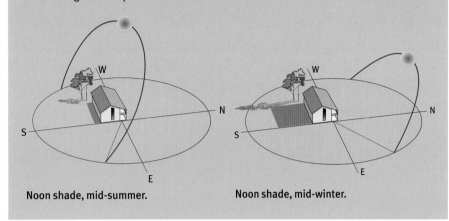

Noon shade, mid-summer.   Noon shade, mid-winter.

A large body of water, such as that found in a swimming pool, helps to maintain a fairly constant temperature by reducing the extremes of air temperature in its immediate vicinity. On the other hand, a small ornamental garden pond will quickly absorb the heat of the sun.

Wind

A windy garden makes it difficult for plants to grow and is unpleasant to sit in. Contrary to popular opinion, a solid windbreak is not the best type. The most efficient windbreak has equal proportions of solid sections and voids. This causes the velocity of wind to be reduced, while the turbulence created by the solid obstruction is avoided.

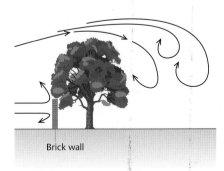

Brick wall

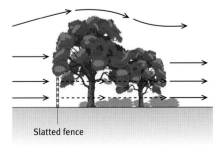

Slatted fence

LEFT   Solid barriers such as trees with dense foliage, brick walls and paling fences, create turbulence on both sides of the windbreak.

RIGHT   Trees and shrubs with light foliage and a slatted fence filter the wind and reduce its speed.

Backyard design basics

Before drawing up your design plan, there are a few important backyard design principles to consider. There are conditions and rules as there are for any other pattern. Understanding the way shapes relate to each other is at the heart of backyard design. A backyard that is well proportioned is harmonious and balanced. Good design depends on using everything to your advantage. Your backyard and the elements you have in it should suit the style of your house and your lifestyle. Fortunately, the process is much more straightforward than you think.

Correct perspectives

When you finally draw up your backyard plan (see Drawing a plan on page 105) keep in mind that, although you are showing everything from a bird's-eye view, you must also visualise the perspectives from eye level. Often sweeping curves made on a graph will look too excessive when seen from eye level, and will need to be drawn less dramatically. Curves should always flow smoothly with changes of direction and not look too obvious. Two important design rules when drawing paths are that lines that diverge as they run away from the eye lessen the sense of distance, while lines that converge make the path look even longer.

There is a practical method for overcoming any perspective problems that may arise after you have outlined the basic layout on paper. Simply mark out the courtyard, paths and garden beds with a length of string, hose or a line of lime or sand. You will then be able to stand back and get the feel of the path or courtyard from different points of view.

Garden shapes

The size and shape of your backyard will determine your garden's pattern to some extent. Long and narrow, rectangular, square, circular or triangular backyards all need to be handled differently.

Tricks with shape

- Long and narrow or rectangular backyards can be made into a series of rooms that you walk through. Divide the rooms by using trellis or hedges. Walking from one room into another creates an element of surprise. For example, one room as the

OPPOSITE   This informal design relies on lush, colourful plantings for its effect. The path beckons you to explore further.

adults' area, one as the children's and one for vegetables.

- You can change the space in square backyards by having the design at 45 degrees to the boundary.
- Circular designs within a square block work well, as do rectangular designs.
- Triangular backyards can be treated simply as such. Rectangles and circles also work well in triangular designs.

Ground patterns

Backyard design is also about patterns and the spaces within the patterns. The character of the garden will depend on its underlying pattern. The curves of garden paths and beds help create this pattern. Gardens are not static as they inspire movement. It's the passage you make through them that makes gardens a delight to be in.

The ground pattern of your garden will depend on various

LEFT   Circular and rectangular designs within a square look good.

RIGHT   Movement can be created in a small, square courtyard by a change of direction. Decking is ideal for creating this effect.

BELOW   A long, narrow backyard can be made into a series of rooms.

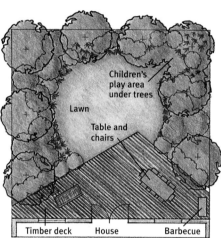

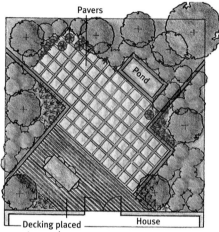

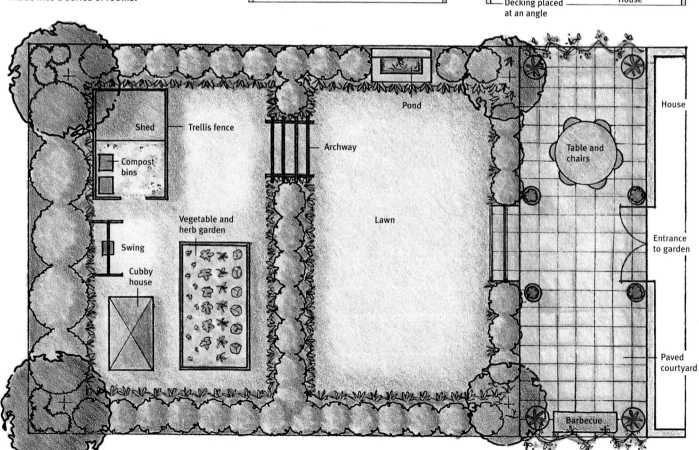

factors, including the shape and size of your land, existing features, and how you want to use your space. Do you want more paving than grass? Do you prefer wandering paths or straight lines? Keep in mind that paths and paving make up the garden's framework and connect its main areas.

Formal gardens are based on symmetrical patterns in which one part of the garden mirrors the other. They are often laid out on a central axis with plants outlining the garden's pattern. On the other hand, informal ground patterns are based on asymmetric patterns with paths winding around the garden.

The ground pattern can be a series of circular shapes, rectangles or squares. Your paths may be ornate and features of the garden or they may be subtle and unobtrusive.

Combining house and garden

Your first step is to establish a link between indoors and outdoors. Taking note of what you see of your backyard from the inside is very important. This will provide you with clues for focal points and vistas, while ensuring that your design will reveal itself from indoors.

First, consider which rooms you use the most, as creating appealing views from these is critical. Think about what your backyard will look like from your dining or living areas, kitchen or bedroom. Can you position a statue, specimen tree, water feature, gazebo or arch where it can be viewed as a focal point? Or do you want to block an ugly view? Do you want to be able

Smart tip

Large gardens with sweeping paths and garden beds can have considerable movement within them. This movement invites you to walk around the garden with the paths leading to a point of interest, view or seating area. On the other hand, small gardens do not need as much movement and should attempt to keep the eye contained within the garden.

An ornate path is the main feature in this small garden.

ABOVE   There is a natural flow from indoors to outdoors in this garden. The waterfall that trickles down the sloping garden is the focal point and also produces a relaxing sound.

RIGHT   Double doors provide easy access to this courtyard. The house walls and paving blend well together. Large pots of cycads add detail.

to keep the children in sight? And don't restrict your plan to the daytime – consider lighting that will highlight a feature tree or statue in the garden during the evening.

It's also important to consider the position of the main access to the backyard. There should be a natural flow from indoors to outdoors. For instance, using paving outside a kitchen or dining/living room will help extend the indoor room into the outdoor room. If you don't have direct access to your backyard (for example, some homes enter the backyard through the laundry), you may have to rethink some aspects of the design of your house. Could you change a window for a door to create better access to the garden? Perhaps French doors could provide improved access and a stronger visual link.

If the style of your backyard is influenced by the style of your house, the backyard will not look like an afterthought. Consider

what sort of exterior paving will link with or be suited to the flooring that you have indoors. The colours you use should also be taken into consideration. If you have strong colours inside, you may wish to extend them outdoors, or perhaps you would prefer a quieter feel. Or would you like to use complementary colours outdoors?

Where possible, use similar or compatible materials to those used in the construction of the house. For example, if you have a timber house, build your gazebo or other structures out of timber.

If you have a contemporary house with an uncluttered look, then a similarly uncluttered look in the backyard will integrate both. On the other hand, a Federation house may be more suited to a pretty cottage garden with an arbour and a profusion of flowers. Many brick houses from the 1950s and 1960s lend themselves to a formal garden design.

ABOVE   A sundial surrounded by perfumed thyme makes a pretty focal point.

LEFT   A seat, cleverly placed at the end of the pathway as a focal point, beckons the passerby.

Focal points

When we decorate indoors, we use a feature as the focal point in the room. This could be a fireplace or a pleasant view from a window. A focal point is just as important in the garden. You may already have such a focal point, such as a beautiful borrowed view around which you can build the garden, a neighbour's tree or a shapely tree in your own garden.

If you don't have an existing focal point, you will have to create your own – a well-placed seat, large urn, gazebo, arch, sculpture, water feature or gate, for example. When you create your own, take into consideration the views from windows, doorways and urban courtyards.

Your focal point should be an integral part of your design. You can make it a feature at the end of a path, or you might like it to create an element of surprise as you turn around a corner or hedge. Or perhaps your backyard is large enough to have several focal points.

Borrowed views

Take note of distant views or neighbours' trees, which can be 'borrowed' and fitted into your garden's design. Borrowing landscape in this way leads the eye from the immediate garden area to the surrounding area and then back again. This has the psychological effect of counteracting boundaries and making small gardens appear large. Sometimes by judicious pruning you can open up the view to reveal a larger panorama. An advantage of borrowing surrounding views is that you can use established trees and shrubs for no cost.

A view can also be framed by a group of trees or shrubs. Framing a view allows you to control the parts of it you wish to see. Pathways may also lead to views, creating an element of surprise at the end of a stroll. A seat or gazebo encourages you to sit and enjoy the view. It can also be framed by a carefully positioned arbour or pergola.

Drawing a plan

Putting pen to paper is an important step in designing your ideal backyard. Don't be alarmed at the thought of drawing plans, however, as you can execute adequate drawings with no formal training. These drawings will allow you to have a thorough understanding of what is involved in creating your backyard and will also ensure that you make the most of every bit of space – whether your backyard is a small courtyard, country garden or an urban block. This chapter takes you through all the steps in a simple, straightforward way.

How to begin

The first step in the design process is to obtain a site plan of your land, including the house if it already exists. Your title deeds should include a site plan, usually drawn to a scale of 1:200. An architect's or builder's plan can also serve as a basis.

If you can't access an existing site plan, you can measure the garden yourself. First measure the boundaries – the length and width of the yard – and then measure the house itself. You will also need to measure the spaces between the walls of the house and the boundaries.

Make an enlarged photocopy of your site plan to give you a scale of 1:100 (1 cm = 1 m), which should be enough to work with. Or you can transfer the information to graph paper at a scale of 1:100. Graph paper will help to keep everything to scale. This enlarged site plan forms the framework of your design.

It's a good idea to have a few copies of the enlarged site plan so that you don't have to worry about making mistakes. A better alternative is to purchase some tracing-paper that you can put over the site plan. This allows you to draw different ideas and try different garden concepts – it's unlikely that your initial ideas will be the same as those you finally use.

A scale ruler – with up to six different scales allowing measurement of 60 m or more – is a worthwhile investment.

The base plan

The following guidelines relate to land with an existing house and certain other features already in

Tools

- Pencils (2H for accurate lines, HB for looser work, 2B for sketching)
- Rubber
- Scale ruler
- Compass for drawing circles and making templates
- Set square for angles
- Tape measure

Materials

- Fresh copy of the site plan enlarged to 1:100 (1 cm = 1 m)
- Tracing-paper for overlays
- Drawing board or substitute (a table will do)
- Tape to stick paper to board and table

place, but the same principles apply if the house is still at the planning stage.

The site plan should show essential features such as fences, services and easements. Mark any trees you are retaining for personal or legal reasons by drawing a solid dot for each trunk, and then draw wavy-edged circles around these dots to represent the canopies. Any attractive, healthy shrubs should also be marked on the plan.

Don't draw any items that might be moved. You may be able to relocate the clothes line, for example, if there is sufficient sun available elsewhere in the backyard.

Gather any further information about the site in a notebook under headings such as sun, shade, slope, wind, views, privacy and wet areas. Make a site analysis using this information by adding the north point to your plan, and then mark sunny areas and areas that are shady most of the time (including those shaded by neighbours' trees or buildings), wind directions, pleasant and unpleasant views, drainage problems and land contours.

The activity plan

This plan is intended to plot the lifestyle of your family. To prepare it, take a pencil and a fresh copy of the site plan. Then copy key elements of the base plan, such as the position of trees and shrubs, and circle and note present or planned areas of activity. You can experiment with positioning by simply rubbing out and replacing these areas.

If you prefer, you can use paper templates with names written on them. These can be taped to the plan to represent different areas of activity – you can move them around until you are satisfied. If you are starting with a bare block, you will have to give the activity plan considerable thought. The important thing to remember is that the activity plan must be tailored to suit your requirements.

Allocating space

Examine the amount of space allowed for each area. Discussion among household members will be needed so that everyone is happy and agrees with the desired outcomes.

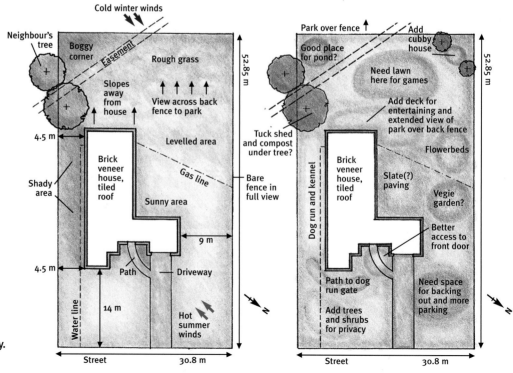

LEFT Your base plan reflects your site in detail.

RIGHT Your activity plan should show the needs and aspirations of your family.

Try to avoid having too many small activity areas in close proximity. Double up if there are problems. For example, the paved area intended for entertaining can have a netball or basketball ring installed at the side, or it can also be used for bike-riding and rollerblading. Consider the size of the activity spaces in relation to each other and to the backyard areas as a whole. This will enable you to decide whether the proportions are reasonable.

Access

Make sure that the driveway and any paths are in the best places. Is there easy access from the front to the backyard? Sometimes a front path and a driveway extending to the backyard are combined, and you are forced to squeeze past cars to reach the house. A separate path is a better option.

Special elements

Positions for water features, lighting, walls, trellises, pergolas and other such items can be added to the basic activity plan. You can incorporate them into spaces that are already allocated. You may be able to direct a floodlight towards feature trees, for example, or you can adapt something that is already in place. A waterfall could be introduced to flow over a retaining wall and into a pond below.

The final plan

When you have mapped out your activity areas to some extent, you should collate design ideas and include them in the final plan. Now that you have specific necessary site information, you can use some imagination and create your own spaces. By using geometry, the loose activity shapes can become more specific.

If you like formal designs, you may choose a pattern in which most lines are straight and either parallel or at right angles to each other. If your taste is informal, you may prefer to incorporate curves or diagonals, which will create more movement in the design. You can add interest by visualising some of the areas in the plan as intersecting circles and other shapes.

Draw in the shapes you have developed from the elements in your activity plan. Check the general appearance of the shapes as you draw them, as they must blend with the character of both new and existing features. Try to maintain the overall scale when including items such as tables, chairs, barbecues and water features, and label the various areas.

Remember to indicate on the plan the finishes you have in mind. You may, for example, have chosen brick for the walls, gravel for paving and lattice for screens. Because there is such a wide range of materials available, you may prefer to do more research before making final decisions.

Smart tip

Computer software is available to help you design your garden. Some are realistic 3-D garden design programs that include libraries of trees, shrubs, annuals, groundcovers and even outdoor furniture. Make sure the program you choose is in metric as many from the United States are in inches and it can be difficult to convert measurements.

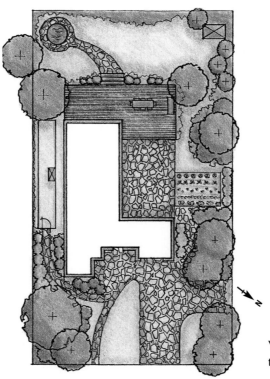

Your final plan should have all the details on it.

Difficult areas

Not everyone is blessed with a flat backyard and perfect growing conditions – most blocks slope to

a certain extent. But you can still make the most of whatever conditions you happen to have and

create a beautiful backyard. This chapter shows you how to transform steep slopes into interesting

terraces, and how to decorate narrow, shady areas. You can turn damp spaces into beautiful bog

gardens, and you will be surprised how easy it is to garden in hot, dry areas using the right plants.

There is also no need to feel limited by small areas, as there are tricks to create the illusion of space.

Sloping blocks

Most blocks slope to a certain extent and it is not unusual for new home owners to get a surprise when they decide to start a garden and find they need retaining walls for areas they thought were almost level.

A sloping site probably offers more interesting possibilities than a flat one. For example, it can be host to many garden features, including rock gardens, terraces, rock outcrops and water projects such as waterfalls, cascades and ponds. Although a steeply sloping site usually needs more earthworks than a flat one, the visual effects created by adding garden features will more than reward you for the effort.

You may need to create flat, outdoor living areas and have retaining walls and steps built (plans for retaining walls more than 1 m high need to be submitted to your local council for approval). A series of flattened areas, one below the other, can be terraced (see diagram next page). You can cut soil from the surface to lower the level of the land (diagram 1) or add soil to fill a dip (diagram 2). An efficient way to grade is the 'cut and fill' method – soil removed from the higher section is pushed forward to raise the surface below the cut (diagram 3). The latter procedure means that you are making good use of your own soil, rather than having it totally removed, which can be very expensive. A retaining wall is often built to hold the vertical edge of each cut.

If, however, the amount of soil to be retained is not great, you can make the transition from one 'landing' to the next by a series of banks. Allow your slopes to flow gently into one another. One terrace can be linked to another by a few steps or a ramp.

OPPOSITE   **This terraced retaining wall adds an interesting pattern to the garden. Plants in the bottom terrace soften the wall.**

Three ways to grade your slope

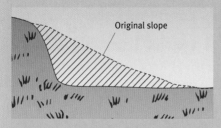

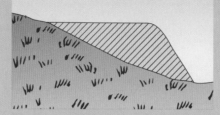

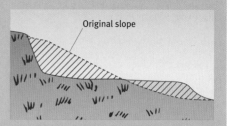

1   Removing soil from the slope and leaving a steep cut to be faced with a retaining wall.

2   Adding soil for an embankment on which to plant.

3   Cutting and filling: combining two procedures to reduce the steepness of a slope.

Smart tip

When cutting and filling, the soil beneath the cut is stable because it's already well compacted, but areas of fill are relatively unstable until the soil has been allowed to settle. Although you will need to allow plenty of time for the soil to settle, you can speed up the process by trampling the ground from time to time (for large jobs, hire compacting equipment).

Where steep slopes are treated as a series of terraces at right angles to the slope, space permitting, you could make one of these terraces wide enough for a lawn or sitting area. If you don't have a large budget, choose cheap, concrete blocks or the like for retaining walls and cover them with trailing plants or climbers.

You can take advantage of the natural contours of a block of land by building retaining walls to follow their shape. The retaining walls can also work as edging for garden beds. Using this approach will save time and money as very little earthworks will need to be carried out.

Drainage

Drainage needs to be considered carefully on a sloping site, especially if you are undertaking earthworks. If you are building retaining walls made from bricks, concrete or concrete blocks, ensure you incorporate correct drainage (see Installing drainage pipes on page 141) to avoid pressure against the wall from water build-up. Check with your local council before building a retaining wall of any size.

Retaining walls constructed from railway sleepers, treated logs, crib systems, interlocking systems and dry-stone walls allow water to run through and therefore do not need drainage.

A sloping garden has many possibilities. In this garden, feature stone walls surround the entertaining area. Steps lead you further into the garden.

The use of light-coloured gravel helps give the illusion of widening narrow passageways. The blue walls make a delightful backdrop for Japanese maples and ferns.

Narrow, shady areas

Many old terrace houses, townhouses and even new houses or small urban blocks have a narrow passageway running down the side of the house. Some of these are actually entries into houses. These areas need not be dull and lifeless, as there are many design techniques that can brighten them up.

You can, for example, make a focal point at the end of a passageway – a dramatic sculpture, a water feature, a large urn or, for those with an artistic touch, a *trompe l'oeil*. A simple, inexpensive and effective touch can be created by some white pebbles surrounding a water bowl.

You can widen the appearance of the area with a pathway of white gravel, pavers or pebbles and low-growing plants on each side of the path. These plants will draw the eye from side to side and give the path more breadth. A clipped hedge of Japanese box (*Buxus microphylla* var. *japonica*) or pots of box will provide evergreen foliage.

You can erect a pergola over the area to provide privacy if it is possible for neighbours to look down into your passageway. Grow a climber over the pergola and attach hanging baskets to the beams.

Adjoining walls

If your narrow passageway has an adjoining boundary wall or tall building, this can produce a rather unpleasant 'chasm' effect. To overcome this, you can paint the wall a light colour or you can brighten it up with a climber. Attach chicken wire or trellis and grow an evergreen such as Chinese star jasmine (*Trachelospermum jasminoides*) on it. Chinese star jasmine's glossy, evergreen foliage looks good throughout the year, especially when covered in its white, perfumed, late-spring and summer flowers. Camellias can also be espaliered on the wall or pruned to form a tall, narrow hedge in front of it.

Plants for shady passageways

- Acanthus
- Aspidistra
- Bergenia
- Clivia
- Coleus
- Dietes
- Hosta
- Liriope
- Lobelia
- Lomandra
- Ophiopogon

Dealing with shade

- Damp, densely shaded soil can become dank and sour because the circulation of the air is restricted. This is easily corrected by turning the soil a couple of times. Leave a break of at least a week between each turn to allow air circulation.

- Shaded soil often becomes very acidic but is easy to check with a soil-testing kit.

- The soil in shaded areas is often lacking in nutrients and needs supplements of fertilisers. Mulches of cow or chicken manure and compost are ideal as they attract earthworms, which in turn help to aerate the soil. As the mulches break down they also add structure to the soil, encouraging better drainage. This is most important in dry, shaded areas as organic matter will help to retain moisture.

- If a tree has a mass of surface roots that make growing conditions difficult, you can always limit your plants to containers.

Succulents are ideal plants for dry gardens.

Hot, dry gardens

Do you live in a climate that receives little rain and experiences extremes of hot weather? Don't despair, as there are many plants – especially low-water-use perennials – that thrive in such conditions.

If you have the space, plant trees for a cooling effect – there are plenty of trees that suit hot, dry conditions, such as *Schinus molle* and *Amelia azederach*. The best are often those that are indigenous to your area. There are also many other trees, shrubs and perennials that do not require a lot of water, so ask your local nursery. Pergolas attached to the house or free-standing pergolas covered in climbers can add shade.

Don't bother with lawns in hot, dry areas as they can be a waste of money and water. An alternative is to grow ornamental grasses that require little water such as *Festuca glauca*, *Helictotrichon sempervirens* or *Lomandra* species. These grasses make effective tall lawn subjects. Better still, try to find a grass indigenous to your area.

You could also make a gravel or pebble garden and plant low-water-use perennials and succulents. Use large stepping stones as pathways through the gravel or pebbles. Many herbs thrive in dry conditions and can be planted in gravel gardens. Consider using sage, thyme, golden oregano, oregano, rosemary and lavender, all of which have culinary uses.

A water feature is also a must for hot, dry areas. Water has a cooling effect, especially the sound of running water.

A drip-irrigation system on garden beds will deliver water to where it is needed without waste.

ABOVE   This hot, dry garden relies on succulents for form and foliage shapes. A mulch of pebbles prevents the soil losing moisture through evaporation.

LEFT   Gravel gardens planted with ornamental grasses are ideal for hot, dry areas.

Give plants a deep watering once a week, rather than a little each day. As plants mature, gradually reduce the frequency of watering. Learn to identify when plants require water by noting signs such as drooping leaves and flowers.

Mulching
Mulching is essential in hot, dry areas. Organic mulches have two important functions. They reduce the amount of moisture lost through evaporation and keep the soil cool during summer. They are also biodegradable, so continue to be of benefit even when they are breaking down.

Undemanding succulents
The popular emphasis on low-water-use gardening and a wonderful diversity of leaf shapes and colours have ensured the place of succulents in modern landscaping.

You can make some beautiful hot, dry garden beds with succulents and pebbles. Use the pebbles as a mulch and interplant with succulents. Place a few pots among the pebbles for height and interest. Their low water demands mean that they are the perfect container subjects for hot, dry areas.

Pot plants for dry areas
A good potting mix is the key to success with pot plants for hot, dry gardens. You can buy mixes for specific purposes, such as those formulated especially for terracotta pots.

Because of their porous nature, line the inside of terracotta and stone pots with black plastic. Don't line the bottom, however, or drainage will be impeded. Alternatively, you can spray with Pot-A-Seal™. Adding water storage granules to a mix will also promote water retention.

Succulents for hot, dry gardens

- *Aeonium* species
- *Agave attenuata*
- *Agave filifera*
- *Aloe* species
- *Echeveria* species
- *Kalanchoe* species
- *Sansevieria trifasciata*
- *Sedum* species
- *Sempervivum* species
- *Senecio serpens*
- *Yucca* species

Plants for damp areas

- Blue flag iris (*Iris orientalis*)
- Cardinal flower (*Lobelia cardinalis*)
- Drumstick primrose (*Primuladenticulata*)
- Elephant's ear (*Alocasia* species)
- Giant ornamental rhubarb (*Gunnera manicata*)
- Goat's beard (*Aruncus dioicus*)
- Japanese flag iris (*Iris ensata*)
- Louisiana hybrid iris
- Marsh marigold (*Caltha palustris*)
- Meadowsweet (*Filipendula ulmaria*)
- Plantain lily (*Hosta* species)
- Purple loosestrife (*Lythrum salicaria*)
- *Sanguisorba tenuifolia*
- Siberian flag iris (*Iris sibirica*)
- Tall sedge (*Carex apressa*)
- Tannia (*Xanthosoma sagittifolium*)
- Taro (*Colocasia* species)
- Tassel cord rush (*Restio tetraphyllus*)
- Tufted sedge (*Carex gaudichaudiana*)
- Yellow skunk cabbage (*Lysichiton americanus*)

Damp areas

How can an area of the backyard be one gardener's dream, while the same area is a nightmare for another gardener? This is often the case with damp areas. You can, of course, drain a damp area (see Drainage on page 110) and that can be the end of the problem. But you can also turn such an area into a feature spot and grow some wonderful moisture-loving plants.

You can also incorporate a pond into a damp area and could consider a stream leading to it. Some people actually channel water to areas in their garden, so that they can create a feature bog garden with attractive, colourful plants and foliage.

How to make a bog garden

If you have an overwhelming desire to grow moisture-loving plants but find yourself bogless, don't worry. Creating a bog or damp garden is quite easy. Simply dig out a section as if you were making a pond, keeping in mind that it has to be deep enough for large plants. Once you have done this, measure out a length of butyl pond liner or black plastic and cut it to size. Puncture the liner with a fork to provide drainage holes, which will prevent the soil from going sour. Lay the liner in the excavated area, and replace the soil. Firm down the soil and water it thoroughly before planting. Extra water usually needs to be added to the garden in very dry spells.

ABOVE   Some plants, such as *Iris ensata* and pink-flowering *Sanguisorba*, thrive in moist conditions.

RIGHT   In nature, damp-area plants occupy the transitional zone between a pool or stream and high ground.

Small backyards

The limitations imposed by small backyards are part of their appeal and also part of the challenge. In small areas details become important because any mistakes will be very obvious. Space should be carefully allocated and the selection of materials to be used is a major consideration. While you can't physically increase the space of a small garden, you can certainly employ a few visual tricks to create the illusion of space.

Small-backyard ideas

- Light paving creates the impression of space.
- A change of level – even if it's only one step – can produce the illusion that there are two gardens.
- Laying paving in a geometric pattern creates the illusion of lengthening and widening the space.
- Allocate more space to sitting and walking areas than to plants.
- Wide, raised beds look particularly good and provide extra sitting space.
- When you link the garden to the kitchen or family room, you break down the division between inside and outside and make the space appear larger.
- A pergola or arch can be used to introduce height into a small garden in situations where a tree may not be suitable.
- Don't use too many plants in small spaces. Because every centimetre of space counts, each plant should fulfil its purpose well. Limited space means that plants should be chosen for their year-round appeal. There is no point growing plants that flower for a couple of weeks and then look dull for the rest of the year. Make use of handsome foliage plants that hold their own throughout the year.

This small but well-balanced backyard allows for movement, seating and plants.

Improving your backyard

You may be lucky enough to have moved into a house with a well-established, beautiful backyard garden. But there is generally something in the garden that one wants to change. Perhaps the garden's tone does not suit your taste or maybe the outdoor living area needs to be enlarged to suit your family's needs. It may be too contrived and may need to be softened, or it may have too many – or not enough – trees. Or it could just need some simple additions, such as lighting, a walkway, bower or hedges to create a couple of garden rooms.

Evaluating a backyard

The main point to keep in mind is to be patient and wait until all the seasons pass so you can see what appears in each one. That uninteresting tree may burst into spring blossom and multitudes of bulbs may appear underneath it.

Make a list of all the aspects of the garden you are unhappy with in order of their irritation value. The checklist on the following page will help you to determine the current state of your backyard.

Restoring a garden

Before you do anything to your backyard, you need to assess your site, make a plan and mark all the trees, shrubs and elements on it (see Drawing a plan on pages 105–7). Place tracing paper over the top and try out different ideas. Once you have a finished plan and have added to it all the elements that fulfil your household's needs, you can decide which plants to keep and which to remove.

Pruning everything back in old, neglected backyards will often reveal a new picture. Don't be too quick to remove shrubs and trees as these form the backbone of the garden and it will take years to replace them. Instead of removing old fruit trees, for example, use them as supports for growing climbing roses or clematis.

Clearing pathways and steps will also help to reveal the framework of the backyard. Sometimes a simple trick, such as removing a straight path and replacing it with a more meandering one, can change the whole tone of the backyard. Pick out the features you like best in the backyard and build your new design around them.

OPPOSITE   A makeover need not cost the earth. Some paint, a new path and several new plants will make all the difference to your backyard.

A backyard makeover

Over the years you may find that your needs in relation to your backyard have changed. For example, your children may have grown up and don't use the backyard any more, so areas that were allocated to them can be altered to suit another purpose. Or you may simply be tired of the way your garden looks and want to introduce some new elements.

If your children have left home and you have more time to garden, you may wish to reduce that large expanse of lawn by extending garden beds. On the other hand, you may be tired of mowing the lawn and want to turn it into a lower maintenance gravel garden or large garden beds with paths in between.

If there is a children's area that is not used any more, now is the time to turn it into that pond you have always wanted but haven't built for safety reasons. Alternatively, you could surround the area with a clipped hedge and create a quiet reading or sitting room.

Make a site plan of the backyard (see How to begin on page 105) and, using tracing-paper overlays, allocate new elements to various positions until you get the required result.

Easy makeovers

Walkways and arbours

These add height to gardens and also create interesting focal points that pull the garden together. A pergola covering the length of a pathway and covered with climbing plants will transform the path. You can change the look of a seat by building a simple arbour around it and by painting both the same colour. Grow a perfumed climbing plant over the arbour to enhance the sensual pleasure.

You can make a simple walkway or bower by using large, lime-washed concrete plumbing pipes as supports for timber arches. Position the pipes upright on the edges of the walkway or bower, concrete them into place and attach timber across the top. Grow perfumed climbers over both pipes and timber.

A simple arch can add height to the garden. A perfumed rose climbing over it enhances the sensual pleasure.

Creating garden rooms

Using hedging to divide the backyard into different rooms can also change its look. Hedging can be used to break up a long, thin backyard, and a square backyard can be divided into four compartments with a fountain or sculpture as a centrepiece. You can also create a room for growing herbs and vegetables.

A touch of paint

Don't be afraid to use paint boldly in your makeover. Paint is cheap and can transform your garden. Paint wooden poles or garden stakes in bright red, blue or yellow and make tripods for upwardly mobile plants. Tripods provide support for small climbers such as sweet peas, edible peas or small climbing roses. If you prefer a more natural look, make tripods from wattle, willow, hazel, bamboo or anything that will stand on its own. Tie the structure together with wire.

Seats, pine table settings, arches, gates and pergolas come alive with a coat of paint.

Effective lighting

If you enjoy entertaining, seriously consider dressing up the backyard with outdoor lights. Correct placement of lighting will turn trees, shrubs and statuary into late evening and night features. If your budget doesn't extend to permanent outdoor lighting, make use of the many attractive candles or outdoor lanterns available. These can be hung from trees or placed around table settings.

Adding a seat

Often just placing a seat at the end of a path or in a central spot in the backyard can change the feel. The garden seat has a dual function – when it ceases to be a seat, it becomes part of the view and a feature in itself. The shape, size, colour and setting are important and should relate to the style of your garden. When locating a seat, take into account the view when you're sitting on it. A wooden seat built around the base of a large focal tree creates an alluring, shaded feature.

Perfumed climbers for walkways and bowers

Consider planting the climbing moonflower (*Ipomoea alba*) – its huge, 15 cm pure-white flowers unfold at dusk. Fragrant herald's trumpet (*Beaumontia grandiflora*) is another possible choice as it reaches a height of 8 m and produces large, white, trumpet-shaped flowers. The heavily perfumed white flowers of Madagascar jasmine (*Stephanotis floribunda*) contrast beautifully with its waxy, deep-green leaves. It grows best in partial shade and well-drained soil in a frost-free climate. You may also wish to consider summer flowering jasmines such as poet's jasmine (*Jasminum officinale*) and Arabian jasmine (*J. sambac*).

LEFT   A garden seat allows you to sit and enjoy your garden. The seat's bright-blue edges and colourful pots add a nice finishing touch.

BELOW   Thoughtful placement of lighting will extend the time you can remain outdoors.

Doing the groundwork

With the completed plans for your ideal backyard in hand, it's time to turn your dreams into reality. But where do you start? Taking a little time to plan the right order in which to proceed will ensure that everything progresses smoothly. Consider the timing of each step so that you can have materials on site and can co-ordinate the work of tradespeople. It's also time to start preparing the site – removing obstructions, excavating, putting in services. You may have to apply for local council approvals and decide what's easy enough to do yourself and when to call in the experts to give you a hand.

The order of work

The most important aspect of getting going on your backyard is deciding the right order for doing all the projects that are part of your final plan. The aim is to ensure that the creation of your backyard progresses in a logical way, avoiding situations where you have to 'undo' work already done. For example, you don't want to pull up paving when you realise you need to install irrigation pipes, or discover that the post for a pergola is right where the edge of a raised garden bed is supposed to go. Of course, there will always be situations where part of one project may upset some other job, but with your final plan in hand, you should be able to minimise the disturbance, and get things happening quickly and smoothly. If you are in any doubt about the order, ask an expert.

The typical order of work will run as follows:

1 Checking for and obtaining local council approvals – a lot of the work won't need approval but it's always safest to ask. If you get all your approval applications under way early, it means the approval for many things should be ready when you want to start building them.
2 Site preparation – most sites require some heavy-duty work at the beginning, including contouring the ground according to your plan, removing obstacles and demolishing unwanted structures.
3 Installation – essential drainage; watering-system pipes; and electrical-system wiring.
4 Construction – in-ground swimming pool; structural basics, such as footings for walls and pergolas; and paving, paths, steps and walls.

OPPOSITE **Before you build and plant your backyard, you will need to prepare the site.**

Smart tip

If your backyard makeover is going to take several months, try to schedule heavy work so that it takes place in the cooler months of the year. For example, laying pavers in spring is a lot easier than doing so in the fierce heat of summer.

Understanding the order of work for this courtyard garden allows you to have the necessary materials on site in the correct sequence.

5   Planting of large trees – especially if the positioning of trees could damage structures. Big trees may even need to go in at an earlier stage, especially if the construction of walls limits the amount of space available for manoeuvring them into position.

6   Carpentry – for timber structures such as decks, verandahs, pergolas, arbours, summerhouses, carports, fences and gates.

7   Topsoil, soil rejuvenation (see The soil on pages 223–7), installation of light fittings and power outlets, and finishing the watering system.

8   Planting, grassing and mulching. At this point you also need to finetune the watering system.

You can, of course, adapt this basic order of work according to the specific requirements of your backyard. If you think about your site and what you're going to build, it should be obvious when

to construct, say, pools, water features, garages and sheds. You'll probably find that the more detailed your plan becomes, the easier it will get to assess what needs to go where and more importantly when it should go there. For example, electrical cables and pipes should be laid before paving or walls. Edging should be done at the end of paving.

The timetable

If the work in your backyard is going to be extensive, you may also find it useful to work out a rough timetable for the work. This will not only give you an idea of how long the whole process should take, it will also give you advance warning of when you'll need to order materials and have them delivered. It can also help you plan when you'll need money on hand to pay the bills! A timetable doesn't need to be accurate to the minute, but it should be able to track when things can start, when they should be finished and critical points along the way.

Site preparation

The amount of work involved in getting the site ready to execute your grand plan will depend on how many things are unwanted or in the wrong place – buildings, walls, soil, boulders, trees and shrubs. If your block is being cleared for a new house, retain any topsoil for later use. Unless you're very lucky, you'll usually have some excavation, demolition or tree felling to do. You may need to remove stumps or move boulders carefully so they won't be damaged and you can reuse them elsewhere. Finally, you may need to lay services and mark out the site.

Excavation

Some shifting of soil is almost always necessary, as it's quite rare to have a perfectly level block. See the discussion on sloping land on pages 109–10 for the methods you can use to create a level area and changes of level. At this point, however, the question you need to ask is how much excavation is involved. Can you do it with a barrow and shovel, or do you need to call in a bobcat operator?

You'll be surprised how often a bobcat is the answer. For example, in a small backyard, you may be able to do the digging by hand, but you may find you then have to deal with a small mountain of soil that gets in the way of everything until it's removed – at which point the bobcat operator with a truck to take the soil away may come into the equation. The other thing to take into account is that what will take you days will only take a skilled bobcat operator a couple of hours.

If you do need to call in earthmoving equipment, there must be adequate access to the backyard. If there is no room for the machines to get down the side of your house, or no rear access, major earthworks can become extremely expensive or time consuming as the equipment may have to be craned onto the site.

Smart tip

If your entertaining area needs expanding and you can't obtain the same pavers that have been used already, you can extend by adding a different but complementary paver around its edges as a wide border.

Smart tips

- Don't try to do everything at once. If all the big jobs are at the start, intersperse them with easier ones.
- When materials are delivered, try to have them dropped as close as possible to the job at hand.
- Use a wheelbarrow with pump-up tires for easier pushing.
- Wear gloves to prevent blisters, scratches, splinters and spider bites.

BELOW Use a lever to move heavy rocks.

BOTTOM A hand trolley can be very helpful around the garden.

Remember, whenever planning excavation, always check for services such as pipes and electrical cables before commencing digging.

Demolition

This goes hand in hand with excavation, certainly in terms of removing material from the site. The other similarity is that of ensuring all services to the building are disconnected before commencing demolition. In the case of any building (no matter how basic it might be), check and double-check that there are no electrical cables to the building. If there are, call an electrician to disconnect and properly terminate them. The same must be done with plumbing. If you have a backyard lavatory, the pipes should be capped properly before demolition. You may think it won't matter if rubble blocks a pipe you no longer need, but it'll be a different story if it turns out the pipe also carries waste from your house.

Tree felling

Before felling a tree, check with your local council's tree preservation officer to determine if you need permission to do so. If it's a big tree, consider calling in experts to do the job. It can be expensive, but you should weigh this expense against the cost of injuring yourself or having to repair a dozen roof tiles and a ceiling. Falls are the most common form of DIY injury, and tree felling is often the culprit.

If you decide to fell the tree yourself, firmly prop an extension ladder against the trunk, and consider tying a rope around your waist and to the tree. Lop branches from the top, working your way down the tree. Cut under branches first, then cut from above. Removing stumps is the really hard part. You can chop them off below ground level, grind them down (you can hire grinders) and use the grindings as a mulch, or bury them and let them rot away slowly.

With a little hard work you can physically remove a small stump. To remove a stump, retain as much trunk as possible (for use as a lever). Dig down at least half a metre all around the stump, cutting all the supporting roots you can find. Place a rock against and, if possible, under the stump to act as a fulcrum. Then use a hand winch connected to the top of the stump and a solid anchor to pull out the stump. A crowbar can also be used to help lever out the stump.

Moving rocks

Boulders (and sandstone blocks) present plenty of challenges in the backyard due to the fact that even seemingly small ones can be surprisingly heavy. A few simple techniques make them a lot easier to manage. A hand trolley is cheap to hire or buy and can prove invaluable, especially if you have a lot of rocks, blocks, trees and large pots to move. And never underestimate the power of levers. They help you shift even the heaviest objects a little at a time, to achieve the desired position. To protect boulders during movement, place a block of wood between the rock and the metal of the crowbar, trolley or bobcat. If you need to move heavy objects between levels, wherever possible construct wooden ramps so you can slide or roll them up the slope rather than lift them. A hessian sack or heavy canvas can make objects easier to slide.

Laying services

Once excavation, demolition, tree felling and the heavy work has been completed, the next step is to lay pipes for drainage and irrigation systems, and cables for lighting. If drainage is to be connected to the sewer or stormwater system and electrical cables are to be connected directly to mains power (that is, you're using 240 volts rather than a 12-volt system), then qualified plumbers and electricians must be used. Your backyard plan should have the positions where you want cables and pipes to go marked on it. When they're actually being laid, though, mark any variations from the plan as accurately as possible for future reference.

Marking out

As the site preparation progresses, it makes a lot of sense to peg out the positions of the various features you intend to construct. This is especially the case where there will be changes of level, but it can also let you see where paths, paving, walls, stairs, utility areas and so on will be going. Marking out (using pegs, stringlines and spray-painted lines) can give you an indication of the dimensions of the backyard and let you confirm the ideas and measurements from your plan. If you are going to make some adjustments, this may be the last inexpensive opportunity for doing so before the real work begins.

Calling in experts

If you decide that some jobs in your backyard are best left in the hands of experts, the first step is to locate the right people for each job. Your local landscaping association is a good starting point and any tradespeople with the skills you require advertise their services in local papers under landscaping. A handyperson may also be able to do simpler jobs.

Engaging a tradesperson's services will be more effective if you have a clear plan of what you want to achieve. It doesn't matter if your plan is drawn roughly, as long as it

offers a starting point to put your idea into effect. Often a tradesperson will suggest better ways to do things or solutions to problems you didn't realise would arise. But you shouldn't agree to anything you don't really understand. 'That sounds OK, but give me time to think about it' is a perfectly reasonable response to a suggestion, especially one that involves large amounts of your money. When you've digested what you've been told, discuss it again.

Ideally, you should get three quotes on any medium to large job you want done, and you should let the people quoting know that is what you're doing. Don't be surprised if the quotes vary widely, but don't take the lowest quote as a matter of course. While price is important, you need to assure yourself that the work will be done to your satisfaction. Ask if it's possible to inspect some previous jobs done by a particular tradesperson and if possible talk to the clients to ensure they were happy with what was done.

When asking for quotes, ensure that each contractor is quoting on the same work and that the quoted price includes everything necessary for the job. What appears to be a cheaper quote may turn out to be more expensive when items that weren't included are added in or unforeseen difficulties are encountered.

Once work has begun, try to avoid making changes to your plan. As ideas take shape, the temptation to change your mind can be overwhelming. In some cases, changes may be sensible and necessary. But in all cases, changes will cost more money and time. That's why planning is so important. If you're ninety-nine per cent sure of what you want before work begins, the extra one per cent shouldn't break the bank.

Employing a skilled bobcat operator may be the best option when you have to move large amounts of soil.

Backyard
projects

Creating your ideal backyard also involves putting your plan into action. This section provides practical, step-by-step instructions that show how easy it is to lay pavers, build a pergola, construct a classic brick barbecue and much more. There are projects you can make for your kids, such as a birdhouse or cubby, and challenges for the enthusiast, such as a deck or garden steps. And what's more, if you tackle some or all of these projects, this section could end up saving you a fortune.

Putting your plan into action

Employing a skilled tradesperson to undertake projects in your backyard isn't cheap. You can choose to save money by using your own time and effort. Even if you have limited experience as a home handyperson, with care and patience you will be able to tackle a number of projects that are sure to enhance your lifestyle.

Planning

With the following projects, the best way to ensure a good result is to plan. Take the time to ensure you have everything you need to complete a project (both tools and materials).

Have a good look at the entire project and read right through the instructions. Sometimes there are alternatives or hints that will influence what you buy or when you do something. Do you understand all the steps, and how the components come together to produce the finished product? Look at how, say, A fits into B and how A needs to be cut to just the right size. When you're sure you understand how the project works, you're ready to begin.

There's an old builders' saying: measure twice, cut once. If you're a real beginner, to paraphrase Lewis Carroll: what you measure three times is true. To get a project to work perfectly, measure it, check that your measuring is straight, mark it with a pencil. Then measure the marks. Then measure them again. And after you've cut, you can even check that the cut was right and won't throw out measurements elsewhere. It sounds like a lot of measuring but it's really about slowing down and making sure before you proceed to the next step.

Tools

The second way to ensure a good result is to use the right tools. Some essential items such as a set of screwdrivers, shifting spanner, hammer, handsaw, spirit level, tape measure, pliers and drill are relatively inexpensive and form part of any home's basic toolkit. But when you're buying these items, don't go for the cheapest; buy the best you can afford. Even items such as quality screwdrivers can make a huge difference to the ease and comfort of constructing a project.

If you're unsure about what to buy, talk to the staff at your local hardware store. Most are only too willing to provide information that will guide you to the right choice for your needs. The drill is the only really complicated purchase. Make sure you get one with forward and reverse, hammer action, sufficient power for domestic applications, and a good selection of bits for drilling wood, concrete and brick.

Once you have good tools, look after them. Protect them from rust, keep them sharpened and lubricated, and use them sensibly. Take extra care with power tools: check for frayed or damaged cords, and never work in rain or wet conditions.

In some cases, buying expensive specialist tools isn't warranted if you'll only need them for one project. In such a case, it can be more economical to hire them. But always look for quality in the tools you hire, just as you would with the tools you buy. Poor tools can be worse than useless.

Getting the result you want

Most of these projects have been designed to be as simple as possible to make them accessible to any home handyperson. In many of them, suggestions are included on extra touches that aren't critical but will enhance the finished project. A confident home handyperson should feel free to adapt a project to suit their tastes or to ensure it's in keeping with the rest of the backyard. It pays to look around at the homes of friends and neighbours to see how they've done things and the touches you'd like to include in your projects.

Finally, if you've looked at a project and decided your involvement should go no further than your chequebook, it's still worth taking the time to look through the project and understand what's to be done. This will provide you with background information that will enable you to clearly explain what it is you want; help you understand what your tradesperson is planning to do; and help you check that the work is being done correctly and to a satisfactory standard. It will also help you assess whether quotes are reasonable.

Building a garden

Simple things like edging, walls, paths, lattice and steps give a backyard its essential structure. They connect areas, or divide them; they can contain, support or shelter plants and soil; block wind, provide privacy, screen unsightly views, and mask utility areas. They can be formal or informal, they can be unobtrusive or they can make a statement on their own. They set the mood and style of your garden, and when you build them yourself, they can add personal touches that give you a great sense of satisfaction.

Building jarrah edging

Edging goes hand in hand with paving and paths, in defining styles and creating effects. One choice is to have none at all with bordering plants doing the job perfectly well. Edging can be flush with the paving or path, which allows leaves to be easily swept into the garden, but may also allow garden soil to spill onto paving or gravel. Edging can also be raised, defining and containing garden beds around the paved area. Edging can be constructed with the material used for adjacent paving, and is often laid in a different pattern to define the limit of the paved area. However, using different materials can provide an interesting contrast, for example, wooden edging works well next to gravel paths.

Stooped edging refers to a trimmed edge of bare soil between a garden bed and the lawn. It can be made easily and cheaply with a spade (and a garden hose if a curved edge is required). The main expense is the time it will cost you in keeping the lawn trimmed and the soil weeded.

Flush and raised edges are necessary where pavers have been laid on a dry bed, in order to keep the pavers at the edge in position, or where you simply want a more clearly defined border or a 'mowing strip' beside a lawn.

Timber can be used to create a raised or flush edge. A durable timber that's widely used for edging is jarrah. It's ideal for low-key edging in, for example, an

Jarrah edging can be an understated yet durable method for containing a gravel path.

Difficulty: Easy

Time: 2–3 m of edging
per hour

Tools

- Steel mallet
  (or small sledgehammer)
- Garden hose (or rope)
  for marking curves
- Stringline
- Straightedge
- Spirit level
- Saw
- Power drill and driving bit

Materials

- Rot-resistant stakes 300–450 mm x
  50 mm x 25 mm (metal stakes can
  also be used)
- Jarrah 75 mm x 10 mm,
  length as required
- Bugle-head screws
  (approximately 30 mm long)

Australian native garden, a vegetable garden or informal cottage garden. Jarrah has the advantage that it can be used in many areas of the country because it is both hard-wearing and termite-resistant.

These instructions are for building a raised, curved, jarrah edging fixed with timber stakes, which can contain garden soil or separate paving from garden beds. (For flush jarrah edging, you would need to excavate a trench to take the timber then backfill the trench after the edging is in place. For raised, freestanding edging, you should use thicker timber, from 20 mm to 50 mm depending on the variety.) For straight lines and moderate curves, a stake every 1–1.5 m is sufficient. On tight curves, you may need extra stakes.

Peg out the boundaries of the proposed edge with timber stakes. For curved edges, lightly knock in the stakes then adjust them until the curve looks right. You can use a garden hose or thick rope to indicate informal curves.

1   Once you've marked out the curve, hammer in the stakes firmly. Fix a stringline 75 mm above ground level to indicate the intended top of all the stakes. Set up the stringline close to the curve and use a straightedge and spirit level to mark the correct height on each stake.

2   Remove the stringline to keep it out of your way when positioning the timber. Place a piece of edging in position and start

driving in extra stakes (their broader side adjacent to the jarrah) to help form the required line or curve. Only knock them in far enough to hold them in place, as some will be removed once the edging has been attached permanently. When the edging is in position, decide which stakes should remain. Their tops should be 15 mm below the top of the edging. You can have stakes on both sides of the edging to ensure it stays in place.

3   Attach the edging timber to the stakes using bugle screws: drive them through the edging into the stake. Hold the jarrah firmly against the stake as you insert the screws (one screw per stake is normally sufficient). If the edging timber or the stakes are prone to splitting, use a thinner screw and drill pilot holes first, or use thicker stakes.

4   Where edging timbers overlap, drive in a stake centred on the join so both timbers will be attached to it. This will help maintain a smooth curve or line.

5   Mound soil against the edging to a level that hides most of it.

Laying brick edging

Brick edging is superb for straight edges or an impressive flowing curve. You can lay bricks end to end (stretcher-bond fashion) or side by side (header bond), either on their sides or bases. They can be laid without mortar, especially if they're in a saw-tooth fashion or simply side by side.

- As the final appearance depends on the accuracy with which the bricks are laid, you should set everything out before placing a single brick. Set a stringline at the height you want the edging to be.
- For a one-course edging with the bricks laid flat end to end, mix only a small quantity of mortar to begin with, taking care to avoid making it too wet. Shovel a generous amount of mortar into position and roughly level it with a trowel. Place a brick on the mortar so that it sits 10–20 mm above the stringline. Gently tap the brick down to the level of the stringline with the handle of the trowel or brick hammer.
- Leave some mortar sticking out at either side of the edge as the bricks are laid. Once you've completed a section, or about every half-hour, use the trowel to remove the excess on the lawn or pavement side of the brick and add it to the opposite side to make a haunch (a triangular piece of mortar that abuts the brick to provide extra support). See Building a brick wall on pages 139–40 for more on laying bricks, and Smart tip on page 137 for a mortar mix.

Plants to soften edges

Name	Position
Aubretia cultivars Rose-red or purple flowers depending on the cultivar	Sun or part shade
Catmint (*Nepeta* × *faassenii*) Violet-blue flowers	Sun
Fan flower (*Scaevola aemula*) Mauve-blue flowers with yellow centres; coarsely toothed deep-green leaves	Sun or part shade
Golden oregano (*Origanum vulgare* 'Aureum') Bright greenish gold edible leaves	Sun or part shade
Mondo grass (*Ophiopogon japonicus*) Green grass-like leaves	Sun or part shade
Sandwort (*Arenaria balearica*) White flowers	Sun
(*Arenaria montana*) White flowers	Sun
Snow-in-summer (*Cerastium tomentosum*) White flowers	Sun
Swan River Daisy (*Brachyscome iberidifolia*) Mauve-blue flowers	Sun
Yellow alyssum (*Aurinia saxatilis*) Bright yellow flowers	Sun

This single-brick-rimmed path provides a solid yet attractive edge to the lawn.

Making a lattice screen

Difficulty: Moderate

Time: 4 hours

Tools

- Stringline (or chalk-line)
- Straightedge
- Spirit level
- Line level (optional)
- Post-hole shovel
  (or post-hole digger)
- Square
- Pencil
- Tape measure
- Wheelbarrow (for mixing concrete)
- Crowbar, or broom handle or rod
- Claw hammer
- Power saw
  (preferably 185 mm blade)
- Gloves, safety glasses and earmuffs

Materials

- Posts
- Cement and soil mix
  (1 part cement to 5–6 parts soil)
  or pre-mixed concrete
- Railings
- Galvanised nails
- Battens
- Lattice

Screens can separate areas of the garden, provide privacy or give plants something to climb on. This project also can be adapted easily to 'cap' a paling fence.

Before you start, check that you will not be digging near any services such as water or gas pipes, or telephone cables. Mark the proposed points for the two post holes. Note the location of trees and any structures that might interfere with the installation of posts. Note ground levels, as any variations may require longer or shorter posts.

1 Set up a stringline at, say, 300 mm above the ground. Check that it is level using a straightedge and spirit level or line level hung in the middle of the stringline.

2 Mark then dig the post holes. Their width will depend on the dimensions of the post, but there should be no more than 75 mm on either side of the post. The depth, typically 600–750 mm, will depend on the height of the screen.

3 Cut each post to length (measure the depth of the hole plus the height above ground of the posts). Using the pencil and square, mark a line (measuring from the top of each post) at 300 mm above ground level.

This lattice screen supports a climbing rose, divides the garden and is a feature in itself.

4 Place the posts in the holes. Fit the end posts first (if building a screen with more than two posts) and any that mark a change in the ground angle. Align the pencil marks with the stringline.

5 If you are using a cement and soil mixture, half fill the end holes and ram the mix down around the posts using the flat end of a crowbar. Check the alignment of each post to the stringline and also check for plumb with a spirit level. Continue to ram the hole until it's full. (Alternatively, add enough water to the cement mix in the wheelbarrow to make a damp but firm paste. Shovel it into the holes and poke it down using a broom handle or rod to remove any air bubbles. Check the alignment of each post and use a spirit level to check for plumb.) Then check the other posts are straight and the correct height and concrete them in. If using pre-mixed concrete, poke it down with a broom handle or rod to remove air pockets.

6 Now measure the distance between the posts and cut the bottom rail to that length. Skew-nail it to them, ensuring it is level.

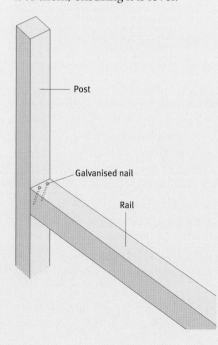

7 Nail battens on both sides of the bottom rail and to the posts to form a groove to hold the lattice.

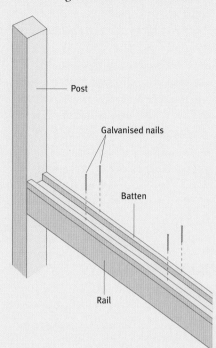

8 Position the lattice, leaving space at the top of the posts for the capping rail to sit flush.

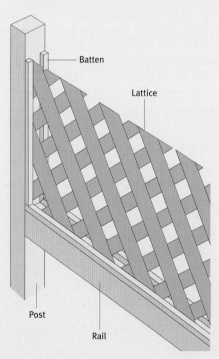

9 Cut and skew-nail the top rail, ensuring it is level.

10 Fix battens on both sides of the top rail to finish containing the lattice.

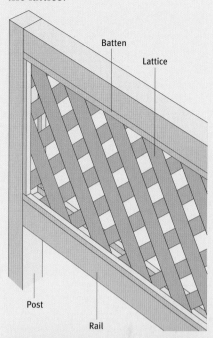

Climbers for lattice

Name	Position
Arabian jasmine (*Jasminum sambac*) Perfumed white flowers	Sun
Bleeding heart vine (*Clerodendrum thomsoniae*) Crimson and white flowers	Sun
Bower vine (*Pandorea jasminoides*) Pale-pink flowers	Sun
Cape honeysuckle (*Tecomaria capensis*) Scarlet-orange flowers	Sun
Chinese star jasmine (*Trachelospermum jasminoides*) Perfumed white flowers	Sun or part shade
Clematis cultivars Colours depend on the cultivar	Sun
Madagascar jasmine (*Stephanotis floribunda*) Perfumed waxy white flowers	Filtered sun
Potato vine (*Solanum jasminoides*) White flowers	Sun
Purple coral pea (*Hardenbergia violacea*) Purple flowers	Sun or part shade
Sweet pea (*Lathyrus odoratus*) Perfumed flowers in a variety of colours	Sun

Constructing brick garden steps

Difficulty: Hard

Time: 0.5–1 hour per step

Tools

- Stringline and stakes
- Wheelbarrow
- Long-handled shovel
- Rubber gloves
- Bricklayer's trowel and mortarboard
- Spirit level
- Bolster or cold chisel and mash hammer

Materials

- Bricks as required (suppliers can help calculate quantities)
- Concrete (see Smart tip on page 137)
- Mortar (see Smart tip on page 137)
- Timber offcuts for formwork (optional)

Make steps wide enough so that they are comfortable to walk on.

Steps are one of several ways of changing levels in a garden (ramps and paths are alternatives), but while they serve a functional purpose they can also create lots of visual interest. If you have the space, steps can be made wide enough to display pot plants. Steps can be formal or informal and constructed from a wide variety of materials, most commonly brick, stone and timber sleepers. The techniques used in building walls with these materials can be employed in similar ways when building steps and stairs.

There are many designs for steps but there are some recognised ways of planning and constructing them that ensure they are safe and comfortable to use, and look good, too.

Planning steps

Consider the basic elements of steps first. A step consists of a vertical riser and a horizontal tread. The generally accepted formula for workable steps is as follows: twice the riser height (r) plus the tread length (t) equals about 650 mm ($2r + t = 650$ mm). The degree of the slope will determine the riser height and this in turn allows you to calculate the tread length (from the front to the back of the step). Generally, risers should be 100–180 mm high, preferably about 150 mm. Thus the tread should be about 350 mm. Each riser in a flight of steps should be the same height but tread lengths can vary, especially if the stairs are meandering up a slope. Even then, though, it's good if the risers remain less than one stride apart.

When planning steps, you should also consider who is going to use them. Young children and the elderly may find risers over

150 mm high either too difficult or, at least, somewhat uncomfortable to use. At the same time, very low risers should be avoided, as the eye does not distinguish them easily, especially in shade or at night, which makes people more likely to trip and fall. Another consideration is the width of the steps. Space may be a limitation but, as with paths, it's always good if there is enough room for two people to walk side by side.

The slope will affect how you prepare the site: the steps can either be set back into the slope or sit on the face of the slope or somewhere in between. At the very least you may need formwork across the front of each step area when you pour footings, or you may require formwork for the entire footing.

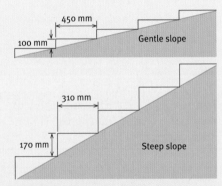

Steeper slopes require higher risers.

1 Decide on your materials: both tread and riser can be built of bricks laid flat or on their edges, or compacted gravel can be used for the tread. If you use gravel then, for strength, lay bricks side by side for the riser, which forms the top leading edge of each tread. Select bricks for steps that won't retain moisture, which will promote mould and make them slippery.

2 Decide on the appropriate riser height and tread length (see

Planning steps above). Depending on the slope, excavate the area for the steps to the depth of the bricks plus the concrete footings, or level the site of each step.

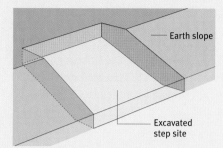

Earth slope

Excavated step site

3 Set out the tread height and position of each step using a stringline and stakes. Position each stringline to mark the top leading edge of each step, and make sure it is level. (You will use this stringline to place bricks accurately.)

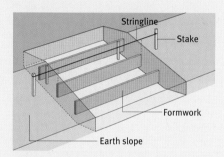

Stringline

Stake

Formwork

Earth slope

4 Construct formwork for concrete footings as required (see Laying a concrete slab on page 197).

5 Mix enough concrete to pour footings at least 100 mm deep for all the steps (see Smart tip) and allow it to set.

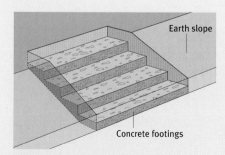

Earth slope

Concrete footings

6 Start with the bottom step, laying the bricks on the footing of

concrete. Bricks for the leading edge of each step should be laid in line with the axis of the step and not across it. Scoop some mortar from the mortarboard with the trowel and place it on the footing. Spread it over the width of two or three bricks, taking care to keep as much mortar as possible within the line of the step.

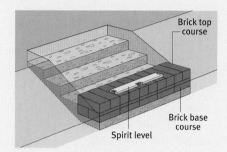

Brick top course

Brick base course

Spirit level

7 You can lay bricks for the riser end to end (unless the tread is gravel, in which case they should be laid side by side). Use a spirit level to check that the riser is horizontal.

8 Pick up a little mortar with the trowel and spread it, with a buttering motion, on one side of a brick. Gently lower the buttered brick into position. Repeat with the next brick, pushing it against the side of the last brick laid. Use a spirit level and the stringline to check that the leading edge of the step is horizontal as you work, but allow a slight slope downward from back to front so that it sheds water. If necessary, use a mash hammer and cold chisel to cut any bricks to size.

9 You can fill the tread area with broken bricks and mortar to bring it to the right level.

10 Continue building remaining steps.

11 Scrub off any mortar spills with a damp rag. Allow the mortar to dry for at least two days before you walk on it, or four days before you wheel a barrow over it.

Bricks for risers can be laid end to end.

Difficulty:	Easy to moderately hard
Time:	0.5 hour per step

Tools

- Circular saw (or chainsaw)
- Stringline and stakes
- Spirit level
- Narrow, long-handled shovel (or spade)
- Mash hammer and flat timber
- Crowbar (optional)
- Power drill and driving bit

Materials

- Railway sleepers (or landscape timber) for risers
- 350 mm x 50 mm x 50 mm rot-resistant stakes
- Gravel, pavers or bricks
- Bugle-head screws at least 50 mm long

Smart tip

To vary the dimensions of steps, use the formula $2r + t = 650$ mm (two times the height of the riser plus the length of the tread = 650 mm). See Planning steps on page 136.

Smart tip

Where garden steps divide a retaining wall, extend the broken ends of the wall inwards, at an angle or in a curve. These wall returns may reach only part of the way up the steps, or they may extend to the top. For a sleeper wall, the returns could consist of a couple of courses of sleepers lying on their narrow edge, with the lower ones half embedded in the adjacent soil.

Timber steps suit this natural style garden.

Constructing timber garden steps

Second-hand railway sleepers and new landscape timbers are both suitable for steps. However, it's best to use timber only for risers because wooden treads can become very slippery when wet and encourage the growth of moss and algae. For treads, compacted gravel, bricks or pavers can be used (the latter two set on a base of sand, mortar or concrete).

1 Establish the height and positions of the steps and level each step area with a spade or shovel.

2 Mark the top leading edge of each step with stringlines attached to stakes, and check that they are level. Some timber may have to be cut. Only experienced operators should use a chainsaw.

3 Use a mash hammer to drive two stakes vertically into the ground behind the position of the first riser. The finished height of the stakes should be below the finished height of the riser.

4 Start with the bottom riser, firmly screwing the timber to each stake in two places, and ensuring that the step is level.

5 After the first riser is constructed, shovel crushed rock into the area behind it up to the level of the base of the next riser. Do the same for the remaining steps.

6 When the steps are finished, add more crushed rock to bring the tread to the correct level. Compact using the flat end of a crowbar or a flat piece of timber and a mash hammer. Alternatively, brick pavers may be laid on a sand or mortar bed to form the tread. In any case, while the step should be horizontal across the front, it should slope slightly from the back down to the front to spill water.

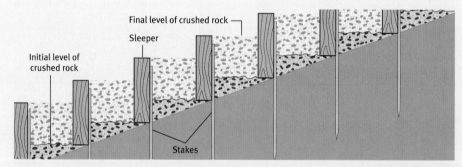

Final level of crushed rock
Sleeper
Initial level of crushed rock
Stakes

Sleepers form the risers; crushed rock forms the treads.

Building a brick wall

A single layer of bricks, braced with piers, is suitable for a freestanding wall or a retaining wall up to about 450 mm. Higher retaining walls should be of double-brick cavity construction (or you can use hollow concrete blocks) and usually require local council permission, engineering diagrams and construction by a licensed builder. A cavity wall consists of two single-brick walls held together with wall ties: a total wall width of 350 mm leaves a cavity about 130 mm in width. The following instructions can be adapted for either type of wall, or for edgings, barbecues, brick or stone steps, etc.

The concrete footing for a retaining wall should have a width about two-thirds of the wall's height. So, for a wall 1 m high, the footing should be about 650 mm wide and 250 mm deep. For a freestanding wall 1 m high, a suitable reinforced footing could be 250 mm deep and twice the thickness of the wall (at least 300 mm). To construct a footing, excavate a straight-sided trench and remove all loose material. Place trench mesh on trench-mesh supports then pour concrete into the trench. If you're building a cavity wall, you'll also need to insert L-shaped reinforcing bars about every metre along the wall, connected to the trench mesh. Allow at least 48 hours for the concrete to set.

Bricks and blocks are almost always laid in horizontal lines called courses. A course is the thickness of a brick plus the mortar layer on which it sits. You can construct a simple course guide using stakes set vertically at either end of the wall and in line with it. Set a stringline between the stakes to ensure evenly spaced courses.

It's important to lay the first course as accurately as possible.

A weathered brick wall provides a mellow backdrop for wisteria.

Difficulty: Moderate to hard

Time: 1 hour per metre

Tools

- Stringline and 2 course guides
- Bolster and mash hammer
- Pair of line blocks (course guides)
- Wheelbarrow
- Short-handled, round-mouthed shovel
- Rubber gloves
- Bricklayer's trowel and mortarboard
- Spirit level
- Scrap of iron bar

Materials

- Bricks as required (suppliers can help calculate quantities)
- Mortar
- Wall ties as required
- Runny concrete mix for cavity walls

Smart tip

For bricklaying, it's worth equipping yourself with one or two specialist tools. A bricklayer's trowel is ideal for picking up and spreading mortar, and for quickly scraping any excess from joints (use a pointing trowel when tidying mortar and for stone walls). If you want to rake the joints, you'll need a jointing tool.

Bricklaying tools: bricklayer's trowel, pointing trowel, jointing tool.

1 If this is your first attempt at bricklaying, mix only a small amount of mortar. Then, holding the trowel in your working hand, pick up a brick in the other. Scoop up some mortar from the mortarboard with the trowel and place it on the footing. Spread it over the length of two or three bricks, taking care to keep as much mortar as possible within the line of the wall.

2 Pick up a little mortar with the trowel and spread it, with a buttering motion, on one end of the brick you're holding. With practice you'll work out how much mortar to pick up each time and get better at placing it.

3 Gently lower each buttered brick into position, pushing it against the end of the last brick laid. The brick is correctly positioned when its edge nearly touches the stringline, it is horizontal (check with the spirit level) and there is a 10 mm gap between it and the last brick laid.

You can move the brick slightly by tapping it with the end of the trowel handle. If the brick will not sit in position but sinks instead, the mortar is too soft. If you have to force a brick into its final position, the mortar is too firm or you've used too much.

4 Once the first course is complete, move each end of the stringline up to the next mark on the course guides. For low, single-brick garden walls of only a few courses, simply repeat this process until the job is complete.

5 If you're building a cavity wall, you must join the two sides of the wall with the ties – about four per square metre of face, staggered along the wall – as you go. Embed the outer parts of each tie in a newly spread layer of mortar, with the centre of the tie crossing the cavity. The next course of bricks on each side will secure the tie. You may have to adapt this method to suit the ties you buy, because styles vary.

6 Now fill the cavity with a concrete mix containing 7 mm screenings. Keep the mix reasonably wet so that it runs easily into all the spaces. Use the iron bar to poke the concrete into position and remove any air pockets.

Installing drainage pipes

Retaining walls and walls forming garden beds require drainage of some kind to prevent any build-up of water that could destabilise them or at the very least cause unsightly damp and mould. Even walls less than a metre in height can be affected, especially if they have a large area of potential run-off behind them. Timber walls are particularly at risk of damage from moisture so they should always be provided with adequate drainage.

- Before building walls and laying paving, you should work out how excess water can be drained. It could run off, or into a stormwater drain (requiring connection by a licensed plumber), or into soakholes. But you also need to provide effective drainage behind the wall itself.
- To determine how much piping to buy, measure the length of your proposed wall and add an extra 150 mm or so. When buying the screenings, tell your supplier the size of the job and ask for an estimate of the quantity you will need.

- Remove any dirt and debris from behind the wall, leaving a smooth base for the pipe. Clear all weepholes (gaps left in the fabric of the wall so that water can leak through). Position the pipe behind the wall and as close to it as possible, sloped towards the end you want it to drain to. Keep it in place by gently shovelling screenings on either side every metre or so.
- Stand plywood sheets next to the pipe and screenings. If you have a helper, one of you can be backfilling the embankment side of the plywood with excavated soil while the other shovels screenings into the space between the plywood and the wall. You need to keep raising the plywood so that only a few centimetres remain buried at any time. When the screenings are about 150 mm below the finished level of the ground behind the wall, pull out the plywood. Cut builder's plastic to fit over the compacted screenings before you backfill with topsoil.

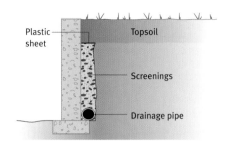

A drainage pipe installed behind a retaining wall.

Drainage piping comes in various sizes and its flexibility makes it easy to lay.

There should be adequate drainage behind all retaining walls, especially timber ones.

Building a timber retaining wall

A timber wall is probably the easiest kind of wall to construct. Once excavation is complete there are no special tools or equipment needed and you can build a section at a time. Timber walls can either be formal in style or more casual and rustic.

Landscape timbers for walls (such as redgum, spotted gum, ironbark and treated pine) can be rough-sawn or dressed and come in a variety of lengths including 2.4 m, 2.7 m and 3 m. They're usually 200 mm wide with varying depths of 50 mm (for low walls or short lengths between supports), 75 mm (most commonly used and suitable for walls up to 800 mm) and 100 mm (for walls up to 1 m or where the pressure against the wall may be strong due to, say, wet soils).

Trim timbers to the lengths required, squaring off the ends. Saw uprights to length, ensuring that the exposed end (top) is cut neatly. As a general rule, the length of the upright should be twice the planned height of the wall – so about half will be embedded in concrete. The horizontal timbers are intended to meet end to end behind each upright and can be fixed with either bolts or nails.

1　Fix a stringline to indicate the position of the wall. Mark the location of each timber support.

Excavate a hole for each support, allowing about 100 mm clearance all around the timber. The depth of the hole depends on the height of the wall. Stand the upright in the hole. (You can set the uprights at the correct height at this stage by adjusting the depth of the hole. However, it may be easier to cut the uprights to height when the wall is three-quarters built, especially if you are using sleepers of different widths.)

A timber retaining wall can be softened with plants.

2 Ideally, have a helper hold each upright in position, while you check with the spirit level that it's both vertical and aligned with the stringline. Carefully place a little concrete all around the upright and poke it with a length of steel rod or broom handle to compact it and get rid of any air pockets. Progressively fill the hole with concrete: if you use a fairly firm mixture, the timber should remain in position without the need for props. The concrete at the front needs to be 50–75 mm below the base of the wall so that it can later be covered by soil, lawn or paving.

3 Once the concrete has set (at least 48 hours) start installing the horizontal timbers. They should butt against each other behind each upright and be fixed with zinc-plated or galvanised coach bolts.

Drill a hole of the same diameter as the bolt, tap the bolt through and locate the washer and nut behind the wall. As the nut is tightened the head of each coach bolt is drawn firmly against the support timber.

4 Alternatively, if using nails, skew-nail from the top of the lowest horizontal timber and into the upright. Drill a pilot hole if you find the timber hard to penetrate. Skew-nail each of the remaining horizontals into both the horizontal below it and the vertical timber.

Trailing plants to soften walls

Name	Position
Coprosma × kirkii Green shiny leaves	Sun
Dalmation bellflower (*Campanula portenschlagiana*) Deep purple-blue flowers	Part shade
Dusky coral-pea (*Kennedia rubicunda*) Deep-pink to dark-red flowers	Semi-shade
Grevillea ('Poorinda Royal Mantle', 'Bronze Rambler', 'Forest Rambler' and *G. gaudichaudi*) All four suit large banks	Sun
Ground morning glory (*Convolvulus sabatius*) Blue flowers	Sun
Native false sarsaparilla (*Hardenbergia violacea*) Purple flowers	Sun
Prostrate rosemary (*Rosmarinus officinalis* 'Prostratus') Lavender-blue flowers	Sun
Rose daphne (*Daphne cneorum*) Rose-pink flowers	Sun
Serbian bellflower (*Campanula poscharskyana*) Mauve-blue star-like flowers; mid-green slightly hairy leaves	Shade
Snow-in-summer (*Cerastium tomentosum*) White flowers	Sun

Laying a gravel path

You can use gravel to create a durable paved surface suitable for nearly all garden styles provided that the area to be gravelled is flat. If the soil base is solid and well drained, you can lay the gravel directly onto it. The gravel in pedestrian areas should be no thicker than 50 mm or the area will be too soft and difficult to walk upon, while driveway gravel should be 75–100 mm thick.

But if the soil base is badly drained, or if you wish to create a gravel driveway, you will need to lay it on road base. Crushed limestone (if available) is ideal as it compacts well and sets very hard because of its lime content, but there are other suitable kinds of road base. Ask your local landscape supplier about availability.

In most situations it is advisable to provide a permanent edging to keep the gravel in place, exclude soil and help restrict invasion by weeds (see Building jarrah edging on pages 131–2). The main difference between laying gravel for pedestrian use and laying gravel for vehicular access lies in the thickness of the gravel.

Maintaining your gravel is simple. All you need to do is regularly rake up leaves and

Gravel can look superb in paths that are solidly built and well maintained. Note how raised edging contains any loose stones and divides the gravel and the garden.

garden litter, and hose away any spilt soil after scraping up what you can with a shovel.

First make sure that the area is well drained. Then install an edge around the area to be gravelled. Choose the type of edging carefully. For a footpath, 75 mm x 25 mm treated pine or jarrah screwed to stakes of the same material would be suitable. Mortared bricks also make good edgings.

Before installing brick edging, you will need to excavate to allow for the correct thickness of gravel. Once the edge is finished, allow three or four days for mortar (if you used bricks) or any concrete to harden. Next, clean up and roughly level the area you plan to gravel. Collect any rubbish and rake smooth.

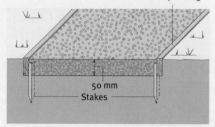

Treated pine edge

50 mm
Stakes

Edging for a gravel path.

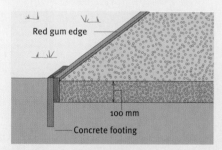

Red gum edge

100 mm
Concrete footing

Edging for a gravel driveway.

Laying gravel on road base

This method is ideal for driveways or areas that are badly drained. Road base can be obtained from your local landscape suppliers.

1 Hose the area thoroughly before you begin. Lay 25 mm of road base for a pathway and 50 mm of road base for a driveway. Using a rake turned upside down, push the road base against edges and into corners.

2 Moisten with a hose. Use a compactor and run it three or four times over every part of the road base. Take care not to damage the edging.

3 Add the gravel when the road base ceases to sink into the soil. Place 50 mm of gravel on top of the road base for a driveway and 25 mm for a path.

4 Rake the gravel evenly over the area.

Difficulty: Easy

Time: 3–4 hours

Tools

- Long-handled shovel
- Rake with strong tines
- Bricklaying tools, if building brick edging
- Vibrating plate compactor (can be hired)

Materials

- Road base
- Gravel (there are different colours)
- Edging materials (timber or brick), as required
- Rustproof screws (or bolts), as required
- Stakes
- Concrete for footings, if required
- Mortar for brick edgings, if required

Smart tip

Laying gravel on shadecloth prevents it being trodden into the soil.

Gravel suits the style of this house and the formal garden.

Other materials for paths

Paths shouldn't just get you from point A to point B – they should entice you into your backyard, create structure by dividing areas (no matter how large or small), and allow access for every kind of activity you can envisage. So when choosing materials, consider where they will be used and for what purpose.

Try to keep the materials used for paths consistent throughout the backyard to create harmony and unity in the design. The path material should match the style you want to create. For formal gardens, for example, this means clean-looking materials such as sandstone, paving tiles, paving bricks, concrete pavers and reconstituted stone. For informal gardens, bricks, paving bricks, cobblestones, gravel, wooden rounds, stepping stones and even compacted dirt can be used. In some areas with light traffic, you may even find that grass may still be the ideal surface.

While you're looking, bear in mind the colours and materials already used in your house. Whatever you use for paving and paths should match the buildings, walls and paving around them (and the plants, for that matter) to create a harmonious connection.

Another good technique is to mix materials. A popular and dramatic effect is to use large pavers (for example, concrete pavers) surrounded by pebbles. Groundcovers around pavers achieve the same result while softening the use of stone and some groundcovers such as thyme will release aromas when walked on that further add to the enjoyment of your backyard.

The clean-looking paving used for this path suits the contemporary style of the house and the pergola.

Bringing the indoors outdoors

Our temperate climate lends itself to an outdoor lifestyle, so it's little wonder a great backyard often becomes a favourite place for relaxation and entertaining. A number of features can enrich the experience. Paving and decks, especially in high-use areas, can help bring the indoors outdoors, while pergolas and shadesails can take the edge off a hot, summer day and protect you from the sun. The following projects will help you to create, with a little care and effort, backyard features that will enhance your lifestyle.

Laying pavers on a dry bed

Difficulty: Moderate

Time: 1–1.5 hours per square metre

Tools

- Long-handled shovel
- Stringline
- Spirit level
- Screed board and short lengths of wood 25–30 mm thick, as guides
- Wooden float
- Planks (or plywood sheets) to walk on newly laid pavers
- Broom
- Vibrating plate compactor (can be hired)

Materials

- Washed sand (for bedding)
- Pavers
- Concrete or timber for edge restraint
- Very fine, washed sand (to sweep into cracks)

Paving is often the easiest way to deal with areas where there will be a lot of activity: entrances, around barbecues, around dining and seating furniture, in play areas and courtyards. It can provide a low-maintenance answer for areas where it's too dark or damp for groundcovers such as grass. Paving can create beautiful effects that further enhance your backyard. Sandstone, paving tiles, paving bricks, concrete pavers and reconstituted stone work well for formal backyards, whereas bricks, paving bricks, cobblestones, packed earth and gravel give a more informal look.

The technique of laying pavers on a dry bed works best for small pavers such as bricks or cobblestones, especially pavers of regular thickness. Some pavers (such as second-hand bricks) have irregular thicknesses and may need to be individually set into position using a rubber-headed hammer and spirit level.

1   Calculate how deep you will need to excavate by adding up the planned depth of the base and bedding layer plus the thickness of the pavers. Excavate the area, then prepare the sub-base and base.

2   There are three parts to the structure of a pavement. The underlying sub-soil supports the pavement. Trim this smooth and ensure it is free of soft or wet areas and preferably sloping gently for good drainage. If the sub-base includes fill, compact it thoroughly.

A paved patio can be ideal for a practical, low-maintenance entertaining area.

3 The next layer, the base, is usually compacted crushed rock. Pedestrian pavements generally require a base 75 mm thick, while paving for vehicles needs 100–150 mm. The bedding layer sits immediately beneath the pavers. It is usually of sand, sometimes mixed with cement, and its maximum thickness (when compacted, in the case of sand) should be about 30 mm.

4 Erect a stringline at the finished pavement level and check it with the spirit level.

5 Spread the sand for the bedding layer and level it, using a screed board resting on the guides. Their thickness represents the depth of sand you need considering the sand bed will become about 5 mm shallower for every 25 mm of compacted depth (this must be taken into account when setting the stringline).

6 Remove the guides. Use sand to fill the channels left by the guides, and smooth off the surface with a wooden float until it is level with the surrounding areas.

7 Set up another stringline to mark one edge of the area to be paved. While you probably don't need a stringline for every row of pavers, a few lines will help keep the pattern straight. Place the first

row of pavers along the stringline. Continue, working from the sides to avoid walking on the prepared sand bed. To avoid disturbing newly laid pavers, place planks or plywood sheets over them. Cut pavers as required to fill small or irregular spaces.

8 Once all the pavers are laid, install permanent edges of mortar, concrete or timber and place them below pavement level so they can be disguised with plants or mulch (see Building jarrah edging on pages 131–2). This ensures the stability of the pavement.

9 Sweep very fine, washed sand into the spaces between pavers. When the edging is complete, sweep off surplus sand, then put the compactor to work. To protect the pavement, use a neoprene mat under the plate or spread and maintain a thin layer of sand on the pavement during compaction. Pass the machine several times over the paving, being careful not to let it overhang the edges.

Paving patterns

Rectangular pavers such as bricks are ideal for a variety of patterns that create interesting overall effects. Rectangular pavers can also be laid in a number of patterns including (top, left to right) herringbone, stretcher bond, basketweave; (bottom, left to right) two styles of bedding faces and soldier courses. Note how some designs hold your eye, while others lead it on, perhaps to another feature you want to accentuate. Different patterns or directions for patterns can make a garden appear longer, or a narrow garden wider.

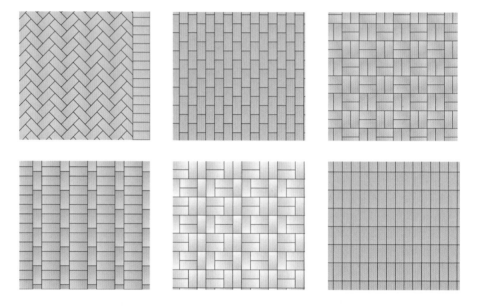

RIGHT   Brick paving patterns.

BELOW   Cobbles form a pattern on the floor in this minimalist courtyard.

Laying pavers on a wet bed

A wet bed of mortar is used for large unit paving such as concrete slabs and for smaller unit pavers covering limited areas. This method is also used for laying pavers on a concrete base. You need to set up a stringline for each row of pavers, allowing a 10 mm gap per row for grout.

1 Use bricklayer's mortar for the bedding. It should be wet enough for a large slab to settle into position after a few light blows with a rubber mallet, but not so wet that the slab sinks. If the mortar is too firm, you will need to hit too hard and may break slabs. Put enough mortar on the base to support several pavers at a time, then spread it to a depth of about 25 mm.

2 Wet the base of each paver to help it adhere. Leave the mortar a little high so that as pavers are positioned the bed can settle without too much oozing out.

3 To finish bedding the slabs, erect a stringline at one edge of the paving to give you an overall guide to levels. Then take a spirit level or a straight piece of moderately heavy timber (around 100 mm x 50 mm) two to three times the length of a single paver. Place the timber on top of recently laid slabs and lightly tap with the rubber mallet until the slab tops line up with the stringline and each other.

Difficulty: Moderate to hard

Time: Depends on the size of the job

Tools

- Shovel
- Straightedge or spirit level
- Soft but heavy mallet
- Rule
- Stringline
- Bolster or tile-cutting machine
- Broom

Materials

- Mortar (1 part cement, 1 part lime, 6–8 parts concrete or propagating sand – without clay fines)
- Pavers

A formal paved area with an angled pattern. The paving is edged with a border and surrounded by box hedge.

Erecting shadecloth

| **Difficulty:** Moderate |
| **Time:** 4–6 hours |

Tools

- Tape measure
- Scissors
- Sailmaker's needle/sewing machine
- Saw
- Power drill and bits
- 10 mm timber or steel rod
- Stringlines
- Plumb-bob
- Square
- Spirit level
- Shovel
- Wheelbarrow

Materials

- 6 brass grommets (with grommet kit)
- Rope (length as required)
- Shadecloth or canvas as required (approximately 2.5 m x 3.5 m)
- Sailmaker's thread or whipping twine
- Two 3 m posts of treated pine or cypress pine 75 mm x 75 mm
- 4 large rustproof cuphooks
- Concrete
- 2 large rustproof eyehooks

In the heat of summer, one of the greatest needs in any backyard is shade. If you are fortunate to have large trees, you may have plenty of shade. If not, you may need to erect some sort of shade – a market umbrella or shadecloth or shadesail. The advantage of erecting shadecloth or sail is that you don't need to keep putting it up or down when you need it, but it can be dismantled as the cooler months approach, giving you fuller sun when you want it.

There are shadecloth kits available from hardware stores, but these can be quite expensive. Do-it-yourself shadecloth can be a lot cheaper and is just as easy to set up as many kit versions. It's really just a matter of assembling all the necessary components. The added advantage is that while kits come in standard sizes, if you do your own shadecloth, you can tailor the size to your exact shape and area. The only hurdle is the hemming, which may prove too much for the average sewing machine and may need to be sewn by hand. Alternatively, you can call a sailmaker (they're listed in the Yellow Pages) and ask them to hem your edges on a heavy-duty industrial sewing machine (usually for a small fee).

This project keeps things simple with a small rectangular shadecloth attached to the fascia board of your house and two posts. If you have appropriately sited trees, you may substitute them for the posts. And if you decide you want a triangular shadecloth, you'll only need one post.

1 Determine the size and density of the shadecloth you want to erect. In this project it's 2500 mm x 3500 mm. Cut the shadecloth to size

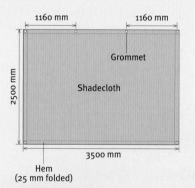

Shadecloth provides welcome shade for outdoor meals in hot weather.

(allowing 25 mm extra for the hem). Hem the edges, ensuring the hem is wide enough for the grommets to penetrate through doubled-over shadecloth. This will make the shadecloth stronger. Position grommets in the corners. Position two more grommets along one of the longer sides of the shadecloth, 1160 mm from the corners.

2   Mark out the positions for the cuphooks on the fascia board, with the second cuphook 1160 mm from the first, the third at 2320 mm and the fourth at 3500 mm (3.5 m). Drill starter holes into the fascia for the cuphooks. Screw in the cuphooks.

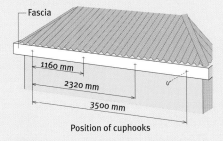

Position of cuphooks

3   Estimate the position of the outside corners of the shadecloth (using stringlines, a plumb-bob and a square if necessary) and mark the positions for the posts approximately 250 mm further from each corner.

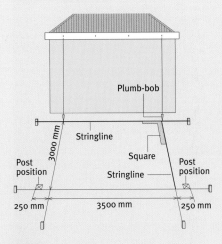

4   Dig post holes 300 mm wide and 600 mm deep. Set the posts in the holes and ensure they are vertical. Half fill the holes with

concrete, and poke it down using a rod to remove any air bubbles. Ensure the posts are still vertical then fill the holes with concrete to slightly above ground level. Slope the concrete away from the posts so that water runs off. Allow the concrete to set for at least two days. If you use quick-set concrete, allow a couple of hours or follow the manufacturer's specifications.

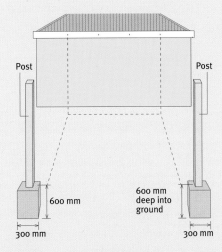

5   Cut the posts to a suitable height. Drill starter holes for the eyehooks in the posts. Position the eyehooks on top of the posts or on the side. Screw the eyehooks to the posts.

6   Attach the shadecloth to the cuphooks and tie the two ropes to the grommets on the outside corners of the shadecloth.

7   Loop the ropes through the eyehooks, adjust the tension as required and tie off the ropes.

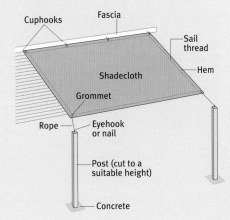

Building a low, freestanding deck

Difficulty: Moderately hard

Time: 2.5–3 days

Tools

- Measuring tape
- Stringlines
- Hammer
- Square
- Plumbline
- Spirit level
- Shovel
- Power drill and bits
- Power saw or handsaw
- Socket wrench
- Shifting spanner
- Chisel
- Plane
- Paintbrush

Materials

- Timber and nails (for profiles and temporary bracing)
- Nine posts 90 x 90 mm treated pine or 100 x 100 cypress pine or 75 x 75 mm hardwood, length as required
- Three 3600 mm bearers 190 x 45 mm treated pine or 125 x 75 mm hardwood*
- Nine 3600 mm joists 140 x 45 mm treated pine or 100 x 50 mm hardwood*
- Galvanised steel stirrups
- 50 mm coach screws
- Pre-mixed, quick-set concrete (approximately 1 bag per post hole)
- 75 mm galvanised bullet-head nails (or galvanised nail plates or brackets) for fixing bearers
- 75 mm galvanised nails (or galvanised framing anchors or hangers) for fixing joists
- Decking boards as required (19 mm hardwood or 22 mm softwood)
- 50 mm galvanised annular ring or twist-shank nails (for fixing decking)
- Primer and paint (or sealer)

* To determine timber sizes, check Australian Standard 1684.4.

A timber deck can provide an attractive outdoor area to complement your garden, pool or barbecue. When attached to the house, it extends your living space outside, essentially giving you another 'room' (especially if it is also covered by a roofed pergola).

Because timber decks can be constructed on almost any site with no need for excavation, retaining walls or drainage, they are a great solution if your house is on a steep slope and you need an additional outdoor area but don't want the expense of moving or levelling soil. (It's wise to have your soil type tested so you know how deep to dig post holes and footings.)

Designing a deck

Most councils require decks to conform to both building regulations and Australian Standard 1684, so an experienced builder or draftsperson should draw up your final plans and specify all materials. However, you can do the groundwork for the design and calculate most of your costs.

A deck is made up of posts (stumps), bearers, joists and boards. To calculate the amount of decking you need, simply measure the intended floor area in square metres and add a further 10 per cent. To calculate how many timber pieces you will need, work out the spacing and span of the structural members. Spacing means the distance between two structural members of the same type (for example, two joists) and is usually measured from the centre of each joist. Span is the distance between members that support another structural timber (for example, two bearers supporting a joist) and is usually measured from their inside faces.

Determine the position and size of the posts, bearers and joists, by drawing up a scale plan of the

Ground-level decking is a reasonably easy type of decking to build.

deck. First mark in the position of the corner posts (a). Next draw a line (or lines) connecting these posts in the direction the decking boards will run (b); this line represents the positions of the bearers. On the plan measure the length of these bearers and mark the position of intermediate posts (c) to reduce the span between the supports to a suitable distance: a span of 1800 mm is recommended for decks less than 1000 mm off the ground, and up to 3000 mm maximum for elevated decks, depending on the type of timber. Next draw in the joists, spaced 450 mm apart. Joists (d) will run at right angles to the bearers. Again, draw in intermediate bearers where the span of the joists is too great. Using your scale drawing, you can now calculate the approximate size for posts, bearers and joists of your chosen timber.

If deck posts are more than 1000 mm high and supported in brackets, or more than 1800 mm high and embedded in concrete, you will need to brace them permanently to prevent any sideways movement. The braces should be of either 90 mm x 45 mm treated pine or 100 mm x 50 mm hardwood.

The best size

This project is for an average sized deck 3600 mm x 3600 mm sited within a metre of the ground. It's large enough for a small family gathering or for entertaining a small group. You can vary the size to suit your needs but be aware that for larger spans than are detailed here you should consult the experts at your timber supplier to get the correct sized timber to ensure your deck is safe. Higher decks may also require additional bracing. When planning your deck, you should consult your local council to ensure it complies with all regulations.

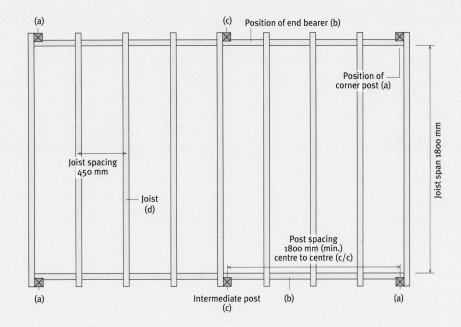

Determining the position and length of posts, bearers and joists.

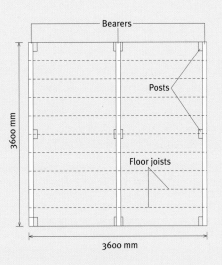

Deck and post bearer plan.

Preparing the site

Clear surrounding areas of any roots, logs and tree stumps, especially if there is a risk of termites. Termites will seek out and rapidly destroy any wood left lying about and may be drawn towards the timbers of your deck. Make sure there is adequate drainage and ventilation. Stuffy, damp areas are more attractive to termites than dry, airy ones. In cool, dry climates (without termites), posts are commonly installed directly in the ground. Otherwise, follow the instructions for installing the posts in stirrups as described below.

1   Decide whether you will install posts directly in the ground or in stirrups (this is important if you live in an area that is termite-prone or warm and humid). Decide whether posts will continue up from the ground to support a pergola.

2   Set out the positions of the posts using stringlines attached to existing walls or fences or to setting-out profiles (hurdles). Use the 3:4:5 method to check for square (see the Smart tip on page 157). Set all the stringlines at the finished height of the posts.

Setting out six of the nine posts for a timber deck with the help of stringlines.

Stringline

Use a 3:4:5 triangle or equal diagonals to check for square

Post spacing

Post spacing

Profile (hurdle)

Use a spirit level and square (or plumbline) to mark post corner

3   Dig post holes 300 mm square and 600 mm deep (if your soil is stable). If the soil is particularly dry, pour a litre or so of water into the hole and allow it to soak in.

In the ground

1   Establish the length of posts by measuring from the bottom of the hole to the stringline (or from the top of the layer of gravel). Deduct 150 mm so that there is at least 150 mm of concrete under each stump. Use a power saw to cut posts.

2   Add water and quick-set concrete as per the manufacturer's instructions. (To obtain the correct consistency you may prefer to add the concrete in batches rather than all at once. However, it is important to keep in mind that quick-set concrete hardens in 15 minutes, so there is not much time for experimentation.) Fill to between 150 mm and 180 mm.

3   Place the post into the hole and swivel until it is at the correct height and alignment. Use a spirit level or plumbline to check for plumb.

4   Backfill the hole gently with concrete or soil, checking for position as you go.

5   Install all posts this way and leave to set for 24 hours.

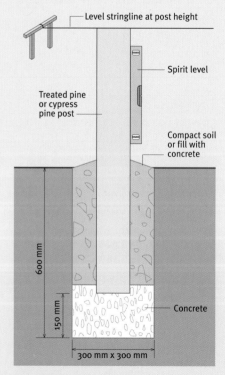

Level stringline at post height

Spirit level

Treated pine or cypress pine post

Compact soil or fill with concrete

600 mm

150 mm

Concrete

300 mm x 300 mm

Installing a post in the ground.

In stirrups

1 Add water and quick-set concrete as per the manufacturer's instructions. (See step 2 on page 156, right column.)

2 Fill the post hole with concrete to just below ground level. Place the post stirrup in the concrete, checking that it is plumb and level. Allow the concrete to dry (at least half an hour; more time will ensure maximum strength).

3 Measure and cut the posts to size using a power saw. Backfill the holes with soil and place a post in each stirrup.

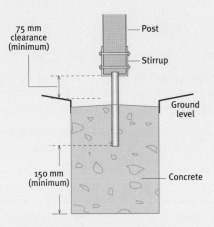

75 mm clearance (minimum)

Post

Stirrup

Ground level

150 mm (minimum)

Concrete

Installing a post in a stirrup set in concrete.

4 Nail temporary bracing to support each post and check for plumb using a spirit level or plumbline. (Fix bracing in opposing directions and make sure it will not obstruct later work.)

5 Fix posts to stirrups using 50 mm coach screws.

Fixing bearers to posts

1 Cut the bearers to length (3600 mm). Sit them on top of the posts. Drill pilot holes for skew-nailing and fix bearers with two 75 mm galvanised nails. Alternatively, use galvanised nail plates or brackets.

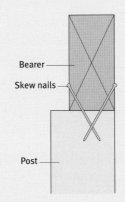

Bearer

Skew nails

Post

Bearer positioned on top of post.

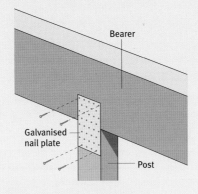

Bearer

Galvanised nail plate

Post

Bearer supported on top of posts.

2 To attach the joists, cut them to length and lay them over the bearers at 450 mm intervals. Fix joists to bearers by skew-nailing them with 75 mm galvanised nails, or supporting them in galvanised framing anchors or hangers.

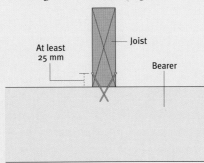

At least 25 mm

Joist

Bearer

Fixing joist to bearer with skew-nailing.

Smart tip

Ensure the set-out area is square by measuring diagonals (they should be equal) or using the 3:4:5 right-angle triangle method: if one side of a measured triangle is 3 m long, another 4 m long, and the remaining side 5 m long (or 300 mm, 400 mm and 500 mm), the triangle is right-angled and the outer lines are square. Use a spirit level or plumbline to locate the post positions below the intersections of the stringlines.

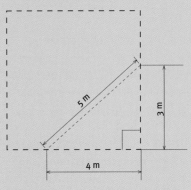

5 m

3 m

4 m

Determining a 3:4:5 right-angle triangle.

Smart tip

To make profiles (hurdles), cut three pieces of scrap timber, such as 50 mm x 25 mm hardwood. Cut one end of each of two pieces to a point so it can be hammered into the ground. Nail these stakes to each end of the third piece of timber.

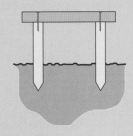

Making a profile.

Smart tip

Before installing decking boards, give all surfaces (including their cut ends) and the top surface of the joists one coat of primer, stain, decking oil or water-repellent preservative. This is an effective way to extend the life of your deck. (Alternatively, fit flashing to the tops of the joists.)

Smart tip

Where posts continue up to support railings, or to form part of a pergola, partially house and bolt the bearers approximately 10 mm into the posts. To fix bearers to posts, use two 12 mm diameter galvanised bolts. Drill the holes and position the bolts at least 25 mm from the upper and lower edge of the bearer, in the middle of the posts.

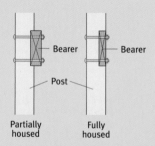

Bearers housed into posts.

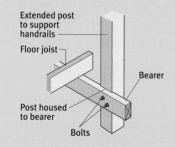

Post extended to hold handrails; bearer housed into post.

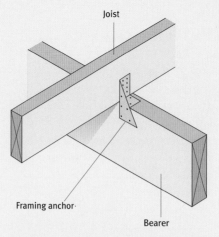

Fixing joist to bearer with framing anchor.

3 Fix any bowed joists with the curve upwards. Plane the tops of joists if necessary to create an even surface (that is, to remove bowing or adjust slight differences in joist depth); this is preferable to packing gaps.

4 Lay the decking boards across the joists (the best faces uppermost), making sure that each board is supported on at least three joists. Stagger the joints so that there are never two end-to-end joints next to each other on the same joist, and leave a gap of 3–5 mm between boards to allow water to drain away. (However, regulations for fire-designated areas state that there should be no gaps between decking.)

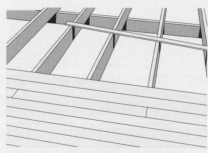

Laying the decking boards across the joists.

5 Allow board ends to project beyond the edge of the joists, to be trimmed after fixing. To straighten bowed boards, attach them at the ends first, then drive a chisel into the joist at mid-span and lever the board straight before nailing.

6 Fix the boards to each joist with two 50 mm long galvanised nails. (Use annular ring or twist-shank nails.) Leave the nail heads flush with the surface, not punched, so that there are no nail holes where moisture can enter the timber and hasten decay.

At the ends of boards and at butt joints, drill holes 80 per cent of the nail diameter, approximately 12 mm from the ends of the boards, to prevent the boards splitting as you are nailing.

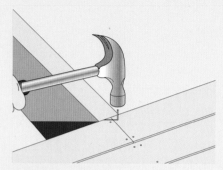

Fixing boards to a joist.

7 Periodically check the remaining distance and, if necessary, adjust the width of the gap to keep the boards parallel and to ensure that the last board does not have to be sawn lengthwise to fill a tapered gap. When all the boards are in place, mark the overhanging ends with a chalk line and trim with a power saw set to the depth of the decking.

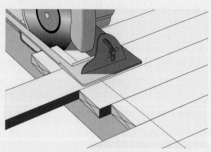

Trimming boards.

8 Once the decking boards are fixed and the ends are all neatly trimmed, you can apply additional coats of your chosen paint, stain, oil or clear finish as recommended by the manufacturer.

Low-level decks

Even if you live on a flat block in a single-storey house you can still extend your outdoor living area by building a very low timber deck (less than 150 mm above the ground). This not only provides a clean, grit-free entrance to your house, but links indoor and outdoor areas. There are a number of things you should do.

- Keep the perimeter of the deck open to allow plenty of air to circulate underneath. Also space the decking boards at least 5 mm apart (unless you are in a fire-designated area).
- Ensure adequate surface drainage. Make sure the ground beneath the deck is graded to prevent water from pooling. Place a plastic membrane over the ground and cover it with stones, gravel or sand to assist drainage (or install drainage pipes if water pooling is likely to be a major problem).
- Select the timber for the deck carefully. If timber supports are less than 150 mm above the ground, they should be of cypress, Class 1 hardwood or H5 preservative-treated softwood. Decking boards should be Class 1 or 2 hardwood or H3 preservative-treated softwood. Steel purlins may also be used as bearers or joists, set on brick supports; their advantage is that they won't rot and they cannot be destroyed by white ants, or termites.

ABOVE **A pergola over a deck can support vines and creepers for extra shade.**

LEFT **A low-level deck increases your living area.**

Difficulty: Moderate to hard
Time: 1 day

Tools

- Circular saw (or handsaw)
- Pencil and ruler
- Measuring tape
- Step template (see page 161)
- Hammer
- Spirit level
- Chisel
- Power drill and 20 mm bit
- Spanner
- Paintbrush
- Stringline
- Square

Materials (for stairs)

- Timber for stringers and treads
- 50 mm x 50 mm galvanised steel or aluminium angles for attaching treads
- 65–70 mm galvanised bolts and rustproof screws for fixing tread angle brackets
- 150–175 mm galvanised coach bolts (depending on timber) for fixing stringers to bearer or joist
- Ledger: 100 mm x 50 mm (if required)
- Galvanised brackets and bolts (for fixing steps at ground level)
- Quick-set concrete
- Primer
- Paint (or other finish)

Materials (for handrails)

- Posts: 100 mm x 100 mm to 70 mm x 70 mm hardwood (or 90 mm x 45 mm treated pine) x approximately 1000 mm
- Top and bottom horizontal rails of up to 1.5 m: 75 mm x 38 mm hardwood or treated pine (if required)
- 12 mm diameter galvanised bolts
- 10 mm diameter galvanised bolts or coach screws (for rails installed on edge) or 75 mm galvanised nails (for rails installed flat)
- Galvanised angle brackets, if required
- 75 mm batten screws
- Balusters, vertical rails, lattice (if required)

Constructing timber stairs and handrails

If you've built a raised deck you'll probably need to provide steps up to it. Stairs to areas more than 1 m high are also required to have a handrail. However, a competent handyperson can build both stairs and handrails.

The first decision you need to make when building outdoor stairs is where to locate them. You will need to consider access to the garden as well as to the house, and ease of construction. Another thing you need to think about is the width of the steps: should they be wide enough for one person or do you want to allow for two or more people to walk side by side?

Outdoor stairs consist of two basic elements: treads (the horizontal pieces of timber that you stand on) and stringers (the boards or other structures that run at an angle beside or beneath the treads and hold them in place). However, despite these common elements, every set of steps needs to be designed to suit the actual height between the deck or other raised area and the ground.

The simplest method for building stairs is to support treads on galvanised steel angles that are fixed to the stringers with galvanised bolts or screws. (A more involved method is to house treads into grooves routed in the inside face of each stringer, but unless your joinery is very precise, water can collect in the joints and the timber tread can rot prematurely. This method is not recommended for the home handyperson.) You can use a ledger to attach steps at the top and brackets to attach them at the base.

Calculating step dimensions

There are some basic rules to follow when calculating the number of steps you require and their angle or steepness. Each rise (the

Timber stairs and handrails can be attractive as well as practical.

measurement from the top of one tread to the top of the next) must be identical and should be between 160 mm and 190 mm maximum. The 'going' (the horizontal distance from the front edge of one step to the front edge of the next) should also be identical and be in the range of 240–275 mm (any larger and users may have to take two steps on each tread). The length of the treads should be 900–1200 mm for timber 45 mm thick. Steps wider than 1200 mm will need additional timber supports (called carriage pieces) fixed under the centre of each tread.

To determine the optimal number, size and steepness of your steps, you need to do the following calculations.

- Measure the overall height of the steps (also known as the overall rise or vertical fall). For example: 1020 mm. Then calculate the number of rises by dividing the overall height by an average rise of 170 mm: 1020 mm ÷ 170 mm = 6.
- Calculate the number of treads (one less than the number of rises): 6 − 1 = 5 treads.
- Calculate the going. This could be related to the tread width or, where the overall length (or 'run') of the stairs is fixed, be that length divided by the number of treads. The tread width can be slightly larger than the going: if, say, you have limited space and the maximum possible length of the stairs is 1200 mm with five treads, the going will be 1200 ÷ 5 = 240 mm, and if you use 250 mm wide timber each tread will overhang the one below by 10 mm.
- Prepare a triangular step template out of plywood or stiff cardboard, with the going and rise at right angles to each other. The diagonal (hypotenuse)

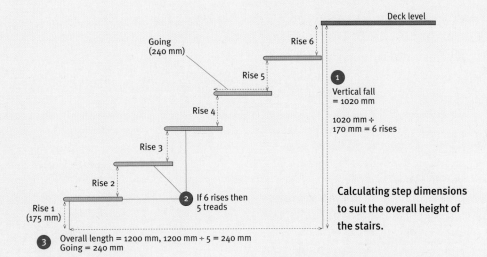

Calculating step dimensions to suit the overall height of the stairs.

represents the 'pitch line' (angle) of the stairs.
- Calculate the approximate length of the stringers by multiplying the pitch line length (take this measurement from your step template) by the number of rises.

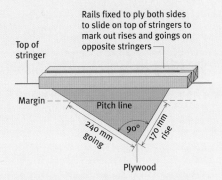

Using a step template to mark out the rises and goings on stringers.

Materials

Hardwood is a popular choice for steps, particularly for treads, because of its durability. But you should note that stairs may bridge termite barriers and, if necessary, take precautions accordingly. Treads and stringers need to be a minimum of 240 mm x 45 mm for hardwood or treated pine. Treads can be made from a single piece of timber (although this can distort when exposed to weather) or from two or three pieces 125 mm x 50 mm or 120 mm x 45 mm installed 10 mm apart to allow water to drain away. These are called built-up treads.

Smart tip

According to the Building Code of Australia the minimum going is 240 mm and the maximum rise is 190 mm in domestic constructions.

Smart tip

Stringers longer than 1350 mm can be bolted together with a 10 mm diameter galvanised rod or bolt ('long thread') positioned below the tread closest to the middle of the stringers.

Smart tip

Built-up treads made from two or more planks allow for water run-off.

A 'long thread' below the middle tread holds the stringers together.

Stairs

1 Cut two stringers to the appropriate length. (Allow some extra if stringers are to extend over the top of a bearer or ledger.)

2 Using the prepared step template, mark the tread positions on the inside face of each stringer, allowing a 50 mm margin along the top edge. Next, mark the horizontal and vertical cut-off lines at each end. The horizontal cut on the bottom will allow the stringer to sit firmly on the ground, while the vertical cut at the top will butt against the front bearer of the deck. Also mark any cut-outs for ledgers or fixing brackets if the stairs are to be fixed to the side of a house, deck or other structure.

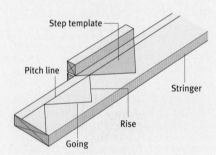

3 Cut the treads to length. Prime the ends with a coat of timber finish.

4 Fix the treads into position on galvanised steel angles using galvanised screws and bolts (the length depends on the depth of the treads).

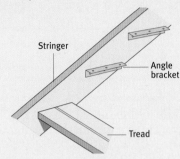

5 Attach the stair assembly to the deck or building by notching the stringers over a bearer or a ledger, or by bolting the stringers to a bearer or joist with angle brackets.

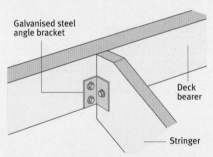

Bolting a stringer to a deck bearer.

6 Fix the steps at the ground by supporting the stringers either on galvanised steel brackets set into concrete, or supporting

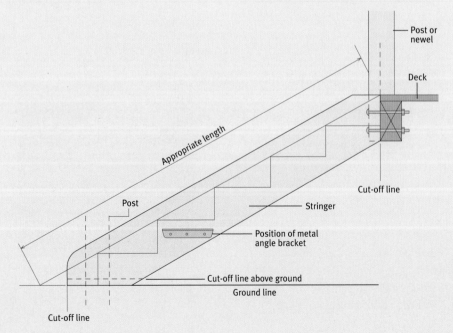

stringers on timber posts sitting in brackets or set into the ground.

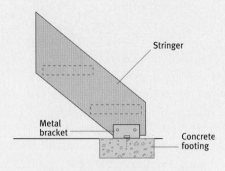

Supporting a stringer on galvanised steel brackets set in concrete.

Handrails

Decks or other structures more than 1 m above the ground must have horizontal handrails at least 1 m high. Stairs to these elevated decks must also have railings, which are required to be at least 865 mm above the front edge of the treads. There must be no gaps more than 125 mm between balusters, handrails, treads, or anywhere in the stair structure.

7 When installing the posts that support an elevated deck, if possible continue them through to the required railing height for the stairs or through to support a roof or pergola. If this isn't possible (or they can't be positioned where the stairs are needed), bolt a 70 mm x 70 mm hardwood or 90 mm x 45 mm treated pine post to the outside of the top of a stringer with 12 mm bolts, ensuring the post is vertical using a spirit level and that the bolts will not interfere with the top stair. Bolt a post to the outside of the stringer at the bottom.

8 Run a stringline between both posts and, using the spirit level and ruler, ensure it is at least 865 mm above the front edges of the tread. It should also be parallel with the top of the stringer.

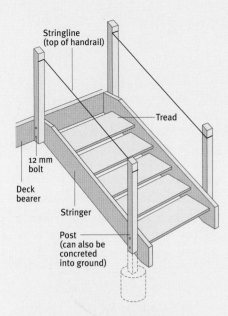

Running a stringline between the posts.

Labels: Stringline (top of handrail); Tread; 12 mm bolt; Deck bearer; Stringer; Post (can also be concreted into ground)

9 Using the stringline, which indicates the position for the top of the handrail, attach the rails to the posts. These can be installed flat or on edge. To fix them on edge, attach them to the posts with two 10 mm diameter galvanised bolts or coach screws. To install them flat, either tenon the tops of the posts into the underside of continuous top rails, or house half the width of the rails into the sides of posts that continue up to a pergola or roof. Skew-nail two 75 mm x 3.75 mm galvanised nails at each joint. Never use simple butt joints with

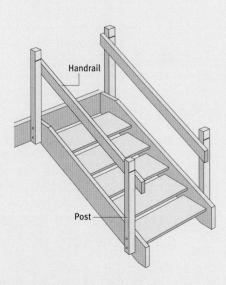

Handrail attached to the posts.

Labels: Handrail; Post

skew-nailing to fix rails to posts. In some States legislation requires rail joints to be strengthened by adding angle brackets. These are fixed with batten screws to the post and to the underside of the abutting rail.

10 Install bottom rails (if required) in the same way as for the top rails. You can infill between the top and bottom rails (or the stringer) using vertical balusters skew-nailed to the rails, additional horizontal rails, timber lattice, a solid surface such as timber boarding, plywood, safety glass or acrylic, or a colonial-style design with dowels, diagonal members and decorative boards.

Vertical balusters skew-nailed to rails.

Label: Baluster

11 The rails can be trimmed flush with the posts, the posts can be trimmed flush with the rails, or they can be decorated with post capitals and the like. When installing the rail on the opposite stringer, ensure it is the same height as the first rail. To do this, measure the distance from the top of the first stringer to the top of the first rail, and mark this on the posts for the second rail. To attach rails to the deck, the principle is the same, except you should ensure the rails between posts are at least 1 m high and horizontal.

Building a simple three-post pergola

Difficulty: Moderate to hard

Time: 1–3 days

Tools

- Pencil and ruler
- Tape measure
- Hammer
- Spirit level (or plumbline)
- Stringlines
- Profiles
- Shovel
- Power saw (or handsaw)
- Safety glasses and earmuffs
- Power drill and 10 mm drill bit
- Spanner
- Adjustable bevel (or protractor)
- Paintbrush

Materials

- 3 posts: 2400 mm x 90 mm x 90 mm treated pine (or 100 mm x 100 mm durable hardwood)
- 4 bags pre-mixed, quick-set concrete
- Galvanised post stirrups
- 50 mm coach screws
- 2 beams: 3600 mm x 190 mm x 45 mm treated pine
- 50 mm galvanised bolts (10 mm diameter)
- 10 rafters: 1800 mm x 120 mm x 45 mm
- 75 mm galvanised nails
- Roofing timber: up to 50 lengths of decking 3600 mm x 70 mm x 19 mm (or battens 75 mm x 38 mm hardwood or 70 mm x 35 mm treated pine), depending on shade preference
- 50 mm galvanised twist-shank nails
- Primer and paint (or stain and clear finish)
- Shadecloth, lattice or polycarbonate roofing, if desired

A pergola can make a deck, patio, courtyard or other outdoor area more attractive and comfortable during the summer months and, with the addition of a lattice screen or timber fence, it can provide privacy as well. If covered or roofed, a pergola can also help keep the interior of your house cooler by shading walls that would otherwise be in full sun. The location and orientation of your pergola will determine its style and the degree of weather protection required.

One of the simplest pergolas to build is an unroofed two-post or three-post pergola that is attached to the eaves fascia of a house. If your house has a sturdy fascia, the job is even more straightforward.

The materials listed for this project are for a long, narrow pergola, but it would be easy to alter the height of posts and the lengths of beams and rafters to suit your particular needs. If you plan to roof your pergola, there are several options, ranging from installing shadecloth to fixing UV-treated polycarbonate sheeting.

Before you start, make sure that your plan complies with all council regulations and that you have any necessary building permits.

Roofing a pergola with polycarbonate sheeting provides protection from the elements but allows the sun to shine in.

1   Set out the positions of the posts using stringlines attached to existing walls or fences or to setting-out profiles (hurdles). Use the 3:4:5 method to check for square (see Smart tip on page 157).

2   Dig post holes 300 mm square and 600 mm deep. If the soil is particularly dry, pour a litre or so of water into the hole and allow it to soak in. This will ensure that the concrete does not set too quickly.

3   Add water and quick-set concrete as per the manufacturer's instructions. (To obtain the correct consistency you may prefer to add the concrete in batches rather than all at once. However, it's important to keep in mind that quick-set concrete hardens in 15 minutes, so there is not much time for experimentation.)

4   Fill the post hole with concrete to just below ground level. Place the post stirrup in the concrete, checking that it is plumb and level. Allow the concrete to dry (at least half an hour; more will ensure maximum strength).

5   Determine the height of the posts using the fascia position. Allow for a gentle slope, then measure and cut the posts to size using a power saw. On the outside of the posts at the top cut a housing for the beams 190 mm x 45 mm. Backfill the holes with soil and place a post in each stirrup.

6   Nail temporary bracing to support each post and check for plumb using a spirit level or plumbline. (Fix bracing in opposing directions and make sure it will not obstruct later work.)

7   Fix posts to stirrups using 50 mm coach screws.

8   To join two beams over the centre post, mitre the joining ends and prime them before placing them onto the centre post notch. (This is known as a scarf or 'splay' joint.)

Drill clearance holes (for the bolts) through both beams. Fix the beams to the post using 50 mm galvanised bolts.

9   Drill clearance holes through the outer ends of each beam and fix to the end posts using 50 mm galvanised bolts.

Smart tip

The end-grain of timber is most susceptible to decay, and shaping the projecting ends of rafters and beams reduces the amount of end-grain exposed to the weather.

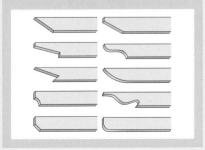

10   Use a bevel or hold the rafter up at one end to mark and measure the angle at which the rafter will meet the beam at one end and the angle at which it will meet the fascia at the other. Trace this rafter onto all the other rafters. Use a power saw to cut the ends of each rafter to the correct angle. Prime all joints before fixing them together. Knock the end rafter into position and skew-nail to the fascia using 75 mm galvanised nails.

11   Nail the rafter to the beam using 75 mm galvanised nails. Nail the remaining rafters to the beams (at 750 mm intervals) and fix with skew-nailing at the fascia end and regular nailing (face-nailing) at the beam end.

12   To roof the pergola, nail decking timber or battens to the top of the rafters at 20 mm intervals (or more, depending on the degree of shade preferred). If using 20 mm intervals, place a length of decking offcut between each piece for easy marking. Fix with 50 mm galvanised twist-shank nails.

13   Prime and paint (or stain and clear finish) the timber. If desired, attach shadecloth or lattice instead of decking timber or battens. Or, if using other roofing material, attach it according to the manufacturer's instructions.

This newly built pergola will last many years if it is finished with a quality exterior paint.

Entertaining

The backyard is usually a place where you can retreat to unwind and relax in informal surroundings with family and close friends. Often outdoor socialising involves cooking and eating a meal, typically a barbecue. It's easy to create an outdoor entertaining area: a barbecue, a couple of chairs, and perhaps an outdoor table is all you'll need. But no cook wants to work in isolation, so site the barbecue near the table and chairs. Once you have places to sit, cook and eat, you and your friends can do the rest.

Building a brick barbecue

Difficulty: Hard

Time: 8 hours

Tools

- Chalk (or stringline and pegs)
- Square-mouthed shovel
- Wheelbarrow
- Bricklayer's trowel
- Rubber gloves
- Raking tool or pointing trowel
- Sponge
- Spirit level
- Hammer drill and masonry bit
- Bolster or cold chisel and mash hammer

Materials

- Four 30 kg bags of dry concrete mix for footing
- 150 solid bricks
- Bricklaying mortar
- Cement sheet, 500 mm x 500 mm x 12 mm
- Angle brackets
- Screws and plastic wall plugs
- Gas cooktop

The traditional Australian barbecue was once a simple brick affair incorporating a firebox below a grate, sometimes with a benchtop and an area for storing wood. These days, many people find a portable barbecue more convenient and flexible. In some gardens, though, there may be only one spot that is suitable for a barbecue, and building your own permanent barbecue in brick is both economical and satisfying. A solid, permanent barbecue can provide a focal point for your backyard entertaining.

The brick barbecue in this project accommodates a gas-fired cooktop and has a handy bench. Before starting, make sure that the design will not need to be modified to fit the selected gas barbecue, and that the gas inlet will be accessible. You may prefer to use concrete blocks or stone for the barbecue.

The following project can be adapted easily. The barbecue can be made wider, topped with timber or integrated into a brick wall or brick paving. When choosing the bricks for the barbecue, remember that it may be a key feature of your entertaining area, so try to use bricks that will enhance the look of the finished product. You may also choose to bag or paint the brickwork (if you are bagging, do not point or rake the mortar). The only things to bear in mind as you express your creativity are that you should ensure the dimensions will still fit the cooktop and that you check and recheck that brickwork is straight and level as you go.

1 Lay out a test pattern of bricks in the desired location and mark around them with chalk or a pegged stringline; then excavate a footing 150 mm deep and 150 mm wide. Fill with concrete to just below ground level. Allow the concrete to set for two or three days.

2 Carefully lay the first course of bricks (depressions or 'frogs' up) checking that they are straight and level. Two half-bricks will be needed in each course. (Use a

A well-sited barbecue blends in with its surroundings and is near enough to the table and seating to keep the cook happy.

bolster and mash hammer to break bricks cleanly.) Then spread a layer of mortar on top of the first course.

3 Follow with additional courses in a stretcher bond. After every few courses, tidy up the mortar line with a raking tool or pointing trowel and sponge off excess mortar before it dries. If you plan to bag the bricks, simply remove any excess mortar with your bricklaying trowel and do not rake or point the joints.

4 Place a little mortar on the benchtop end of the second-last course, and position the cement sheet on it. Lay a full coverage of bricks in the last course, with frogs down to leave a smooth surface. Fill the gaps between the bricks with mortar.

5 If the cooktop does not have built-in wings or brackets for fitting over a brick framework, drill holes at the correct level for angle brackets and plastic plugs. (Do not hammer drill the brickwork until the mortar has dried thoroughly or the bonds between brick and mortar may break. Allow at least a week.)

6 Fix the brackets with appropriate screws, then fit the cooktop according to the manufacturer's directions.

Building your own permanent barbecue is both economical and satisfying.

Making an outdoor table

Tools

- Pencil
- 1000 mm steel ruler
- 200 mm square
- 120, 150 and 220 grit carborundum sandpaper
- G-clamps
- Power drill and bits
- File
- Tenon saw (or power saw)
- Hex head bits, 8 mm and 10 mm (or socket spanner set)
- Workbench and vice (useful but not essential)
- Paintbrush

Materials

- Legs: 4 pieces timber (kiln-dried hardwood [KDH]), each 765 mm x 140 mm x 35 mm
- Tabletop rails: 2 pieces timber (KDH), each 800 mm x 120 mm x 35 mm
- Seat rails: 2 pieces timber (KDH), each 1560 mm x 120 mm x 35 mm
- Seats: 4 pieces timber (KDH), each 2000 mm x 120 mm x 35 mm
- Tabletop: 7 pieces timber (KDH), each 2000 x 120 mm x 35 mm
- Galvanised round head bolts, washers and nuts, 90 mm long x 10 mm diameter
- 50 mm and 70 mm rustproof hex head screws
- 2 metal brackets to join tabletop to tabletop rails, each 780 mm long x 30 mm wide
- 25 mm and 50 mm rustproof countersunk screws
- Cleat (to match tabletop width)
- Diagonal table braces: 2 pieces timber (KDH), each 700 mm x 90 mm x 35 mm
- Suitable external timber oil

Simple and strong bolt-together outdoor furniture can usually be completed in an afternoon or two, if you have the correct equipment and materials, plan each step carefully, and remember the old saying 'measure twice, cut once'. Choose kiln-dried hardwoods such as jarrah, red gum and spotted gum. If money is tight, the tabletop, rails and braces can be 25 mm instead of 35 mm.

Cut all timber to length first. Sand ends smooth, rounding over exposed corners.

1 First prepare to fix the legs to the tabletop rails and seat rails. The tabletop rails should sit flush with the top of the legs. The seat rails should overhang the legs and be set up 400 mm from the base of the legs. Two bolts for each connection will be adequate.

To determine the position of the bolt holes, draw a line diagonally across each join from corner to corner. Then measure 40 mm from each corner for the bolt

holes. Note that the position of the top bolts will need to be lower to allow for fitting the metal brackets. Clamp the timber together, checking for square, and drill through both pieces of timber with a 10 mm drill bit. Fit the bolt through with a washer between the head and the timber, and between the nut and timber. The bolt head should be on the outer, visible side and the nut on the inside. Cut and file the bolt ends if they protrude too far.

2 Fix the seats to the seat rails using 50 mm hex head screws. Use two pieces of timber for each seat with a 5 mm gap. Ensure each seat rail is set 300 mm in from the

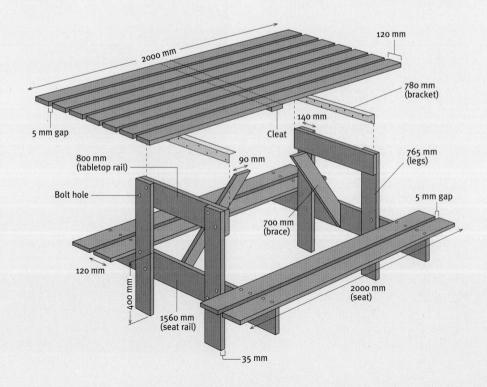

end of the seat. Countersink the screws so that the heads sit flush with the seat to prevent clothing from catching on the screw heads.

3 Assemble the tabletop upside down on a flat work surface, leaving a 5 mm gap between the lengths of timber or planks. To ensure even spacing between the planks, position three 5 mm spacers between each plank, one in the middle and one at each end.

Clamp the planks and spacers before fixing the brackets and cleat. The number of planks required will depend on how much overhang you allow for the tabletop. An overhang no greater than 70 mm is recommended.

Position the metal brackets across the underside of the tabletop, so that they will fit neatly inside the tabletop rails. Fix the

brackets in place using 25 mm rustproof countersunk screws.

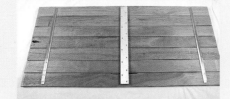

4 Fix the cleat to the underside of the tabletop with 50 mm countersunk screws, after first drilling clearance holes. Before fixing the tabletop you will need to measure and cut the diagonal table braces, which are to be fixed underneath the tabletop.

Make a 45 degree cut to one end of each of the braces using a tenon saw. Stand the table leg and seat structure up on flat ground without the tabletop. Place a straight piece of scrap timber on its edge on top of the leg rail (sight along the edge of the timber to check that it is straight). Place the 45 degree cut end of the brace on the inside of the seat rail with the other end pointing upwards. Mark carefully on each brace where it crosses the bottom edge of the scrap timber and cut carefully with a tenon saw.

Drill a clearance hole through the 45 degree downward edges of each brace, set back 35 mm from the pointed end. Fix the braces into place once the top is positioned.

5 Fix the tabletop in position from the underside with screws through the metal brackets. Don't let the screw points penetrate the surface of the tabletop.

6 Fix the diagonal braces into position with 70 mm hex head screws.

7 Sand and clean the timber. Finish with a suitable external oil or UV-resistant polyurethane. (check with your local hardware shop – some break down when exposed to weather).

This timber table is ideal for a backyard lawn area.

Making a garden bench

A bench or day bed made from rustic timber is a great addition to any backyard. It's a place where you can pause to rest and enjoy your garden, read or snooze. Heavy timbers mean that this project not only looks good, but will last for years, even if left untreated. Just throw some big canvas cushions over it and relax.

This project is for a garden bench or day bed 1800 mm x 500 mm, but you can vary the size to fit some extra people, or a particular area, or the timber you've managed to scavenge.

1 With a pencil, ruler or tape measure and square, measure all timbers to size. Remove any old nails or screws, then cut with a saw.

2 Pre-drill two holes at each end of the shorter rails using a bit slightly smaller than the coach screws. Screw rails to the posts so the ends finish flush with the edge of the posts.

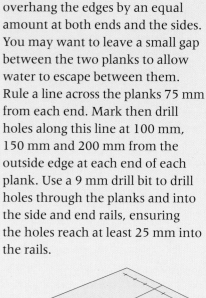

3 Pre-drill two holes at each end of the longer rails and screw them to the posts so the ends are flush with the edge of the shorter rails. This now forms the base of the bench.

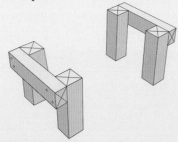

4 Lay the planks on top of the base and measure to ensure they overhang the edges by an equal amount at both ends and the sides. You may want to leave a small gap between the two planks to allow water to escape between them. Rule a line across the planks 75 mm from each end. Mark then drill holes along this line at 100 mm, 150 mm and 200 mm from the outside edge at each end of each plank. Use a 9 mm drill bit to drill holes through the planks and into the side and end rails, ensuring the holes reach at least 25 mm into the rails.

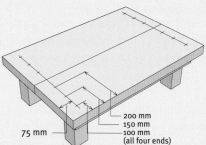

75 mm

200 mm
150 mm
100 mm
(all four ends)

5 Cut dowel into 75 mm lengths (you may be able to buy wooden plugs for this). Apply wood glue to drill holes and dowel pieces. Hammer the dowels into the holes to fix the planks into position. Use the sandpaper and block to round off any rough or sharp edges on all exposed timbers.

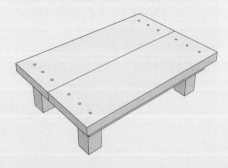

Water features

Water features bring sound and movement to your backyard. The pleasurable sound of water can be gentle and relaxing or crisp and invigorating. And having a water feature to enhance your backyard is not difficult. No matter how large or small the space you have available, there is always a way to incorporate a water feature somewhere in the backyard. Whether you choose a lion head, a wine-barrel, a distinctive wall fountain or a small pond, made with a plastic liner and clay, every type and size of water feature will add a new dimension to your backyard.

Installing a pond

Ready-made ponds of fibreglass or glass resin are available in a multitude of different sizes and shapes. They are easy to install and ideal for creating an instant effect. The addition of a fountain or fish will further enhance the pond.

One of the easiest ways to construct a water feature is to begin with a prefabricated, fibreglass pond available from outdoor centres. Measure the area for your pond, then check the selection for the pond size and shape that will suit your needs. In choosing a pond site, you should ensure that the excavation will not disturb any pipes or electrical services.

1   Dig the hole for the pond, checking the size and shape as you go by putting the shell in the hole every so often.

2   Sit the pond shell onto a 25–30 mm layer of sand so that it's firmly in place. Add a little water to the bottom of the shell until it's well covered and stable.

3   Use a straightedge or stake to measure from the top of the water to the top edge of the pond in several places around the pond to make sure it's level. Having part-filled the shell, backfill the outside of it by hosing a slurry of sand between it and the surrounding soil. This will ensure that the shell remains stable and will not be subjected to uneven pressure when full.

4   Hide the edges of the pond by packing topsoil around the edge and planting suitable groundcovers or shrubs, or by using paving slabs or bricks.

Choosing a water pump

When water falls or tumbles it mixes with air, adding oxygen to the system, which is of great benefit visually, audibly and ecologically. A fountain or waterfall will, of course, require a water pump. Most use 240 volt electric power so you'll need a power supply with a safety switch or earth leakage switch installed along the line. Submersible pumps are best as they can be disguised easily, maintained without difficulty and are available in many sizes.

Select a pump that:
- is designed for continuous running
- is predominantly plastic
- has no corrodible alloy parts.

You also need to ensure that it will pump sufficient water for your needs. Base your calculations on pumping the total volume of water in your pond once every two hours. Waterfalls and fountains oxygenate the water and improve its quality, but they require a stronger pump. For example, a pump's capacity can be reduced from 60 litres per minute to only 8 litres per minute if it has to lift the water 3 metres above the pond surface. When buying piping, it's best oversized, as this will minimise friction. PVC pipes of 25 mm to 32 mm diameter are used commonly (25 mm is suitable for most applications, but 32 mm should be used for large volumes of water).

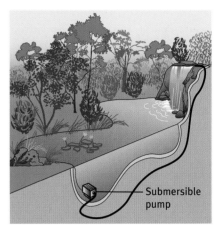

Placement of a submersible pump.

Water features not only provide a soothing focal point in a backyard, they introduce sound and movement to any setting.

BELOW   Fish can bring your pond to life, literally. Some varieties will even help keep the pond clean. While goldfish are popular, you should select a variety that will thrive in your climate, especially considering they will be outdoors all year round.

BOTTOM   Plants can provide cover and food for frogs and tadpoles.

Stocking your pond with fish

Usually you should only place one species of fish in a single pond. Goldfish are very hardy and easy to look after, but can be an environmental hazard if they escape into waterways; they also eat frog spawn and tadpoles. However, 'goldfish' is an umbrella term referring to a variety of fish, including shabunkins, calicoes, golden orfes, comets, orandas and veil tails. Your supplier should be able to give you information about suitable types for your area and advice on cultivation. If you live near a waterway and fish might escape, choose small, local, native species.

Green or golden tench are worth considering as they help keep the pond clean by eating all the detritus on the bottom. Many native varieties of fish, such as the hardyhead family, golden perch and types of catfish, also clean up waste in pond environments.

If you want lots of fish, you'll need a biological filter and a small air bubble pump to keep oxygen circulating. And always provide protection against predators such as birds and cats. If possible give the fish somewhere to hide (such as clay pipes or an overhanging rocky shelf). When putting new fish in the water, submerge their container almost to the rim for ten minutes so there is gradual adjustment between the two temperatures.

Choose native or local water plants if there is any chance of their being washed into waterways.

Creating frog-friendly ponds

Frogs need food, humidity, hiding spots and cool places to breed, so choose a shady position for your pond. Make the pond no more than 30 cm deep with sloping sides so frogs can move in and out easily (otherwise they could drown). Surround parts of the pond with thick foliage and groundcover, rocks and leaf litter so adult frogs can hide. Fill the pond with rainwater or allow tap water to stand in the sun for five days to remove chlorine.

To deal with mosquito larvae, add some native white-cloud minnows. These small fish will not eat frog spawn or tadpoles, although other fish will. However, you could collect the spawn and rear the tadpoles away from the fish until they reach about 15 mm in length.

In some states it is illegal to collect frog spawn, tadpoles or frogs. If you have to collect them to save their lives, release them where you found them when it is safe to do so.

Tadpoles eat daphnia and frozen lettuce leaves (freezing breaks down the structure and softens the leaves); nardoo provides food and cover for frogs in many areas.

Keeping it green

If you have plenty of water and live in a suitable climate, lawn and lush greenery may be for you. You don't have to be a horticultural genius to keep your backyard looking fantastic. One of the most obvious ways of keeping your garden green is to ensure that it is well watered – the right amount, in the right place, for the right amount of time – and well mulched. And when it comes to getting a great lawn, a lot of the secret lies in the preparation. Take care of the basics and keeping your backyard green is a breeze.

Installing a lawn watering system

Difficulty: Easy
Time: 1 day

Tools

- Short stakes
- Chalk (or lime or string)
- Spade
- Trenching shovel and mattock
- Tape measure
- Pipe cutters (or secateurs)
- Multigrips

Materials

- Poly piping
- Poly fittings and clamps
- Pop-up sprinklers
- Connectors
- Tap-adaptor
  (for simple manual systems)
- Solenoids (for automatic systems)
- 24 volt cable, valve box and
  controller (for automatic systems)

In most backyards, installing an in-ground sprinkler system is easy. Cheap, ready-to-assemble kits are available from hardware and garden centres and are sufficient for the average-sized backyard. Extra components and fancy devices such as automatic watering controllers can also be added. While this project is for installing a watering system in a lawn, the procedure for installing a watering system for garden beds is similar although it involves different components.

In either case, work out whether you need help. If necessary, collect brochures from local irrigation suppliers and ask whether they provide a free planning service. If so, take advantage of it. Doing so should give you an efficient design plus a list of the products you require.

If you are designing the system yourself, try to keep the layout as simple as possible. Straight lines with branch lines are ideal. On a plan, plot where the pipes for the watering system will be needed. Lawn sprinklers are available with a range of heads that cover from 1.5 m to 4.5 m; choose a combination that allows you to space them easily down each side of your lawn and through the middle, if necessary, or along the edge of your garden bed. (Ideally the sprayed areas should overlap 100 per cent; in other words, space the heads at a distance equal to the radius of the sprayed area.) You may need rows of pipes for a large lawn (set the rows at a distance equal to the radius of the spray area). Garden beds usually only need one pipe. If you place this along the front of the bed the sprays can be directed back towards the plants, rather than onto pavers and wasting water.

Once you have the basic layout, it's then simply a matter of connecting the right outlets for each area, usually once the topsoil and plants have gone in – drippers for trees and shrubs, sprays for beds and groundcovers, pop-ups for lawns and so on. (Different types of applicators should not be mixed but should be isolated in their own zones.) Keep in mind your water pressure (see Testing your water flow on page 180). If you have a lot

Sprinkler systems save time and energy, but they can waste water if used in hot or windy conditions, or after rain.

of outlets or a big backyard, one solution is to split the system into zones (there are valves that can do this) and water only part of the garden at a time.

Decide whether you want a manual system (fine for small gardens or people who have the time to water regularly) or an automatic one (for bigger gardens or busy people). A simple, manual system can be connected directly to your front or rear tap, using various fittings. Some automatic systems involve cutting into the mains water supply and installing an isolating valve – a job a plumber or licensed irrigation installer will probably have to do (check with your local water authority). A backflow-prevention valve must also be fitted.

1 Mark sprinkler positions with stakes and, with chalk, lime or string, draw the shortest practical route for the pipelines.

2 Remove sods along the marked lines and put them aside for replacement later. Dig trenches deep enough for the piping, the sprinklers and their connectors. The top of each pop-up sprinkler must be no higher than soil level.

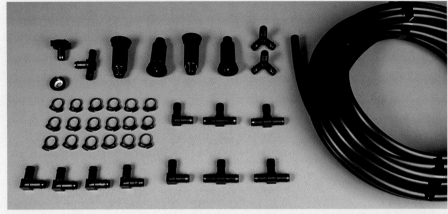

The components of a sprinkler kit.

3 Cut the poly piping to the required size and lay it in the trenches. Coiled poly piping can be made more workable by soaking it in hot water. Push each barbed connector into the pipe, the required distance apart. Secure with the poly clamps, and use the multigrips to check that they are shut tight.

4 When you have connected all the sprinklers, join up the poly piping to the tap.

5 Remove the end sprinkler (or sprinklers if you have more than one line) and turn on the water to flush the pipes. Turn off the water and replace the end sprinkler(s). Turn on the water

again and check all joins for leaks. Adjust sprinklers for coverage. For an automatic system, run electric cable along the trenches to link the solenoids with the controller, using waterproof connectors. (There will be instructions accompanying the controller.) Place the valve box over the solenoids.

6 Fill the trenches with soil, and then cover with the sods and firm down, ensuring that the sprinkler heads remain upright and at the correct level.

7 Finally, if the system is automatic, program your controller to deliver the right amount of water to your garden as often as required.

Testing your water flow

A formula based on the number of seconds it takes to fill a 9 litre bucket or watering can will give you the approximate water-flow rate of your garden taps. At the time of day when you expect to use your new watering system, turn off all taps, inside and out. Then turn the garden tap you intend to use to full pressure and fill the bucket, noting the start and finish times. Calculate your flow as follows:

$$\frac{60 \text{ (seconds) x 9 (litres)}}{\text{time to fill (seconds)}} = \text{litres per minute}$$

Deduct 15 per cent of the total to allow for water pressure fluctuations and friction loss of water within the pipes. As a rough rule of thumb, up to 20 litres per minute is slow but adequate for a courtyard garden, 20–40 is average and sufficient for a typical backyard, and 40 plus is high and could irrigate a farm.

Being waterwise

Whatever equipment you use and wherever you use it, water deeply and less often (to encourage plants to grow deep roots) rather than lightly and more frequently (to encourage root growth near the soil's surface, which dries out more easily). Always group plants with the same moisture requirements in the same bed. Watch plants carefully and water sensibly: be guided by the weather rather than habit (running sprinklers after rain is wasteful). Try to minimise evaporation by avoiding windy conditions and the hottest times of day. Remember that over-watering in badly drained soil may cause root-rot. A moisture meter will help you decide when to water (the cheaper ones are not very accurate). Dripping taps can waste a surprising amount of water. Replace worn washers without delay. Fit dual connectors to your garden taps and attach a hose to one head only, so you can fill a watering can, say, while the hose is running.

A spray is ideal for garden beds although not as waterwise as a drip system.

Preparing soil for lawn

If your block is in a new estate from which the developers have stripped the topsoil, you will have to bring in new soil to enable the grass to establish its root system. If you have kept your topsoil, you may still have to deal with heaps of clay left by builders levelling the site or digging trenches. Lawn requires well-aerated soil and good drainage to develop a thick sward, which in turn helps to prevent attack by diseases and pests.

Lawn grasses grow best in soils ranging from well-drained clay loams to sandy loam with some nutrients in it. If the soil is too sandy, and therefore drains too well, you can add more organic matter ('organic garden mix' or your own compost) to improve its water-holding capacity. If it contains too much clay you can rake in gypsum to improve it, but heavy clay soils are expensive to fix. An alternative solution is to buy some good quality 'turf underlay' (a combination of coarse, washed river sand, soil and organic matter).

The pH of soil – its level of acidity or alkalinity – is also important, and you should test the soil and try to improve it if you are far from the recommended range of 5.5–6.5.

Removing weeds
Use a herbicide that contains glyphosate, following directions carefully, to poison any weeds. (Hand-weeding is not a satisfactory alternative on this scale.) Remove old turf if you are changing to a new variety. Allow several weeks for weeds to die completely and dry off before you prepare to sow your new lawn or lay down rolls of turf.

Aerating the soil
If your area is too large to dig by hand, one way to ensure that the soil has a good, open texture, and also to break up the substrate before adding extra soil, is to go over the area with a rotary hoe. Do this only when the soil is moist, to help protect the soil structure. A rotary hoe is also useful for incorporating organic matter to a greater depth than you can achieve by hand. If you are gardening on a grand scale, you will find it easier to dig up the soil with bobcat teeth or the ripper tines of a tractor. After you have rotary-hoed and added any new soil needed, rake the area as level as possible. Fill any holes with more soil as you rake.

Smart tip

To calculate the quantity of soil, organic garden mix or turf underlay to order, measure the area involved (length and breadth, in metres). Soil depth should be about 150 mm for soil or garden mix, and at least 50 mm for turf underlay. Convert the millimetre measurements to metres (divide by 1000), and then multiply as follows:

$$l \times b \times d = cu. m$$

The number of cubic metres is the amount to buy.

Lawn lore

Here are a few tips to keep in mind when mowing your lawn.

- When designing a lawn, make sure the total lawn area is big enough for easy mowing.
- Don't cut the grass too often or too short as this will allow weeds to invade.
- Mow at a steady pace for the most even results. A hand mower is just the thing for a really small lawn.
- For efficient cutting, maintain the engine speed that is recommended by the manufacturer.
- Change direction every time you mow so that each cut is in the opposite direction to the last one and the grass does not lie only one way.
- Don't put lawn clippings straight on the garden because they may heat up and burn the plants; mix them into your compost bin or heap first.

Growing lawn from seed

Difficulty: Moderate
Time: 1–2 days
Tools
• Nail rake • Light roller (or hand-held rammer) • Hose with sprinkler nozzle
Materials
• Lawn starter (fertiliser) • Lawn seed

A lawn provides the focal point for this tree-rimmed garden.

A good lawn requires quite a bit of time, attention and water, but many people consider it worth the trouble because of its unique contribution to a garden. It provides the most pleasant surface of all for playing, walking and sitting on, and its cool tones soothe the eye in hot weather. A lush, green lawn often seems to pull the whole garden together, linking trees, shrubs and colourful smaller plants in a most harmonious way. It's important to choose a variety of lawn grass that suits your locality.

Growing lawn from seed is much cheaper than buying turf, but caring for the new grass in the early stages takes more time, and you may have to re-sow some sections. Your local nursery should be able to advise you on the quantity and best seed for your area (it may be a mixture of two or more varieties). It's best to sow lawns between spring and mid-summer in subtropical and tropical zones, and in either spring or autumn in temperate and cool areas.

1 Ensure that your soil is well prepared (see Preparing soil for lawn on page 181), and give it a final raking to complete the levelling.

2 Scatter lawn starter at the recommended rate.

3 Once you know your sowing rate, divide the bag of seed into two. Scatter the first half of the seed over the entire area as evenly as you can. Repeat, using the rest of the seed. Rake it in.

4 Run the roller over the sown seed, or press it into the soil with your rammer.

5 Water well, without allowing run-off.

6 Mow very lightly (with blades high) when the grass is around 6 cm tall, and lower the blades only gradually thereafter.

Laying rolls of turf

Turf rolls cost more, but produce an 'instant lawn'. It's particularly helpful when children urgently need a play area, or when the house is new and you don't want dirt carried inside. What's more, you can lay turf at pretty much any time of year. With the help of your supplier, calculate the quantity you need and order the rolls for delivery on a day when you can immediately do the work.

Prepare the soil as previously described on page 181. Scatter lawn starter at the recommended rate, or use turf underlay, which incorporates fertiliser. To make the task easier, try to find a second person to help you lay the turf.

1 Start in the furthest corner and use the fence or a garden bed as an edge from which to work. Lay out the rolls with the edges butted together well: in warmer weather there will be some shrinkage, and you won't want to leave any bare ground. Stagger the joins as you would if you were laying bricks. Walk on the newly laid turf as little as possible.

2 Cut excess turf at the edges with a steak knife or sharp spade.

3 Hire or borrow a roller to press the turf firmly into the soil below.

4 Water by hand during laying – after only a third of the job has been done if the weather is hot or the total area large.

In the next few days you will have to continue to water well, morning and evening, lifting one of the rolls from time to time to check moisture levels. If both the underside and the soil below are just moist, and the roll does not dry out during the day, the turf will thrive.

Top up any indentations when the grass is established by filling them with coarse washed river sand. Don't cut the lawn until the grass is firmly established, and then take off only the top third of the leaves. Lower the blades gradually.

Difficulty: Easy
Time: 1 day

Tools

- Wheelbarrow
- Steak knife (or sharp spade)
- Roller
- Hose with sprinkler nozzle

Materials

- Lawn starter (fertiliser)
- Turf underlay (a combination of coarse, washed river sand, soil and organic matter; optional)
- Rolls of turf

Smart tip

The Australian climate is not kind to lawns and a lot of water is necessary to keep them looking good in summer. Consider reducing the size of your lawn and replacing some of it with native grasses and other small plants.

Fun for kids

For children of all ages, the backyard is often the home base from where they begin to experience

the world around them. It's where they grow up and, as they do, their needs and desires change.

In their early years, a cubby house or sandpit is what they're after; when they're a little older,

it could be a swing and slide, or play centre; older still, and basketball rings are on their wish list.

These projects are well within the abilities of the average home handyperson, and your kids

can certainly help build them.

Building a cubby house

Cubby houses come in every shape and size but there are some basic rules governing all of them. A cubby must be safe, with no sharp, protruding edges or points (nails, screws or pieces of wood). It should be solid, as small children can be boisterous. Parents should be able to see what children are doing inside it, even though it is their 'private space'. It should also allow quick access in the case of an emergency. (An adult can lift this cubby or climb through the windows.) Part of the roof can also be hinged but take care that screws and bolts don't protrude into the cubby itself.

This project is ripe for variations: the roof can be extended over the front and sides, but round the corners to prevent injuries. You may also want to frame the windows and door with battens (this prevents the plywood splitting).

Before you start, make a list of all the timber required. Many hardware stores will cut the pieces to size for you. Some may even cut out the holes for the windows and door. It may be easier to paint or varnish the timber first.

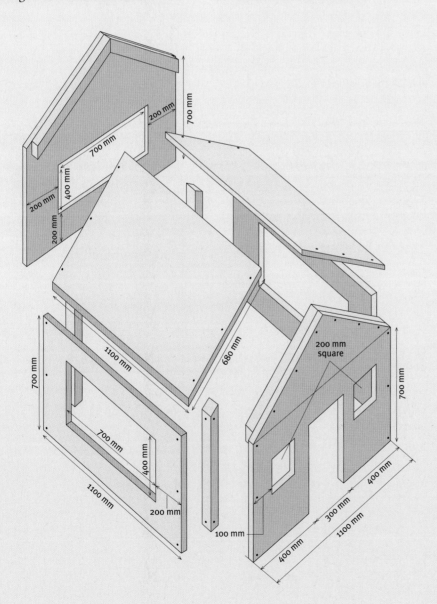

Difficulty: Moderate
Time: 8 or more hours

Tools

- Pencil
- Square
- Tape measure or 1000 mm folding rule
- Panel saw, handsaw or power saw
- Straightedge 1200 mm
- Power jigsaw (or hand keyhole saw)
- Power drill with assorted bits
- Phillips head screwdriver
- Sandpaper
- Paintbrushes

Materials

- 4 kiln-dried hardwood, pine or similar material corner posts: 700 mm x 40 mm x 40 mm
- 4 rafter blocks: 660 mm x 40 mm x 40 mm
- 2 five-ply plywood sheets: 1100 mm x 1100 mm
- 2 five-ply plywood sheets: 1100 mm x 700 mm
- 2 three-ply plywood sheets: 1100 mm x 680 mm
- Forty-eight 30 mm countersunk wood screws
- Silicone sealant (optional)
- Aluminium angle (optional)
- Brightly coloured gloss or semi-gloss paints or varnish

Smart tip

Encourage your children to garden by making a small garden bed outside their cubby. They can plant fast-growing seeds such as sunflowers, marigolds, rudbeckia, pansies, violas, nasturtiums and cosmos. When these plants are in flower, the children can pick them for indoors.

1   Measure and cut all panels to size using a rule, square, straightedge and power or handsaw. Sand and round over all rough edges (the kids can help).

2   Using a square, straightedge and pencil, mark on all four wall panels the positions of the windows and door.

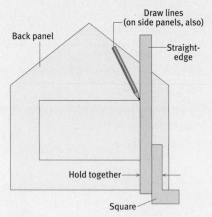

Back panel

Draw lines (on side panels, also)

Straight-edge

Hold together

Square

3   Use a 19 mm drill bit to cut holes at the corners of each door and window, then cut along the lines between the corners using a hand keyhole saw or power jigsaw. Sand off all rough edges.

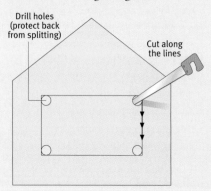

Drill holes (protect back from splitting)

Cut along the lines

Smart tip

Rubbing a little candle wax or soap on the thread of a screw will make driving it in a lot smoother, and will help to protect the screw hole against moisture penetration.

4   Cut the corner panel posts and rafter blocks to size to suit the front and back panels.

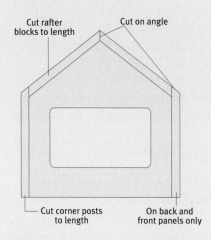

Cut rafter blocks to length

Cut on angle

Cut corner posts to length

On back and front panels only

5   Screw the front and back panels to the corner posts and rafter blocks ensuring that their edges finish flush. Use three screws per post and rafter block, but drill starter holes to guide the screws. The kids can help wield the screwdriver.

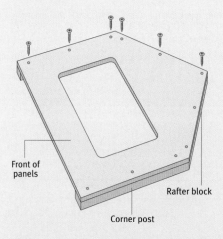

Front of panels

Corner post

Rafter block

6   Stand up one of the side panels and position the front panel so that its edge is flush with the side panel. The kids can help by

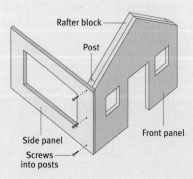

Rafter block

Post

Side panel

Screws into posts

Front panel

holding up the panel while you drill starter holes. Screw the side panel to the posts. Do the same with the other side panel. Then attach the back panel.

7   Drill starter holes for the roofing panels through the roof panel into the rafter blocks on the front and back panels. Screw the roof panels to the front and back panel rafter blocks. If you want to weatherproof the roof, squeeze silicone sealant into the gap between the roof panels. You can also use aluminium angle as a capping but beware of sharp edges.

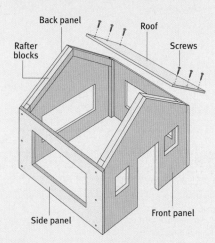

Back panel

Roof

Rafter blocks

Screws

Side panel

Front panel

8   Paint the cubby in bright colours, or colours that will complement your house and backyard. If the cubby is to be sited outdoors, a good paint job will prolong its life for many years.

Planning a tree-house

Children love tree-houses. However, before you start to build one, consider these issues. Some councils have introduced restrictions on tree-houses, due to unsightly constructions ruining the outlook for neighbours. Check your local council's policy before building and, as a courtesy, consult neighbours who might be affected.

Some trees are more suitable for tree-houses than others. Trees that drop a lot of sap can stain clothes and children. Others drop branches, which can be dangerous for children and may damage the tree-house. If in doubt, check with the horticulturist at your local garden centre.

A tree-house should be built solidly. It should have a solid and level deck, and properly constructed railings. Ladders and stairs should also be suitably sturdy. While it may be tempting to attach the tree-house to the tree itself, an alternative that won't damage the tree is to construct the tree-house around the tree, like a deck, although this can be difficult. Remember that the tree-house doesn't have to be high. The sense of being in a tree can be achieved by building a tree-house only a metre from the ground.

When selecting the site for the tree-house, check the ground around it for hard or sharp objects that could injure children if they fall. If possible, use mulch or a sandpit around the tree to provide a soft landing in case of an accident.

This tree-house has been built on the stump of an old tree.

Building a sandpit

Difficulty: Easy
Time: 3 hours
Tools
• Shovel • Drill • Hammer
Materials
• 8 treated pine sleepers: 1700 mm x 200 mm x 100 mm • Four 400 mm reinforcing rods • Two pieces of shadecloth: one 1900 mm x 1900 mm; the other 1500 mm x 1500 mm • Half a cubic metre of screenings or fine crushed rock • Half a cubic metre of sand

One of the most popular backyard areas for children is a sandpit. If it's well made and well maintained, they'll play in it happily for hours. Children aged 2 to 5 years are particularly keen on sandpits, and their interest can last until they are much older.

It's possible to create a sandpit by ordering sand and just spreading it on the ground where you want the sandpit to be. But to prevent problems, it's better to do a little construction to contain the sand and make it easier to use. Good design involves the following considerations: good drainage; weed prevention; partial shade; exclusion of cats, dogs and leaves; long-lasting timber; safe containment of the sand; and the type of sand itself.

Ideally the sandpit should be located where it will get partial shade for most of the day. This will ensure that the children won't get cold or hot and that the sand will dry out reasonably quickly. If there is too much sun you may need to consider erecting shadecloth.

The sand itself should be neither too fine (it will blow about) nor too coarse (uncomfortable to sit in and too loose to make things). It should bind together when wet (to build sandcastles and retain the shapes children push it into). Washed river sand is preferable to sea sand (which can be sticky). Some landscape material suppliers have sand available specifically for sandpits, or they can advise on a suitable type of sand.

1 Select an appropriate site for the sandpit ensuring that it is in easy sight of the house.

2 Excavate an area 1500 mm x 1500 mm to a depth of 150 mm.

Fill with fine crushed rock or screenings and compact lightly.

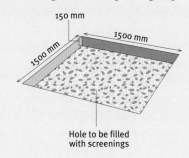

Hole to be filled with screenings

3 Lay the larger piece of shadecloth over the screenings.

4 Drill a hole 100 mm from one end in the centre of each sleeper. The hole must go right through the sleeper and be wide enough for the reinforcing rod.

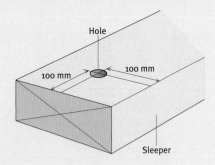

Hole

100 mm 100 mm

Sleeper

5 Position the first four sleepers around the edges of the shadecloth in an interlocking pattern, with the drilled holes in each corner.

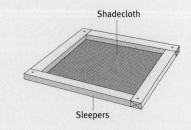

Shadecloth

Sleepers

6 Position the second set of sleepers so that their holes align with the holes on the sleepers below (their interlocking pattern should form a bond with the sleepers below like the stretcher bond in brick walls).

7 Hammer in the reinforcing rods ensuring they sit below the top of the sleepers (to prevent injury).

8 Fill the sandpit with sand. Use the second piece of shadecloth to cover the sand. This will exclude cats and leaves when the sandpit is not in use.

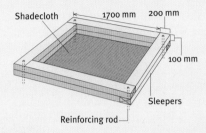

Shadecloth — 1700 mm — 200 mm
100 mm
Sleepers
Reinforcing rod

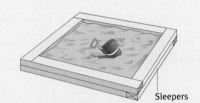

Sleepers

Commercially made sandpits are a quick and easy option and can be covered when not in use.

Installing a basketball ring

From an early age children will want to play a range of ball games and increasingly basketball is one of them. A basketball ring and net is easy to set up. A basket attached to a wall is often sufficient, but make sure the wall is solid and sound (see Safety warning). A proper competition set-up, with space all around the basket, is a job for a specialist.

This project lets you set up a basket in any location and allows you to adjust the height of the basket for younger or older children. For safety, it may be worthwhile to wrap the post in foam rubber, especially if your basketballers are very energetic.

To make the ring adjustable (for children of different ages and heights), choose a backboard that allows you to use U-bolts to secure it to the post. It's possible to make your own backboard using plywood, but, for safety and presentation, commercially available products are preferable. Most allow the backboard and ring to be set out from a post a short distance, reducing the risk of collision. And while backboards come in a range of sizes, smaller ones, still with enough room for rebounds into the basket, will almost certainly look better in your backyard.

When siting your basketball ring, keep in mind that shots for goal will often miss, and choose a spot well clear of windows, fragile plants, washing lines or anything else you value.

A basketball ring and backboard fixed to a pole set in concrete is the safest option.

1   Select the position for the basketball ring and dig the post hole 300 mm wide to a depth of 750 mm.

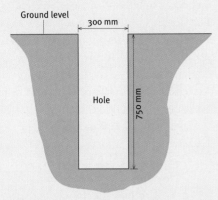

2   Place the post in the hole and if necessary secure it in position using offcuts tied to it temporarily and pegged to the ground. Use a spirit level to check that it is vertical.

3   Half fill the hole with concrete and poke it down with a rod, double-checking that the post is vertical. Continue filling the hole, poking it down as you go. Allow at least two days for the concrete to harden. Quick-setting concrete mix can also be used.

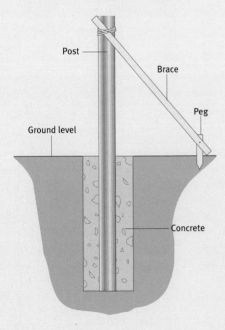

4   Position the backboard at the required height on the post and secure in position with the U-bolts.

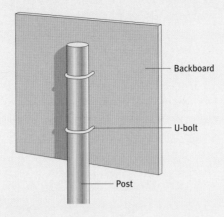

5   Attach the basket to the backboard according to the manufacturer's instructions.

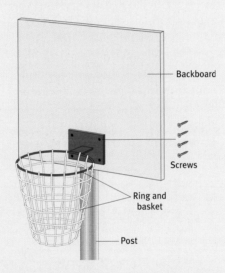

Variation

You can also set up a basketball post that is removable. To do this you'll need a length of steel pipe or plastic plumbing pipe 750 mm in length. Ensure it is slightly wider than the steel post and set it in position in the concrete instead of the post (still ensuring it is vertical). The post can then be slid in and out of the pipe as required. Make sure that no concrete fills the bottom of the pipe, so that the post still sits 750 mm into the ground. Cap the pipe when it's not in use.

Building a climbing frame and swing

Take plenty of time to get the posts in exactly the right positions. Even if you're a little out, it's not a disaster, but you may have to reshape the floor to fit.

You can make a number of variations on this project, because the poles can be moved around into a variety of different positions. Also a slide can easily be made from plywood with pine sides screwed to it and the plywood screwed to the platform. The cubby house project (see pages 185–6) can be added to this structure, using the posts as the supports for its walls. You can also add it to the sandpit (the floor will keep some rain and sun off the sand below).

Site the swing (and slide) over a soft surface such as lawn or mounded woodchips, to provide a soft landing for the inevitable falls. Make sure that a child swinging high will not hit any part of the frame or any hard edges nearby.

1 Carefully peg out the positions for the six posts. The centres of the 75 mm posts should be 1125 mm apart, so the posts are 1200 mm from outside edge to outside edge. Setting up stringlines can help you get this accurate. It also keeps things straight as work progresses. The stringlines are to run along the outside edges of the posts.

2 Dig holes for the posts 300 mm wide and 600 mm deep.

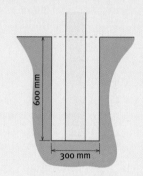

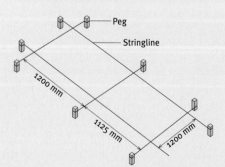

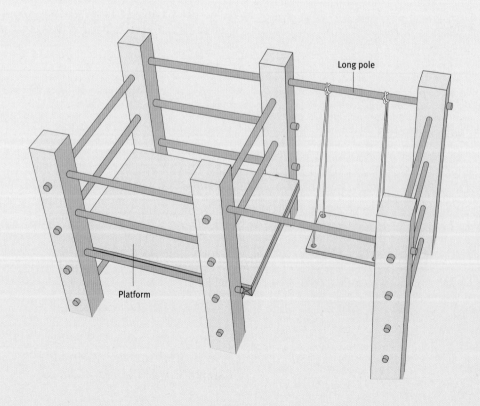

3   It may be possible to site the posts in the holes with a rammed mixture (1:6) of cement and soil holding them upright, otherwise they should be concreted into position. Sit the first post in position, half fill the hole with concrete and check the post is vertical and exactly in position. Prod down the concrete using a rod. Then fill the rest of the hole, continuing to check the position of the post is accurate and vertical. You may use braces to hold the post in position while you work but keep checking that everything remains true. At ground level, slope the concrete away from the post to divert water away. Repeat for the other posts. Allow at least two days for the concrete to set.

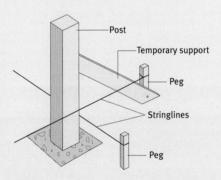

Post
Temporary support
Peg
Stringlines
Peg

4   When the concrete has set, cut the poles to length (1900 mm above ground level) and round off the edges on the ends with sandpaper. Mark the centre-line on the outside and an adjacent side of each post. Measure 250 mm up

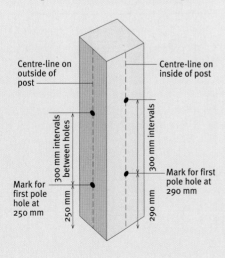

Centre-line on outside of post
Centre-line on inside of post
300 mm intervals between holes
300 mm intervals
Mark for first pole hole at 250 mm
250 mm
Mark for first pole hole at 290 mm
290 mm

from the ground for the first pole hole on the outside of the post, 290 mm up from the ground for the inside of the post. Mark positions for additional pole holes at 300 mm intervals up the post. But move the marks at 1490 mm up to 1500 mm then measure 300 mm further up and mark 1800 mm. Set up a stringline and use a spirit level to check that the holes on all posts are at the same height.

5   Drill the holes for the poles on all posts then slide the poles through the holes.

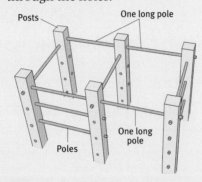

Posts
One long pole
One long pole
Poles

6   Either skew-nail them or skew-screw the poles to lock them in place (screwing them will allow you to easily change the positions of the poles). The two longer poles run through the centre posts to span both gaps between the end posts. If a child is likely to swing high, site both long poles at 1800 mm. If not, you could site one at 1500 mm.

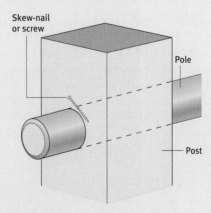

Skew-nail or screw
Pole
Post

7   Check the platform fits snugly in position between the

posts, protruding slightly over the supporting poles at 1150 mm.

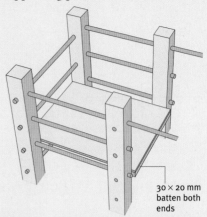

30 × 20 mm batten both ends

8   Remove the platform and nail the battens across both ends. Reposition the platform and nail (or screw) it to the poles.

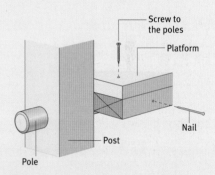

Screw to the poles
Platform
Nail
Post
Pole

9   Drill two holes at each end of the swing seat. Pass the rope over the supporting pole and knot it so that you have two equal lengths of rope. Pass the rope through the holes and knot them so the swing is at the desired height. Trim off any excess rope.

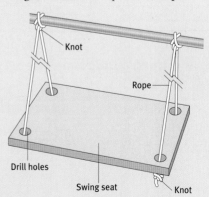

Knot
Rope
Drill holes
Swing seat
Knot

10   For added protection, use a non-slip finish on all poles, posts, the platform and seat.

Utilities

Every backyard has practical uses that need to be addressed – storage, refuse areas, work areas, a place to dry washing. They may seem mundane items but, thoughtfully integrated, they can fit into your backyard without making it any less attractive. And when it comes to the shed, we're dealing with one of the enduring icons of the great Australian backyard. Sheds are not so much a test of your ability as a home handyperson, since they can be very easy to construct; they're often the ultimate expression of a home owner's individuality.

Garden sheds

When planning where to put your shed, find a location that is fairly level so that preparing the site will be less arduous. A flat site is also important to avoid sticking doors.

Garden sheds are commonly available in kit form, and can be easily assembled in a couple of hours. The most popular types are timber (generally cedar or treated pine) or steel (Zincalume or Colorbond). Kits come in a range of sizes, but can also be custom-built to suit individual requirements. Optional extras include aluminium sliding windows; louvre windows; polycarbonate or fibreglass skylights; single, double, roller or sliding doors; gable (pitched) or skillion roofs (a flat roof fitted at a slight angle to draw off water); and, of course, shelves and benches. You can even add period-style features such as a verandah.

Wooden garden shed kits are generally supplied in seven flat pieces consisting of prefabricated walls, a floor and a gabled Colorbond roof, which are bolted together on-site. They can then be stained, painted or sealed to suit your garden.

Metal sheds offer a cheaper alternative and are available in a range of sizes and styles; they can also be prefabricated to individual specifications. The Colorbond wall sheeting is rustproof and comes in a range of colours. Standard heights range from 1800 mm (flat roof) to 2700 mm (gable roof). Add extra height if required.

Some sheds come complete with timber flooring while others require a concrete slab to be laid as the base. You can erect your shed on a 100 mm thick concrete slab with thickened edges into which bolts are cast to hold down the walls. Alternatively, it can be built on a timber deck, with the shed walls bolted to the deck joists. Shed floors can also be paved, or made from concrete blocks.

This tiny bicycle shed provides compact storage with easy roller-door access.

Installing a ready-made steel shed

A garden shed provides secure storage for tools, bicycles, materials and equipment. Ready-made sheds come in a range of designs and sizes and are easy to assemble. Most require a concrete slab for maximum weatherproofing, though some may be supplied with a ready-made timber platform floor.

The steel shed in this project is custom-built to fit into a small, sheltered space, so a treated pine platform floor is adequate. If you wish to install a concrete slab, see Laying a concrete slab on page 197.

You will need an assistant to hold the sides of the shed firm as you screw them together.

1   Clear then level the site.

2   Install a ready-made treated pine platform floor (or install a cement slab). Leave gaps in the floorboards until you provide packing to level the floor framework. Check with a spirit level.

3   Stand or prop the back and sides of the shed in place.

4   Hold the back and one side panel together and fix with 20 mm self-tapping screws and a power drill. There is no need to pre-drill.

The panel edges are squared off so that the sides overlap the back and front. Fit screws at approximately 300 mm intervals. Repeat for the other panels.

5   Fit the roof in the same way.

6   Fix the completed shed to the timber floor using 30 mm screws at 300 mm intervals. If you are installing the shed on a slab, use galvanised metal brackets fixed to the concrete with masonry anchors.

7   Hang the door then fit a padlock if necessary.

Laying a concrete slab

To prepare the site, clear all vegetation from the area the concrete slab will occupy, plus (if possible) an extra metre or so all around to give yourself a clear space to work. Use a pick and shovel to create a level platform and check with a straightedge and spirit level. Hire a small jack hammer if there is a lot of rock. Erect profiles (hurdles) and fix stringlines to mark the edge of the concrete slab (see Smart tip on page 157).

To estimate the amount of concrete you need for the slab, draw up a plan of the slab area and mark off in metres. Multiply the length by the width to obtain the area, then multiply the area by the thickness of the slab (allowing an extra 10 per cent for wastage). For example: 5 m x 10 m = 50 m²; 50 m² x 0.1 m (100 mm) = 5 cubic metres (5 m³). The top of the slab should be at least 100 mm above ground level to prevent flooding in heavy rain; the exposed edge also provides an inspection zone in termite-prone regions.

1 Using the stringlines as a guide, construct boxing ('formwork') for the slab using boards on the edges as a frame. The top of the boards will mark the top of the concrete slab; use the intersecting stringlines to mark its exact corners. Keep the edge boards in place by driving pegs into the ground along the outside edges.

Measure each diagonal to check for square. Nail the boards together using 50 mm nails, then nail them to the pegs when they have been levelled.

2 Position the remaining outer pegs: two pegs per corner and at least one centred along each side, then nail them to the boards. Use inner pegs at intervals to hold the framework square as the outer pegs are driven in. (Remove the inner pegs after the framework is square and level.)

3 Check the boxing framework is level and pack or dig out corners where required.

4 If desired, place plastic membrane over the ground within the boxed area to protect the slab against rising moisture. If the slab is quite large, install reinforcement mesh for extra strength, suspended on 'bar chairs', 50 mm below the planned concrete surface and 50 mm from the edges.

Difficulty: Moderate
Time: 1 day
Tools

- Pick
- Shovel
- Measuring tape
- Stringlines
- Spirit level
- Straightedge
- Builder's square
- Hammer or mash hammer
- Handsaw
- Steel and wood floats
- Screeding board: 500 mm longer than the width of the poured concrete and 100 mm x 50 mm
- Stiff broom

Materials

- Assorted timber offcuts for temporary bracing and profiles
- Boxing ('formwork'): pine or hardwood, 100 mm x 25 mm
- Pegs: pine or hardwood, 25 mm x 25 mm
- 50 mm nails for boxing
- Plastic membrane of 0.2 mm (or 2 microns) polyethylene film (optional)
- F62 steel mesh (if reinforcement is preferred)
- 50 mm 'bar chairs'
- Timber: pine or hardwood, 100 mm x 25 mm for gutter boxing, if required
- Pre-mixed concrete

5 Order ready-mix concrete (20 Mpa, or megapascal, strength) or mix 4 parts screenings, 2 parts sand and 1 part cement. Pour the concrete, working it with a shovel until level.

6 Draw a screeding board across the surface, using a sawing motion, until the concrete is level with the surface of the boxing.

7 Some ready-made metal sheds require a rebate (gutter) on the edges of the slab to assist water runoff. First level the edges of the slab with a float, then carefully place lengths of timber (100 mm x 25 mm) flat on the surface and parallel with each edge. Peg in position. (The rebate is usually 100 mm wide.)

8 Pour more concrete inside the rebate framework and level with a screeding board. Clean up any excess that has spilled over the framework and use a wooden float to level the concrete while it's still wet.

9 Once the concrete begins to 'go off' (in two to three hours, but much depends on the weather) use a metal float to make a smooth surface. (If the slab is for a carport, use a stiff broom to give the surface a rough finish so it won't be slippery when wet.)

10 Allow four days for the concrete to cure. Remove the boxing and trim off any exposed plastic membrane (if this has been used). In very hot weather, cover the slab with plastic to prevent it drying out too quickly.

Smart tip

If your slab requires a rebate make sure you include this when calculating the amount of concrete required.

Concrete is the most practical flooring for a shed.

Installing a ready-made folding clothes line

There was a time when backyards were dominated by a large clothes hoist rotating in the centre of the lawn. Today, most rotary clothes lines have been replaced by clothes lines that fold down out of sight when not in use, often screened off from the rest of the yard. There are several different designs of folding clothes lines, some of which can be bolted to a brick wall. The clothes line can also be supported by freestanding posts set into the ground.

Locate the clothes line in a sunny, well-ventilated area away from trees that will drop sap, which might stain the washing. Check that you have enough space to accommodate the width of the clothes line and that nothing will stop it being folded into position (bear in mind that folding clothes lines come in a range of sizes). Consider paving the area to, from, and under the clothes line.

1　Select a suitable location for your clothes line.

2　Attach the brackets to the posts and back spacer bar using bolts, washers and nuts according to the manufacturer's instructions.

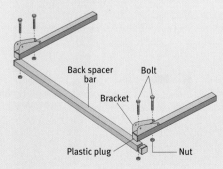

Back spacer bar
Bracket
Bolt
Plastic plug
Nut

3　Assemble the clothes line according to the manufacturer's instructions and lower the frame to its folded position.

4　Determine the positions for the posts (the exact distance the posts should be apart at ground level will usually be specified by the manufacturer, otherwise measure carefully, twice) and mark them.

5　Dig holes for each post at least 200 mm wide and 600 mm deep.

6　Position the posts in the holes ensuring they are the required distance apart at ground level. This is critical to ensuring the clothes line will open and close without hitting the posts. Use a spirit level to check the posts are vertical and that the top of the clothes line is level. Support the posts with props so they remain vertical.

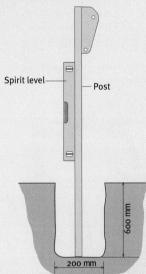

Spirit level
Post
600 mm
200 mm

7　Add or remove soil in the holes so that the height of the point on the posts where the clothes line pivots is 25 mm higher than the head of the tallest person who uses the clothes line. Make some allowance if the clothes line is sited on sloping ground. Recheck that the width between the posts at ground level is still correct, the posts are vertical and the top of the clothes line is level.

Difficulty: Easy
Time: 4–6 hours
Tools

- Shifting spanner
- Selection of screwdrivers
- Shovel
- Spirit level
- Tape measure
- Crowbar
- 10 mm timber or steel rod

Materials

- Ready-made clothes line parts
- Quick-set concrete
- Timber offcuts for props

8 Fill the holes with quick-set concrete as per the concrete manufacturer's instructions. Recheck everything is straight and level then poke down the concrete using a rod. Make sure the concrete is well packed against the posts. Slope the top surface of the concrete slightly away from the posts to direct water away from them.

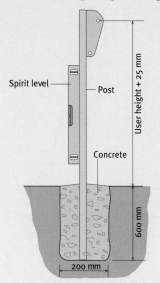

Spirit level — Post — User height + 25 mm — Concrete — 600 mm — 200 mm

9 Allow the concrete to set for at least two days before using the clothes line.

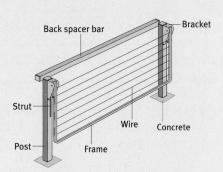

Back spacer bar — Bracket — Strut — Wire — Concrete — Post — Frame

This folding clothes line has been bolted to the brick wall of a house.

Lighting

Lighting is an aspect of backyard design that is often overlooked. Yet it can improve security and safety around your home and add to its appeal. The Australian climate means we can enjoy outdoor living long after the sun has set. And even in the colder months, the garden can still be enjoyed from indoors when it's beautifully lit at night. A great range of lighting effects can highlight plants or garden features, or use water in ponds to create a magical atmosphere. So, even when the sun goes down, your backyard can continue to give you pleasure.

Installing low-voltage lighting

Lighting a path can be attractive as well as practical.

Garden lights have three main purposes: aesthetic (lighting features such as pools, plants or entertaining areas); practical (lighting paths and stairs, street numbers, etc.); and security (sensor lights activated by movement, lighting front porches, doorways, etc.). Lighting that is connected to the mains power supply must be installed by a licensed electrician and this is usually the case with security lighting and floodlighting for entertaining areas. However, many other forms of lighting are available that can create a range of effects to enhance a garden. One of the easiest permanent lighting systems that can be installed is low-voltage lighting, which is well within the abilities of the average home handyperson. Some outdoor lights run on solar energy, doing away with the need for wiring altogether.

Do-it-yourself kits are available from hardware and homeware stores and contain a small range of fixtures that can spotlight plants and illuminate paths. They may be mounted on stakes stuck into the ground, or fixed to walls or fences. Detailed instructions are usually included but there are some additional steps you should take to ensure their safe operation for a prolonged period.

1　The most important thing is to ensure that the cable is kept out of harm's way, as the whole system could be rendered useless if you put a spade through the wiring. If the cable can be unplugged between lights, consider putting it in lengths of conduit (joined where necessary by conduit elbows), available from electrical suppliers and most hardware shops. Light-duty conduit, which is

A garden lighting kit.

white or pale grey, is adequate for this purpose; PVC plumber's piping can also do.

2　Cut the conduit to the required lengths and feed the cable through. If it won't go through easily, tape the cable firmly to a length of wire (such as fencing wire) and use this to pull the cable through.

3　Make sure you run the cable or conduit where there is no danger of it being cut or damaged: you can bury it between lights, run it under garden edging or attach it to a fence or the back of sleepers using U-brackets and batten screws.

4　Make sure the external power point you use for the lights is suitable for outdoor use. If you get a new point installed, make sure it's rated to IP56, which means it's water-resistant. The transformer may be 'weatherproof' but it should still be sited in a cool, dry position well under cover wherever possible. If it can be used to switch lights off and on, the transformer should also be easily accessible.

5　On a plan of your backyard, mark the position of the lights and the route that the underground cable has taken. Refer to this whenever you are digging in the garden or if tradespeople will be doing any work outdoors.

Other types of lighting

- Fairy lights are a perennial favourite, tracing through the branches of trees, defining railings or following eaves. Strings of hundreds of fairy lights also operate on low voltage and can be installed by home owners to create dazzling effects.
- Spotlights can highlight favourite plants or displays of foliage or flowers.
- Floodlights can be used to illuminate a wide area.
- Kerosene lanterns or flares create a play of light and shadow. And, if you fill them with citronella lamp oil, they'll also repel mosquitoes.
- Tea lights (small candles) floating in a pool scattered with frangipani flower create an instant mood of romance.
- Candles set inside glass jars part-filled with sand can create a great effect for entertaining.
- Solar-powered lights have the advantage of not requiring any wiring.
- Sensor lights are usually activated by movement and illuminate the area around the entrance to your house, providing improved security.
- Moonlight is another means of lighting a garden. If you avoid planting trees where they'll cast unwanted shadow at night, you can line paths with white-flowering or silver-leafed shrubs that will stand out in moonlight, indicating the positions of paths.

LEFT Illuminating the area around your house improves security and enables you to entertain outdoors at night.

BELOW Fairy lights have made this freestanding pergola a night-time feature.

Pets in the backyard

Your needs, and those of your children, may not be the only ones that should be considered when you are thinking about your backyard. Your pets could have a wish list of their own. A kennel for your dog, perhaps, or a cattery your feline friends can call their own. A kennel, cattery or dog run may also provide somewhere to keep pets when they can't be supervised or when you're entertaining. They're easy to build and if placed thoughtfully, they can be an unobtrusive addition to the backyard.

Constructing a dog kennel

A basic dog kennel is quick and easy to build, often using materials that are close at hand. This basic design can easily be varied. A peaked roof will involve some extra cuts on the front and back panel and two sheets for the roof (with a ridge cap to exclude water). You can replace the plywood roof with galvanised iron but ensure there are no sharp protruding corners, especially if you have children.

The floor is optional but desirable as it keeps your dog and its bedding off the ground and helps to keep it dry. The floor can also be made separate from the dog kennel, which can then be lifted off the floor to make cleaning it easier.

The measurements for this project are for a kennel to house a small to medium dog. The aim is to provide a place that is snug without being cramped. If you're in any doubt, measure around your dog when it's curled up to see how much space it needs. Then measure the height to its shoulder and ensure the door is at least that height plus 60 mm (to allow for the height of the floor).

1   Cut the front panel of the kennel to size (700 mm high x 600 mm wide) with a handsaw (or if possible get it cut to size at the hardware store). Then with the ruler and pencil mark the position of the door in the centre of the panel. It should be 500 mm high x 300 mm wide. To mark the curve for the top, mark a point 350 mm high on the midline of the panel, hammer a nail in at that point and use a pencil and 150 mm long string tied to the nail to mark the curve.

2   Mark or scribe the shape of the door and cut it out with a jigsaw or keyhole saw.

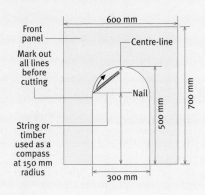

Front panel
Mark out all lines before cutting
Centre-line
Nail
String or timber used as a compass at 150 mm radius
600 mm
700 mm
500 mm
300 mm

3   Position the front panel on top of a length of 45 mm x 45 mm hardwood or treated pine, leaving

Difficulty: Easy

Time: 2–3 hours

Tools

- Ruler
- Pencil
- Handsaw
- Hammer
- Scribe
- Jigsaw or keyhole saw
- String
- Screwdriver
- Power drill
- Assorted drill bits
- Paintbrush

Materials

- One 10 mm plywood sheet 700 mm high x 600 mm wide
- One 10 mm plywood sheet 600 mm high x 600 mm wide
- Two 10 mm plywood sheets 700 mm high x 750 mm wide
- One 10 mm plywood sheet 1000 mm long x 650 mm wide
- Four 580 mm lengths of 45 mm x 45 mm hardwood or treated pine
- Two 610 mm lengths of 45 mm x 45 mm hardwood
- Two 510 mm lengths of 45 mm x 45 mm hardwood
- Enough 750 mm lengths of decking timber or floorboards to cover half a square metre
- 25 mm galvanised nails
- 25 mm wood screws
- Waterproof sealant
- Exterior paint

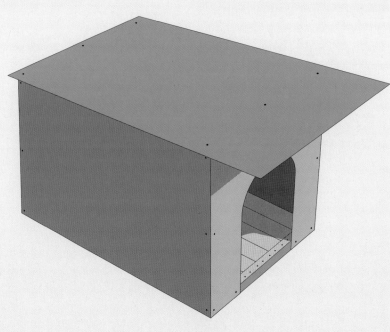

A snug dog kennel is easy and relatively inexpensive to build.

a 10 mm recess at each end. The timber should be flush with the bottom of the panel. Drill a starter hole for a wood screw near each end of the panel and screw the panel to the timber. Repeat the process at the top then fix two 45 mm x 45 mm lengths of timber to the outside vertical sides of the panel, leaving a 10 mm recess at the side and a gap of approximately 2 mm at the top. (The gap at the top will ensure the block of wood won't interfere with the roof.)

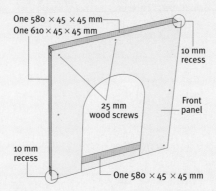

One 580 × 45 × 45 mm
One 610 × 45 × 45 mm
10 mm recess
25 mm wood screws
Front panel
10 mm recess
One 580 × 45 × 45 mm

4   Cut the back panel to size (600 mm high x 600 mm wide). Attach the timbers as for the front panel.

5   Measure and cut the side panels so they are 750 mm wide, 700 mm high at the front end and 600 mm at the back. Position one side panel against the recessed timbers of the front panel, drill pilot holes and screw the panel into position. Attach the back panel in the same way.

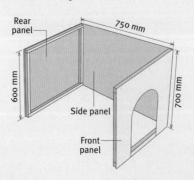

Rear panel
750 mm
600 mm
700 mm
Side panel
Front panel

6   Cut the decking timber or floorboards to length (750 mm)

and nail into position, ensuring there are no gaps between them and the side panel. You may need to drill holes to prevent the nails splitting the timber.

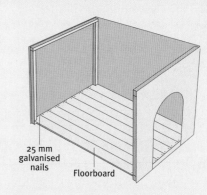

25 mm galvanised nails
Floorboard

7   Drill pilot holes and screw the remaining side panel to the timbers at the front and back panels.

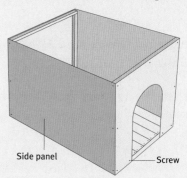

Side panel
Screw

8   Cut the roof panel to size (650 mm x 1000 mm). Drill pilot holes and screw the roof to the timbers at the top of the front and back panels.

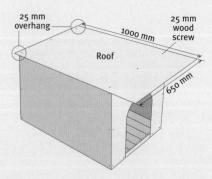

25 mm overhang
1000 mm
25 mm wood screw
Roof
650 mm

9   If there are any gaps along the edges, fill them with an appropriate waterproof sealant. Then paint the exterior, ensuring the roof in particular is well sealed.

Building a dog run

A dog run can be a relatively straightforward project, depending on your requirements and, of course, your dog. Basically, the bigger the dog, the bigger and more solidly constructed the dog run will have to be. If you intend to keep your dog in the run for any length of time (more than a couple of hours) it should have enough room for the dog to move around freely. As a guide, 4 m x 2 m is a good starting point for a medium-sized dog. The fences should also be sufficiently high to prevent the dog jumping out. Dogs such as German shepherds, for example, can jump fences 2 m high.

Many of the skills needed to build a dog run have been covered in other projects. The steps here, therefore, refer you to the relevant pages for further details. This project also assumes that you've set the dog run in a corner of the yard against existing fences. That means you only need to set the posts for the door and to stretch cyclone mesh from the fences to the posts. (Check the position of fence posts – you can attach cyclone mesh to them if you plan your run carefully.) If you wish to site the dog run elsewhere you'll need to set three extra posts. Before starting this project, check with your local council if there are any regulations about slabs and dog runs.

1   Lay a concrete slab 4 m x 2 m (see Laying a concrete slab on pages 197–8).

2   Mark the position for the two posts to be set in the ground. One should be at the corner of the slab. The other should be set on the long side of the slab at a distance that leaves enough space to position the gate or door between

the two posts with clearance for it to open and shut. Set the posts as explained in Building a simple three-post pergola on pages 164–6.

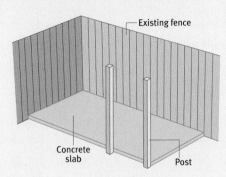

Existing fence

Concrete slab

Post

3   Screw the hinges to the top and bottom of the door or gate. Prop it in position between the two posts ensuring it can open and close freely. Screw the hinges to the corner post. The gate should be hinged so the door opens outwards. This means you'll have to be careful whenever you let your dog out – in a rush for freedom the door and you can get knocked aside. However, if the dog is asleep or unwell and blocking the door, you won't be able to open it if it's hinged to open inwards. Screw a latch to the gate and the U-saddle to the outside of the second post using 25 mm wood screws.

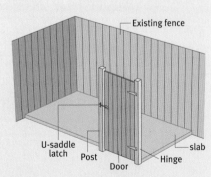

Existing fence

U-saddle latch

Post

Door

slab

Hinge

4   Enclose the dog run using cyclone mesh attached to the posts by galvanised U-staples. If you're lucky, you'll have posts in the right places against the fences to which you can attach the mesh.

Difficulty: Moderate
Time: 1 day

Tools

- Builder's square
- Steel and wood floats
- Screeding board: 2500 mm x 100 mm x 50 mm
- Stiff broom
- Tape measure and pencil
- Hammer
- Spirit level and straightedge
- Stringlines
- Profiles
- Shovel
- Handsaw
- Power drill and assorted bits
- Screwdriver

Materials

- Assorted timber offcuts for temporary bracing and profiles
- Boxing ('formwork'): pine or hardwood, 100 mm x 25 mm
- Pegs: pine or hardwood, 25 mm x 25 mm
- 50 mm nails for boxing
- Plastic membrane: 0.2 mm (or 2 microns) polyethylene film (optional)
- F62 steel mesh (if reinforcement is preferred)
- 50 mm 'bar chairs'
- Pre-mixed concrete
- Up to five posts: 2000 mm x 90 mm x 90 mm treated pine (or durable hardwood)
- Four 10 mm galvanised bolts (for fixing posts to the fence if required)
- Galvanised post stirrups
- 50 mm coach screws
- 1 bag pre-mixed quick-set concrete per post
- Concrete for slab as required
- Cyclone mesh as required
- Wooden gate, second-hand door, or similar with hinges
- 25 mm wood screws as required
- Latch and U-saddle
- Galvanised U-staples
- Corrugated iron 2 m x 1 m

If not, bolt two additional posts to the fence rails and attach the cyclone wire to those. You may find that your dog will distort the wire or try to force its way under it, in which case you may have to reinforce the base, centre or top of the wire with cross-beams skew-nailed to the posts (or tension wires). The cyclone mesh can then be stapled to these as well.

5 If you wish to roof part of the dog run, you will need to fix a timber pitching plate along the fence (90 mm x 35 mm) and a timber plate to the top of the posts (90 mm x 35 mm). You can screw sheets of corrugated iron to the top of the pitching plate and the top plate. For further weather protection, you can enclose one end of the dog run, but make sure that it's still an easy matter to hose it out when necessary.

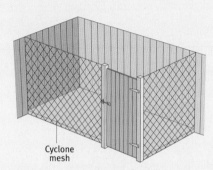

Cyclone mesh

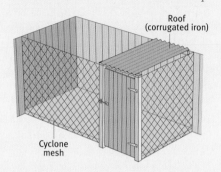

Roof (corrugated iron)

Cyclone mesh

Enclosures for pets are also available in easy-to-erect kit form.

A quiet corner

There's nothing like being able to retreat to a quiet, sheltered part of the garden to read, relax, or to have a cup of tea and a chat. With a little thought and planning, even the smallest backyard can have a private special place for you to enjoy. The secret is in the little touches that define the space – a seat around a tree or an archway may be all that's needed to suggest and mark out your special place. These are simple things that are easy to build and their parts can make a more welcoming whole, adding to the style and appeal of your garden.

Building a seat around a tree

Difficulty: Moderate

Time: 1 day

Tools

- Measuring tape
- Hammer
- Square
- Power drill and bits
- Power saw or handsaw
- Socket wrench
- Shifting spanner
- Paintbrush

Materials

- Timber for four posts 90 mm x 90 mm treated cypress pine or 75 mm x 75 mm hardwood, length approx. 400 mm
- Timber for two 2000 mm bearers 190 mm x 45 mm treated pine or 125 mm x 75 mm hardwood
- Timber for four 1910 mm joists 140 mm x 45 mm treated pine or 100 mm x 50 mm hardwood
- Eight 12 mm diameter galvanised bolts and washers (length greater than the combined thickness of the posts and bearers, minimum 120 mm)
- 75 mm galvanised nails and 8 galvanised framing anchors or hangers for fixing joists
- Seating slats or decking to cover 4 sq. m (19 mm hardwood or 22 mm softwood minimum thickness). The hole for the tree-trunk accounts for roughly 10 per cent of the seating area but allow that much for waste.
- 50 mm galvanised nails (for fixing seating or decking)
- Primer and paint (or sealer)

This project is for a freestanding tree seat of 2 m x 2 m set to a height of 400 mm. It makes allowance for a tree-trunk to a width of 600 mm, large enough for most small to medium trees. Don't forget to make allowance if the tree is young and the trunk will continue to grow. Note also that the positions of the joists can be moved if you wish to have the tree in a position other than dead centre. You may also want to enclose the space around the seat to reduce grass or weed growth under the seat. For this you can use the seating slats or decking as for the top of the seat.

If you want to set the posts into the ground, allow about 300 mm extra length for each and set them in concrete, using stringlines and a spirit level to ensure the tops of the posts are level and each is plumb. This project assumes the seat is being built on a level surface. If it isn't, compacted gravel, house bricks or concrete footings can be used to bring the ground under each post up or down to the required level. Alternatively, you can adjust the length of the posts.

A tree seat under a deciduous tree is sunny in winter and shady in summer.

1 Measure and cut the posts to size (400 mm) using a power saw.

2 Measure and cut the bearers to size (2000 mm) using a power saw.

3 Bolt the bearers to the posts using two 12 mm diameter galvanised bolts for each post so they are flush at the top. Pre-drill the holes, ensuring they are at least 25 mm from the top and bottom edges of the bearer and that the post and bearer are at right angles (using a square).

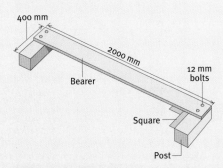

4 The direction the bearers run will determine the direction of the slats. Arrange the posts and bearers according to the desired direction.

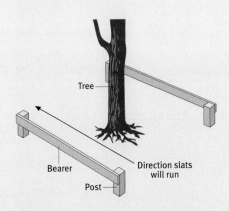

5 Cut the joists to size. The length of 1910 mm allows 90 mm for the thickness of two 45 mm bearers, giving a total width of 2000 mm (adjust length if using hardwood). Using galvanised framing anchors, nail the outside joists to the insides of the posts,

ensuring they are at right angles to the bearers and the top edge is flush with the top of the bearers and posts.

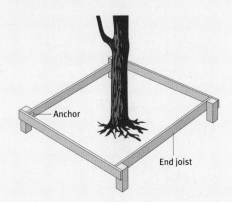

6 Position and fix the two remaining joists at 600 mm intervals along the bearers.

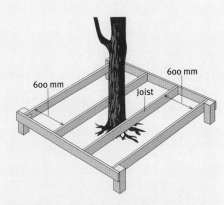

7 Lay two seating slats across the joists 600 mm apart on either side of the tree trunk. Ensure they are at right angles to the joists. And overhang the slats beyond the end joists by enough distance so the slats can be trimmed flush with the ends of the bearers.

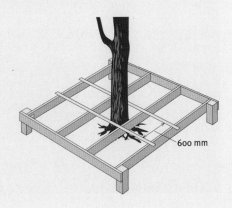

8   Lay the remaining seating slats across the joists (the best faces uppermost). Leave a gap of 3–5 mm between slats to allow water to drain away, and overhang them as with the first two slats. Overhang the slats over the joists around the tree by 50 mm if desired.

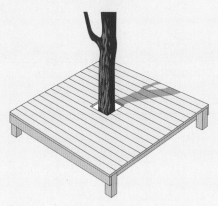

9   Fix the seating slats to each joist with two 50 mm long galvanised nails. (Use annular ring or twist-shank nails for treated pine joists.) Leave nails flush with the surface, not punched, so there are no nail holes for moisture to enter. If nailing at the ends of slats, drill holes 80 per cent of the nail diameter, approximately 12 mm from the ends of the slats, to prevent splitting when nailing.

10   Periodically check remaining distance and, if necessary, adjust the gap width to keep seating slats parallel and ensure the last slat is not tapered. When all slats are in place, mark overhanging ends with a chalk line and trim flush with the ends of the bearers and posts with a saw.

11   Once the seating slats are fixed, you can apply your chosen paint, stain, oil or clear finish as recommended by the manufacturer.

This tree seat provides a perfect view over the garden.

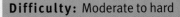

Constructing an archway

An archway should always serve a definite purpose: it could create a view, form an entrance or lead from one part of the garden to another. Generally, the timbers required for an arch don't need to be particularly strong, as the weight they support is only slight. More important is the look, which should lean towards solid rather than flimsy.

This project is for an archway 1500 mm wide by 1000 mm deep (wide enough for two people to walk under it side by side). Ensure the dimensions will fit your planned area, though, and adapt them if necessary. And don't forget that the choice of materials and the way they age will affect the look of your archway. Lattice infills will assist climbing plants, shaped beams or extra beams will enhance the visual appeal, and the project can be roofed if desired. Setting the posts into the ground is the strongest and simplest way of

supporting a freestanding structure such as this. In areas where termites are active the archway may not last as long as it would if it were supported by stirrups, but it will be stronger.

1 Set out the positions of the posts using stringlines attached to wooden stakes or offcuts. They should be 1000 mm apart, 1500 mm on either side of the path or entry point.

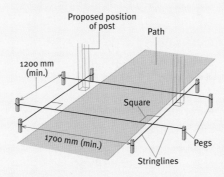

2 Dig post holes 300 mm square and 600 mm deep. If the soil

An archway provides height to the garden as well as supporting plants.

Difficulty: Moderate to hard
Time: 2 days

Tools

- Pencil and ruler
- Tape measure
- Hammer
- Spirit level (or plumbline)
- Stringlines and wooden stakes or offcuts
- Shovel
- Power saw (or handsaw)
- Broom handle or metal rod
- Power drill and 10 mm drill bit
- Spanner
- Paintbrush

Materials

- 4 posts: 3000 mm x 100 mm x 100 mm treated or cypress pine (or durable hardwood)
- 4 bags pre-mixed quick-set concrete
- Temporary bacing
- 2 beams: 2100 mm x 190 mm x 45 mm treated pine
- 50 mm galvanised bolts (10 mm diameter)
- 6 cross pieces: 1000 mm x 90 mm x 90 mm treated pine
- 75 mm galvanised nails
- Primer and paint (or stain and clear finish)
- Shadecloth, lattice or polycarbonate roofing, if desired

Climbers for archways

Name	Position
Bougainvillea cultivars Flower colour depends on the cultivar	Sun
Clematis species Flower colour depends on the cultivar	Sun
Clerodendrum thomsoniae White and red flowers	Shade
Hardenbergia violacea Purple flowers	Sun
Ipomoea alba White perfumed flowers open at night	Sun
Mandevilla × amabilis 'Alice du Pont' Pink trumpet-shaped flowers	Sun
Mandevilla laxa Scented white flowers	Sun
Pandorea jasminoides Pinkish-white flowers	Sun
Pyrostegia venusta Orange flowers	Sun
Thunbergia mysorensis Yellow and reddish- brown flowers	Sun

is particularly dry, pour a litre or so of water into the hole and allow it to soak in. This will ensure that the concrete does not set too quickly.

3 Measure and cut the posts to size using a power saw. (Allow 600 mm for the depth of the post holes.) Cut a 190 mm x 45 mm notch at the top of each post to house the beam.

4 Set the posts in the holes and ensure they are vertical. Half fill the holes with concrete, and poke it down using a rod to remove any air bubbles. Ensure the posts are still vertical then fill the holes with concrete to slightly above ground level. Slope the concrete away from the posts so that water runs off. Allow the concrete to set for at least two days. If you use quick-set concrete, allow a couple of hours or follow the manufacturer's specifications.

5 Nail temporary bracing to support each post and check for plumb using a spirit level or plumbline. (Fix bracing in opposing directions and make sure it will not obstruct later work.)

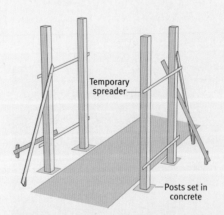

Temporary spreader

Posts set in concrete

6 Cut the beams and shape the ends, ensuring you have a 1700 mm width to fix to the posts after priming. Pre-drill holes through posts and beams then

fix the beams to the posts using 50 mm galvanised bolts.

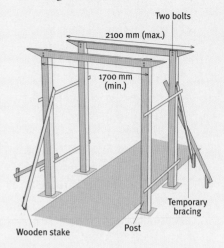

Two bolts

2100 mm (max.)

1700 mm (min.)

Temporary bracing

Wooden stake

Post

7 Cut the cross pieces to length (1000 mm) and prime the ends. Skew-nail between the outside posts at the desired heights.

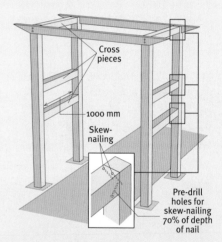

Cross pieces

1000 mm

Skew-nailing

Pre-drill holes for skew-nailing 70% of depth of nail

8 Prime and paint (or stain and clear finish) the timber. If desired, attach shadecloth on top or lattice to the sides and top. If using other roofing material, attach it according to the manufacturer's instructions.

Finishing touches

You've built your great Australian backyard. Now all it needs are the finishing touches: a few ornaments, such as a sundial or a sculpture, perhaps, maybe some feature plants in a planter. You may also want to encourage visitors, and place a birdbath or bird feeder in the garden to attract them. You can go one step further and give them a home with an easy-to-build birdhouse. And for plants, this chapter has two easily constructed planters – one is freestanding for a deck or patio, the other is a window box for flowers or perhaps herbs outside the kitchen.

Making a timber planter

This project is for a wooden planter 350 mm high and 450 mm x 510 mm. It's large enough for a medium shrub or small palm. You can substitute hardwood for pine if you wish, but painting is highly recommended. Sealing the wood to exclude moisture, or lining the project with plastic will also prolong its life. The planter can be used to contain a pot or be lined with plastic (punch holes in the bottom for drainage) or shadecloth and filled with soil.

1 With a pencil, ruler and square, measure battens to size (450 mm) and mark. Cut with a handsaw or power saw.

2 With a pencil, ruler and square, measure slats to size (350 mm) and mark. Cut with a handsaw or power saw.

3 Lay out two battens 350 mm apart (measured from the outer edges) and lay three slats over them ensuring they are at right angles to the battens and finish flush with the ends. They should also finish flush at the top, but if they're uneven at the bottom this can be hidden by the batten. Screw the slats to the battens. If necessary, pre-drill starter holes to prevent splitting. Repeat for the other three sides of the planter.

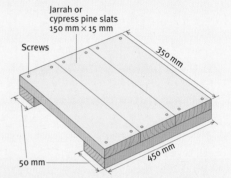

Difficulty: Easy

Time: 2 hours

Tools

- Ruler
- Pencil
- Square
- Handsaw or power saw
- Drill and assorted bits
- Screwdriver
- Hammer
- Paintbrush

Materials

- 8 jarrah or cypress pine battens 450 mm long x 50 mm x 15 mm
- 12 jarrah or cypress pine slats 350 mm long x 150 mm x 15 mm
- 2 narrow jarrah or cypress pine battens 20 mm x 20 mm
- 25 mm wood screws
- 8 jarrah or cypress pine slats 390 mm long x 50 mm x 15 mm
- 25 mm galvanised nails
- Outdoor paint and waterproof sealant

Decorative features can be added to a timber planter to change its appearance.

4 Cut two narrow battens to length (450 mm) and screw each to the bottom edge of the slats of two of the opposite assembled sides.

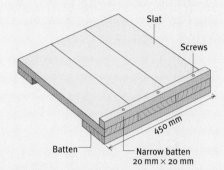

Slat

Screws

450 mm

Batten

Narrow batten
20 mm × 20 mm

5 In the centre of the left and right edges of the slats for these two sides, measure and mark positions for drill holes at intervals of 87.5 mm from the top. Pre-drill starter holes.

6 On the other two sides, measure in 22.5 mm from the left and right edges of the slats and mark the positions for three screws at intervals of 87.5 mm from the top. Pre-drill starter holes.

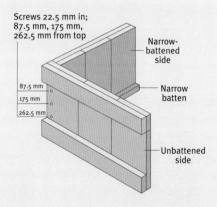

Screws 22.5 mm in;
87.5 mm, 175 mm,
262.5 mm from top

Narrow-battened side

87.5 mm
175 mm
262.5 mm

Narrow batten

Unbattened side

7 Butt one of the first two sides against one of the other two sides so that the pre-drilled holes (hopefully) align. Screw the two sides together.

8 Butt the other two sides to the assembly and screw into position.

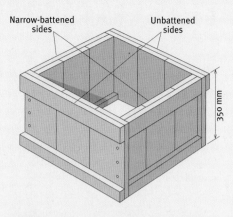

Narrow-battened sides

Unbattened sides

350 mm

9 Measure, mark and cut eight narrow pine slats to length (390 mm) for the floor. Pre-drill two starter holes in each slat 7.5 mm in from each end. Position the slats so they are spaced evenly across the narrow pine battens inside the planter. The small gaps will allow drainage. Nail the slats into position.

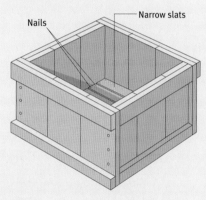

Nails

Narrow slats

10 Seal, stain or paint the planter.

Shrubs for planters

Name	Position
Buxus species Can be clipped to shape.	Sun or shade
Camellia japonica cultivars Flower colour depends on the cultivar	Part shade
Cordyline species Valued for their architectural shape	Sun
Fuchsia species Available in a wide range of flower shapes and colours	Semi-shade
Gardenia augusta Perfumed white flowers	Semi-shade
Laurus nobilis Leaves may be used in cooking	Sun or light shade
Pelargonium cultivars Available in bright colours	Sun
Rhododendron species Rhododendrons and azaleas will tolerate shade	Sun or shade
Rosa species Standard roses are available in a variety of flower colours	Sun
Westringia fruticosa Can be clipped to shape	Sun
Yucca species Strap-like leaves make an architectural statement	Sun

Planters can be used creatively to add character to your backyard.

Building a birdhouse

Difficulty: Easy
Time: 2 hours
Tools
• Pencil
• Ruler
• Square
• Handsaw
• Plane
• Power drill and bits
• Forstner or spade drill bit or hole saw
• Sandpaper
• Hammer
• Paintbrush
Materials
• Jarrah or cypress pine (or plywood), minimum 10 mm thick
• 25 mm galvanised nails
• 10 mm thick dowel x 60 mm long
• PVA adhesive
• Waterproof sealant
• Protective capping (for example, aluminium angle)
• Paint (or stain or oil)

This basic birdhouse can be made from either seasoned jarrah or cypress pine, two timbers that are naturally resistant to decay and insects. Plywood can be used but won't last as long. Timber offcuts can also be used to build a small birdhouse. Pieces of metal can be substituted for the roof as well, as long as they don't let the water in. The birdhouse can be painted, oiled, stained or left to weather to a soft grey colour.

All sorts of things can be used for birdhouses: tin cans, hollowed-out coconuts, old letterboxes and so on. The key is to provide somewhere relatively flat that's quiet, under shelter and inaccessible to cats.

1   Carefully measure and cut all timber to size using a ruler, square and handsaw. Plane and sand any rough edges.

2   To create the bird hole use a Forstner or spade bit (or hole saw) of the desired size, minimum 25 mm. At this point you can drill the hole for the dowel perch below the bird hole, making sure it's slightly narrower than the dowel for a snug fit, but don't secure the dowel just yet.

3   Glue and nail together the base and one side.

4   Glue and fix the front, back and other side to the base. Note that for maximum weatherproofing, the sides must overhang the base.

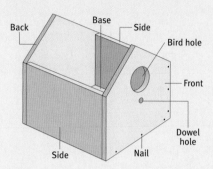

5   Nail the roof pieces tightly together and squeeze a thin bead of silicone sealant into the inside top joint (and other inside joints); or use aluminium angle as capping, stopping short of the ends. For maximum weatherproofing, the roof should overhang the box by at least 20 mm all around. Check that the roof fits tightly over the box without any gaps. Fix it on the sides and gables with nails.

6   Now you can glue the dowel in position. A nice touch is to find a small stick of the correct size to use as a substitute.

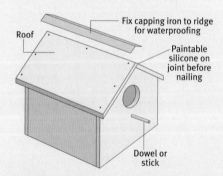

7   Check that all joints are secure. Sand and paint, stain or oil.

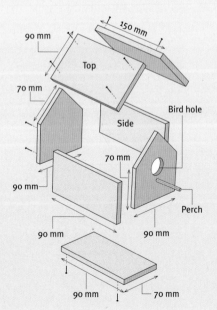

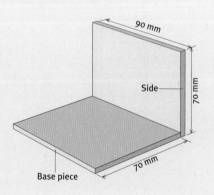

Creating a timber window box

A window box is ideal for flowers or herbs. This window box project is easy to make. It can either be lined and filled with soil for permanent planting or can hold pots – allowing you to rotate plants so you can see them when they're at their best.

1   Using a pencil, ruler and square, mark a piece of timber to a length of 450 mm and cut. Mark the piece at 250 mm along one edge and 200 mm along the other edge, rule a line between the two and cut along this diagonal. This gives you the two ends of the planter with just one cut.

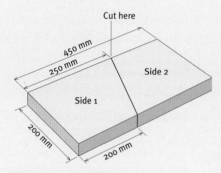

Cut here

450 mm
250 mm
Side 2
Side 1
200 mm
200 mm

2   To increase the life of your window box, prime all raw timber before fixing.

3   Measure and cut slats to length (600 mm).

4   Pre-drill two holes in the ends of each slat and screw three slats to the angled end timbers, butting the slats together to form the front of the planter.

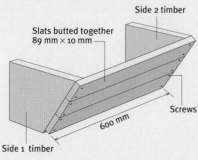

Side 2 timber
Slats butted together
89 mm × 10 mm
Screws
600 mm
Side 1 timber

5   Screw two slats to the side timbers at the back, leaving a gap of 20 mm between them and at the bottom (for drainage).

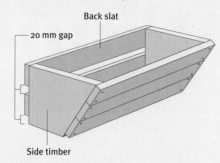

Back slat
20 mm gap
Side timber

6   Screw the last two slats to the bottom, leaving even gaps between the slats and the edges for drainage.

7   Paint, stain or oil to prolong the window box's life.

8   To fix the window box to a wooden window-frame or wall, pre-drill two holes 200 mm apart 40 mm from the top of the back slat and screw it to the wall or frame using 25 mm wood screws. Use a spirit level to ensure the window box is level.

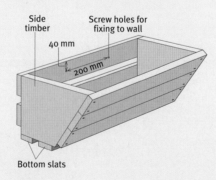

Side timber
Screw holes for fixing to wall
40 mm
200 mm
Bottom slats

9   To fix the window box to a brick wall, pre-drill the holes as before, and on the wall mark two horizontal points the same distance (200 mm) apart and horizontal (using a spirit level). Use a mortar drill bit to drill two holes in the concrete to accommodate plastic wall plugs. Insert the plugs then screw the window box to the wall using 25 mm self-tapping screws.

10   Place flowerpots in the window box or line it with plastic (punch holes for drainage) or shadecloth and fill with potting mix. Plant a selection of colourful flowering plants or sweetly perfumed flowers. Alternatively, plant your favourite herbs so you can pick them fresh without leaving your kitchen.

Difficulty: Easy

Time: 2 hours

Tools

- Pencil
- Ruler
- Square
- Handsaw
- Screwdriver
- Power drill and bits
- Paintbrush
- Spirit level

Materials

- One piece jarrah or cypress pine 450 mm x 200 mm x 20 mm
- Seven jarrah or cypress pine slats 600 mm x 80 mm x 10 mm
- 25 mm wood screws
- Plastic wall plugs and self-tapping screws (if attaching window box to brick)
- Paint, stain or oil

Planting

Planting your garden is a very creative and exciting process. This section takes you through all the necessary steps, from initial site and soil preparation to the finished look and garden maintenance. You are shown how to combine plants in ways that will allow you to get the best from their colour and form. And the comprehensive planting guide will help you to choose plants that are best suited to your particular climate.

Planting your garden

Plants create the tone of a garden. They are the finishing touch. A well-planted garden will reward you for many years to come. But planting is not about rushing out and choosing a few plants and placing them in the ground. You need to consider carefully the overall look you wish to create and how you will go about achieving it. Before you start, it's important to make sure that the soil is healthy. Once you have the right soil, the plants you choose and how you place them become the keys to a successful garden.

The soil

If there is a secret to successful gardening, it lies in the soil. After all, luxuriant growth doesn't occur by chance – it's the product of solid groundwork. So the first and most important step is to ensure that your soil is rich and healthy. A healthy soil not only sustains lush growth, but helps prevent insect and disease infestation. And, unless you are very lucky, you will find that a lot of groundwork has to be undertaken on the soil before you start planting.

What is good soil?

Good garden soil should be full of organic matter and teeming with worms. It should have the correct balance of sand, silt and clay particles and the right amount of air between these particles to promote good drainage and water retention. It must also have a good acid/alkaline balance for healthy plant growth.

Soil consists of inorganic material, organic matter, living organisms, water and air. Although the proportions may vary, the major components remain the same:

- Inorganic materials, such as sand, silt and clay, form the basis of soil components.
- Organic matter improves the structure of the soil, increases the ability of the soil to hold water, retains nutrients and affects the temperature of the soil.
- Organisms such as earthworms, fungi and bacteria break down the organic matter and increase the nutrients (especially nitrogen) available to plants. Organisms also break down the minerals in the soil and certain fungi assist plants in the absorption of nutrients.
- Water transports nutrients, keeps the soil temperature down,

OPPOSITE **Vegetables do not need to be confined to beds of their own. Lettuce, parsley and beetroot look just as attractive as the flowers in this garden bed.**

No matter what type of soil you have, there are plants that are suited to it. Azaleas and rhododendrons thrive in acidic soil.

assists the plants in keeping erect and breaks down minerals.
- Air is essential for the growth of plants' roots and helps to break down minerals. Living organisms in the soil also require air to live.

What is in your soil?
The characteristics of soil change greatly from place to place according to climatic and geological conditions. Soil formed from sandstone, for example, is less fertile and more sandy than soil formed from shale. Soil formed in dry climates has totally different characteristics from soil formed in wet climates, just as soil on a slope is different from soil formed at the base of it. Because of these variations, soil is classified according to its texture and will contain sand, silt or clay in differing proportions and combinations.

Soil texture
Soil 'texture' relates to the proportions of sand, silt and clay it contains. A clay soil is a fine soil as it contains a high proportion of extremely small clay and silt particles. On the other hand, a sandy soil is a coarse soil because it contains a high proportion of relatively large sand particles. A soil that is roughly intermediate, containing both clay and sand, is called a loam.

Soil types
There are essentially three types of soil found in gardens – sandy, clay and loam. Sandy and clay soils usually need some improving, but most loam soils are easy to work and have good drainage. Loam soils need only regular additions of organic matter to provide nutrients and structure.

It's a good idea to test your soil's type before planting, so it can be improved, if necessary. Take a small handful of soil from different areas throughout the garden. Add a little water to each handful to make it slightly moist. Roll this mixture in the palms of your hands until it forms a thread (the shape of a small sausage). Compare the consistency with the chart on page 225 to assess its texture.

How to improve sandy soil
Sandy soil has both advantages and disadvantages. The main disadvantage is that it drains too quickly and nutrients are lost with this free drainage. Fortunately, the

Soil types	Soil characteristics
Sand	A thread cannot be formed as it becomes a fluid mass when moisture is added.
Loamy sand	This will not form a thread but can be rolled into a ball that feels gritty and breaks easily.
Loam	Threads are not easy to form, but can be rolled easily into a cylinder that does not break on gentle bending.
Clay loam	Has a silky feeling and can be rolled into threads that are difficult to bend into a ring.
Clay	Can be rolled into long threads that bend easily.

structure of sandy soil is easy to improve by adding plenty of organic matter, such as leaf litter, compost or animal manure. These will increase its water-holding capacity and supply nutrients to the plants.

It's important to add organic matter continually to very sandy soils found near the sea. This can be done easily by mulching the garden with organic matter at least once a season.

Adding a wetting agent to sandy soil in conjunction with organic matter is very useful. Results can often be noticed after one application.

How to improve clay soil

The main problem with clay soil is its capacity to retain a high percentage of water. Consequently, it needs to be watered less often than sandy soil. Clay or silt soil restricts the normal penetration of the root system because of the slow movement of air and slow drainage. You can balance a clay soil by adding large quantities of organic matter, such as compost, leaf mould or animal manure. Gypsum can also be added, as it coagulates clay particles and this facilitates the drainage and movement of air through the soil.

Smart tip

There is a liquid organic claybreaker on the market, which, when watered into the soil, breaks up heavy clay. The treatment is effective within six to eight weeks of application. It need only be applied every four years, but for best results the claybreaker should be used in conjunction with organic matter.

Sandy soil by the beach can be improved to grow a variety of plants by adding plenty of organic matter.

Soil pH – the vital balance

Soil pH is a measure of the amount of acidity or alkalinity in the soil. The pH of the soil has a significant effect on plant growth. This is because soil pH affects soil micro-organisms, the ability of roots to absorb nutrients, and even the availability of essential nutrients.

The pH level of soil is measured on a scale that runs from zero to fourteen. Zero is on the acidic end and fourteen is on the alkaline end. At the middle of the scale, that is, seven, the soil will be neutral. If you add lots of manure and compost to your garden, you will find that the pH level will probably be suitable for growing most plants. If for some reason your plants are not growing as well as you think they should be and they have been fed and watered properly, then it might be an idea to test your soil. The soil can be tested by obtaining a pH soil-testing kit from a garden centre or nursery.

Changing the pH of your soil

If you find that the soil is too acidic, you can correct it easily by adding dolomite or agricultural lime. Wood ash is also beneficial to acidic soils.

An alkaline soil can be corrected by adding organic matter such as pine needles or decayed oak leaves. Alternatively, use sulphate of aluminium or sulphate of iron at the rate of two tablespoons per square metre.

What to do with a bulldozed site

Before you start building, it is a good idea to get a bobcat to remove the topsoil from the construction area. Place it in a pile elsewhere on the site to be reused when construction is completed and you start to build your garden.

We don't live in an ideal world, and many new home owners are faced with a bulldozed block that has nearly all the topsoil removed and only compacted clay remaining. If your topsoil has disappeared, you are going to have to topdress it with compost mix. Choose a reliable landscape supplier, so that your mix will have the correct pH and will not be full of weed seeds. If you take the measurements of the garden and lawn areas that need to be filled with compost mix, your landscaper will tell you how much compost you require.

If the site is compacted, you will need to turn the soil over to a spade's depth before adding the compost mix. You need to lay the compost mix at least 10 cm thick. Simply lay it over the top of the turned soil and plant into it. No matter how poor your soil is, you can make it into something productive and healthy if you continue to add organic matter regularly.

A successful garden is one in which the plants and positions are well matched. All the plants in this garden bed thrive in a well-drained loam.

Existing garden beds

If you are redesigning a garden and replanting existing garden beds, you should check the soil type and pH. All soils need regular rejuvenation (see Garden maintenance, pages 288–94) and it's a good idea to topdress existing beds with compost mix before planting.

Replacing lawn with garden

There is an easy way to make garden beds over the top of lawn without heavy digging by using the no-dig method or by solarising your soil.

The no-dig method

Lay down at least six layers of newspaper on top of any grass you no longer want. Make sure that all the edges of the newspaper are overlapping. If it is a slightly windy day, dampen the paper before you lay it down. Place at least 15 cm of mushroom compost or well-rotted compost on top of this. You can then plant your seedlings directly into the mix.

If it's difficult to get a supply of mushroom compost or you don't have enough of your own compost, lay down swathes pulled from a bag of lucerne. On top of these place old chicken or cow manure. Make a hole in the lucerne and manure, place a handful of compost mix into the hole and plant your seedling in that. The lucerne and manure will eventually break down and form a rich layer of topsoil to which more compost, lucerne and manure can be added each season.

Soil solarising

Solarising your soil will ensure that the grass and any weeds and their seeds will be killed. Mid-summer is the best time to solarise soil because of the heat needed to make it work efficiently. Simply lay a sheet of black plastic over the lawn area, pressing it down firmly all over. Anchor the plastic securely with rocks or wood and leave it for several weeks. The soil under the plastic will be heated and lawn, weeds and weed seeds will die.

Even an established garden such as this one requires regular soil rejuvenation.

Smart tip

To keep plants healthy, it's important to add organic matter such as manure or compost to the soil at least once a year (see Compost on pages 288–90).

Trees and shrubs form the upper and middle canopies of a garden, while bulbs, annuals and perennials provide interest at ground level.

How to start

Planting your backyard is an interesting task. What and how you plant will set the style and tone. But it's not just about choosing a few plants and placing them in the garden. You can bring out the best in your planting scheme by placing complementary plants next to each other and by choosing the right plant for the right place.

Making a plan

Some people like to add their planting plans to their finished plan. The best way to do this is to take a copy of your finished backyard plan that has the existing trees and shrubs (if any) marked on it. Lay some tracing paper over the top of this plan and trace the existing trees and shrubs onto it. You can now mark where you would like to place any new trees, shrubs and garden beds. Alternatively, you may prefer to walk around your garden and mark places where you wish trees and shrubs to go.

Using trees and shrubs

Think carefully where you place trees and shrubs – consider where the shade will fall and where drains, easements and overhead lines are situated.

Trees form the upper canopy of the garden, shrubs the middle canopy and lower growing annuals and perennials the bottom layer. Don't try to plant everything at once. Start with trees and shrubs (ideal as feature plants or hedges) – you can always fill in the spaces between them with annuals, perennials and bulbs at your leisure.

When starting a new garden, the temptation to overplant is

irresistible. The mature height and width of a tree or shrub, however, must be given full consideration before planting. Plant trees and shrubs with enough room for them to grow to their natural form and potential, otherwise you will have to constantly prune them (or remove some at a later date).

Know your garden's micro-climates

Before embarking on planting your new garden beds you must consider the garden's position. As you have already found out, your garden has many different micro-climates. Some areas may have full shade and some partial shade, while others may be in full sun. These micro-climates can be utilised to their full extent by choosing and planting the correct plant material for the particular conditions (see Your planting guide on pages 251–83).

What you plant is, of course, largely determined by the climate and the locality of the site. A hot, seaside garden has a very different climate from that of a mountain garden. If you are lucky enough to have saved much of the native landscape, you may wish to keep your garden predominantly native. Or if you live near the sea in an exposed situation and wish to keep the view, then you should create garden beds full of plants that will withstand those conditions. There is no point using plants that will not grow in your climate, as they will never thrive.

Using the correct plants and capitalising on the diversity of the garden's micro-climates allows for natural change throughout the garden. And, most importantly, plants placed in the correct positions will grow to full capacity.

LEFT All gardens have a variety of micro-climates and each one should be treated accordingly. The grasses and succulents in the foreground of this garden like it hot, dry and sunny, while the tree ferns in the background are sheltered from the sun by a tree canopy.

BELOW Trees can be used in interesting ways. In this garden laburnums have been trained to form an arch that leads to a statue.

Smart tip

The way plants are used contributes enormously to character. A rounded plant placed between a vertical and a horizontal one will pull the two together visually.

Hostas, spiky foxgloves and Japanese maples all thrive in semi-shade.

Developing character

Every garden has its own character. You can walk into some gardens and immediately gain a sense of harmony. The design of the garden and the way in which plant materials have been used contribute to this feeling. Gardens also change character throughout the year with the change of seasons.

The character of a garden will depend on the particular look that you wish to create, the variations in the block of land and its aspect and outlook. Choosing plants suited to the garden's situation will also have a considerable effect.

Character can also change within a garden. A garden can have a formal outline with neatly clipped box hedges bordering garden beds, but the planting within can be informal. You may wish to have a herb garden bed in a very formal style but then move on to a soft,

informal look elsewhere. Dividing a garden into different 'rooms' allows a great deal of freedom to develop garden character.

Planting for effect

Successful garden beds should have a sense of harmony and provide sufficient internal contrast to make them interesting. There should be enough structure in the garden bed to place plants in context, while simultaneously framing them and accentuating their colours.

Garden beds should be planned to provide a continuity of interest throughout the year. Thought should also be given to the placement of each plant in relation to its partner and the background planting. This book will enable you to understand the main points of

ABOVE   Silver stachys, red-brown *Heuchera* 'Chocolate Ruffles', roses, lavender and the vibrant reds of nicotiana and dahlias combine to make an eye-catching garden bed.

LEFT   Upright conifers provide structure in this garden. Their shape is softened by plants with a much more relaxed appearance.

garden planning, but the sense of creativity and the overall design outcome is, of course, in your hands.

Creating a group planting

Perennials and annuals always look better when planted in groups because groups create strong visual impressions. Grouping plants has other benefits. Because a group of flowers has greater visual impact, it makes you think that the flowerbed is full of flowers. This impression allows scope for the gardener to have a continuity of flowers.

The size of the groups will vary according to the size of the flowerbed. In small flowerbeds, a group of three to five plants makes a good impression without becoming too dominating. Large plants that have a wide spread are best used in groups of three, while smaller, thinner plants can be placed in groups of five. You may need only one plant if it has a large spreading habit.

Always work out the overall width of a particular plant before deciding how many you require for the group. Large, wide flowerbeds can have groups of between seven and twelve plants.

Don't plant groups in even, square blocks and don't make all the groups the same size and shape. Some groups should be broad, while others should be narrow. The number of plants in each group should vary, which is not a difficult requirement given that you are using plants of differing size. Drift each group into the adjoining group, making sure that planting partners are complementing each other.

You can repeat the group throughout the bed. This unifies the planting scheme to some extent, but do not repeat it too many times or it will become dominating. Groups of plants that have different heights should be placed next to each other.

Getting the natural look

Naturalised planting looks wonderful in large gardens where it can be used to imitate nature or in areas of the garden where you desire a natural appearance, such as under trees. It involves large drifts of one or two species used to cover an area.

Simplicity is the secret of success with this type of approach. You can create a naturalised effect in areas of the garden that lend themselves to a woodland theme. Choose permanent plants – such as perennials or bulbs.

Dappled shade under deciduous trees is a good position for bluebells, daffodils, jonquils, primroses or primulas. In deeper shade, drifts of tall-growing honesty in purple or white look spectacular. Large drifts of Japanese windflower planted under trees are striking in autumn.

Blocks of colour

Large blocks of a single colour or a block of foliage will always create a strong impression. For the most interesting effect use one type of plant only. For example, you can create a feature bed containing white groundcover roses surrounded by box or a low-growing lavender hedge. You can also clip and train box or pittosporum to form a mass of greenery and have a feature tree or topiary shrub in the middle.

Blocks of one colour are also used to create a directional effect. Line a pathway with a wide planting of catmint (*Nepeta* species), daisies, irises, lavender, lilies, roses or rosemary.

RIGHT   Successful garden beds should have a variety of leaf and flower shapes.

BELOW   Large blocks of one colour can create a strong impression.

Background planting

Most garden beds have a background, whether it be a fence or hedge. Fences and walls always make better backgrounds if they are covered with climbers. Evergreen shrubs can also provide a backdrop against which the colours of flowers can be set. Flowering shrubs produce a seasonal layer of colour and their leaves provide structure for the rest of the year.

Island beds

Garden beds that can be viewed from all sides need to be structured to emphasise the middle of the bed so they will look good from any angle. Place taller plants in the middle of the bed and taper them down towards the outer edges. Permanent structural plants such as roses and shrubs should be intermingled with taller growing annuals and perennials to create a sense of height.

Alternatively, you can create a border from a structural plant such as box honeysuckle (*Lonicera nitida*) and fill the bed with mixtures of tall flowers so that there is an abrupt falling away to the lower growing hedge.

On with the show

Every garden has its peak periods, but the truly successful garden always has something in flower or on show. Your flowerbeds may peak during spring or summer but this does not mean that there should be nothing in flower afterwards.

There is something very satisfying about wandering through a garden observing which flowers are finishing and which flowers are about to appear. One of the best methods of ensuring flower continuity is planning the distribution of flowering plants throughout the garden by seasons.

A variety of grasses makes an impact in this island bed and looks good from any angle.

Diverse leaf shapes add as much interest in this flowerbed as the flowers. The blue container with upright astelia leaves adds dramatic colour and texture.

Layering

You can layer plants within a garden bed so that as one group of annuals or perennials finishes another nearby group is starting to flower. For example, a semi-shaded woodland bed bursts forth in spring with bluebells and columbines. This is followed by summer-flowering hostas. Autumn produces Japanese windflowers and in winter helleborus and bergenia flowers are the stars.

A sunny bed can start its spring with roses and bulbs. Foxgloves, delphiniums, violas, sweet William and peonies quickly follow. The bed carries on through summer with November lilies, perennial lobelia (*Lobelia speciosa*), perennial phlox, rudbeckia, sedum, achillea and cosmos. When there is nothing in flower, the foliage of plants is the feature.

All of this does not happen overnight, of course, and it can take several years to get it right. It can be frustrating sometimes when you have created a picture and the main subject does not flower until after the rest of the group has finished. This, however, is what gardening is ultimately about – trial and error.

Planting partners

Some flowers bring out the best in each other and this should be taken into consideration when planning your garden beds. In addition to flower colours and shapes, you should be looking for leaf colour, texture and a variety of leaf shapes in a planting partner. Placing different leaf shapes together emphasises their diverse textures and shapes. This also applies to flower shapes. Take, for example, a group of plants with large trumpet-shaped flowers. The large flowers look more pronounced when placed next to a group with smaller flowers. In this way one group is not detracting from the other but complementing it.

A foliage plant placed among a group of flowers will often pull the group together, breaking up what would otherwise be a monotonous scheme. Before the flowers appear, the foliage plant is the attraction, and a new dimension is added once the flowers appear.

Featuring foliage

Although not everybody realises it, foliage is as much a feature of flowerbeds as the flowers themselves. Foliage actually forms the substance of a garden, while flowers are the added attraction. So when flowers are not the main performers, foliage comes into its own and holds the garden together.

Foliage is particularly important in small gardens as it can actually unify the garden. And the foliage of many plants can look just as spectacular as the flowers. The more you consider the highly individual shapes of leaves, the more important they will become to you. It is not just the colour of foliage that should be considered – take into account the leaf texture, structure and the composition of foliage.

Foliage combinations

Placing plants with different leaf shapes next to each other always brings out the best in both. Narrow leaves of ornamental grasses can be used next to large rounded leaves, for example, and rounded leaves used next to deeply divided leaves.

Shades of silver and grey

Silver and grey foliage create soft, shimmering, almost ethereal tones. Silver foliage looks exceptionally good in fading evening light and is even visible at night. When silver or grey foliage is placed in a distant garden bed it creates a sense of extended perspective.

When planted among brightly coloured flowers, silver will tone down the effect of the colours. On the other hand, silver and grey plants will tone up dark colours. You do not need many silver and

Silver and grey plants

- *Achillea* 'Moonshine'
- *Anthemis punctata*
- *Artemisia* species (wormwood)
- *Cerastium tomentosum* (snow-in-summer)
- *Cineraria* 'Silver Dust'
- *Convolvulus cneorum* (bush morning glory)
- *Helichrysum petiolare* (licorice plant)
- *Lavandula* species (lavender)
- *Lychnis coronaria* (rose campion)
- *Nepeta* × *faassenii* (catmint)
- *Perovskia atriplicifolia* (Russian sage)
- *Phlomis italica*
- *Phlomis russeliana*
- *Plectranthus argentatus*
- *Santolina chamaecyparissus* (cotton lavender)
- *Senecio cineraria* (Dusty Miller)
- *Stachys byzantina* (lamb's ears)
- *Tanacetum ptarmiciflorum* (silver lace)

ABOVE **Placing leaves with different shapes, texture and colour next to each other brings out the best in both.**

LEFT **Foliage, rather than flowers, forms the substance of this garden.**

Architectural plants

- *Acanthus mollis*
- *Acanthus spinosissimus*
- *Agave attenuata*
- *Alocasia macrorrhiza* (giant taro)
- *Angelica* species
- Bromeliads (*Aechmea* and *Neoregelia*)
- *Canna* species
- *Colocasia esculenta* (taro)
- *Cycas* species
- *Cynara cardunculus* (cardoon)
- *Cynara scolymus* (globe artichoke)
- *Euphorbia wulfenii*
- *Filipendula purpurea* (Japanese meadowsweet)

The stars in this garden bed are architectural bromeliads with their striking leaves.

grey plants to create an impact. In fact, if you use too many, they actually lose their effect.

Because many of the silver and grey plants are found growing naturally in harsh conditions, such as on shorelines and in deserts and alpine areas, they are suited to dry gardens.

Architectural plants

Some plants have very distinctive, architecturally shaped forms. It may be the texture, the size or the boldness of the leaves or the shape of the plant itself that attracts the eye. Plants with bold forms can draw the eye as much as garden ornaments when distributed throughout the garden. Not all architectural plants are foliage plants – think of the large flowerheads of sunflowers or the interesting bracts of euphorbias.

Architectural plants are best used on their own as a focal point or as feature plants in small areas such as courtyards. They may also be placed next to each other to bring out the best in both. For example, a tall grass like *Miscanthus sinensis* next to the large architectural leaves of cannas or acanthus can look most striking. Or a spiky plant next to a prostrate or domed one will enhance the impact of both. Shrubs clipped to shape or columnar-shaped conifers can also make architectural statements.

Scented foliage

Don't overlook perfumed foliage, as there is nothing nicer than brushing up against a perfumed plant while weeding. Consider geraniums, lavender, rosemary, artemisia, bay tree, lemon verbena, lemon balm and lemon grass.

Gardening with colour

Working with colour is an exciting and creative activity. Colour is one of the most impressive and memorable aspects of the garden and should be taken into account when planting your garden beds. Although there are certain principles underlying the choice of a colour scheme for the garden, the ultimate choice is highly personal. Just as the colour range of your clothes reflects your personality, the colours in your garden reflect your character.

Choosing colours

Many gardeners have the ability to combine colours with flair, while others simply do not think about it and end up with a dazzling array of colours that don't blend or have any relaxing qualities. Although colour choice depends on individual preference, its significance should not be overlooked when it comes to plant choice and positioning. No matter how well planted and designed a garden may be, the wrong use of colour can quickly spoil the effect.

Colour affects the tone of your garden no matter how big or small it is. For example, shady green areas will make you want to slow down or even sit, while a richly coloured planting at the end of a pathway will draw you towards it. Strong tones of yellow and red create an exuberant impact, while softer tones such as blue, pink, lemon and white have a tranquil and relaxing effect.

Smart tip

Keep in mind that strong colours such as yellow, red or orange stand out and advance towards you, while blues, purples and greys tend to recede.

The foliage of yellow and green variegated sage, purple heuchera and dahlias, green hostas and silver euphorbia provide colour in this bed.

The colours you choose, of course, are really a matter of personal preference. It's when you come to co-ordinating those colours that things can become tricky. The initial aim is to try to ensure that the flowers in the colour scheme appear simultaneously, and despite the best research and preparation, this aim is not always achieved. For this reason it is best to use coloured foliage as the reliable element of the scheme in case your attempts at getting flowers to bloom at the same time fail.

Mixing colours

Planning your use of colour doesn't mean that you must limit the scheme to just a few colours. You can always have separate areas containing different colours. To do this successfully, you should ensure that each neighbouring colour scheme blends with the next one. And, of course, your colour scheme can change with the seasons. As the spring layer of the garden finishes the summer layer can produce completely different colours.

Combining colours

Another aspect of successful co-ordination is an understanding of the effects various colours create. One approach is to choose a few colours and keep that mix throughout the garden. You can also use a base colour and employ contrasting colours in particular areas.

One of the first rules to accept when working with colour is that the **green** of foliage is a colour that

RIGHT   Ranunculus, silene and *Bellis perennis* create a 'hot' colour scheme.

BELOW   If you like the idea of using just one colour in the garden, you can expand the theme by adding tints and shades of that colour. In this combination, for example, yellow lightens into shades of cream.

is just as significant as any flower colour. Green is a good background colour and makes a useful filler between other colours. The colour green encompasses a range from pale, yellowish green to a dark, purplish green. Shades of green foliage can be used to create contrasts between light and shadow. Leaf shapes, texture, size and surface sheen all help to enhance the effects of light.

Blue is a cool colour available in many shades that can create a variety of effects. The bright blues lift and enliven the garden, while the soft lavenders and light blues produce a gentle, calm tone. Blue works well with yellow, orange, dark red, purple, pink, lemon, cream or white. Blue is always intensified by grey or silver leaves and white flowers.

Light has a very marked influence on the colour blue. Blue cornflowers or Chinese forget-me-nots produce a sharp, cheerful impression in the midday sun but, as the light fades in the evening, the effect becomes cooler and more mysterious.

Yellow and its various shades are happy garden colours. Yellow combines well with variations of scarlet and orange. It looks extremely attractive with blue or purple and also combines well with pinks, including hot pinks.

Pink is a versatile garden colour but it can look bland when used on its own. Soft pastel shades such as pink need to be darkened by brighter colours. Pink looks especially good with colours of the same range. Maroon, for example, combines well with various shades

Smart tip

When working with colour take into consideration the colour of your house, especially when you are planting directly next to the house.

BELOW Blue and yellow work well together as these blue summer forget-me-nots and yellow achillea demonstrate.

Topiary made easy

Clipping plants into different shapes does take some skill, so if you want the fantasy and whimsy of topiary without the hard work, you can cheat by buying a topiary frame from a nursery. Wire frames are available in many different shapes – dogs, peacocks, birds and ducks as well as spheres, oblongs or circles. While the frame provides the basic shape, you add character and detail in the planting and training stages.

The frame is simply placed in a container filled with potting mix and used as a hollow trellis over which vines growing in the pot are trained. Ivy is the most popular plant for growing over a frame because there are many different leaf forms, sizes and shapes. The climbing potato vine (*Solanum jasminoides*) and creeping fig (*Ficus pumila*) are extremely hardy and do not mind being clipped.

RIGHT   Clipped cylinders of box accentuate the entrance to a pathway and low box hedges emphasise the outline of this garden bed.

BELOW   Red, white and pink work well together.

of pink, blue and white. Purple, lemon and cream can also be incorporated into this scheme.

Very dark, bluish **reds** or shades of maroon are much easier to work into the garden than scarlet reds. Combine them with blue, purple, lemon, white or cream.

Scarlet flowers fit in best with shades of orange and yellow or with blue, pink and white.

White works with most colours. When combined with deep-green foliage it creates a tranquil effect. White looks particularly good in small gardens and creates an illusion of space. White also looks good with shades of silver, cream and lemon and can be used to tone down strong colours such as red.

Purple looks good with shades of maroon or deep red. Add pink to make the effect even more striking. Deep blue will also fit into this combination, as will rusty shades.

Dark colours such as **brown** and **black** combine well with green, apricot, pink and cream.

Techniques with plants

Plants can make interesting decorating statements. These statements may simply involve a fantastic topiary shape or clipped hedge surrounding a vegetable or herb garden. If your garden is small, you can use espalier to your advantage by growing fruit on walls.

Clipped plants

Shrubs that can be clipped to shape are very useful in the garden. Clipped hedges can form backdrops and divide the garden. They can also be used for screening, as architectural statements or to border beds. Some gardens, especially parterre gardens, can consist only of clipped shrubs.

Clipped shrubs can also be used to accentuate the entrance or end of a pathway. Shrubs like box, for example, can be clipped into rounds, squares or other shapes and distributed throughout the garden as features. This approach

also helps to pull the garden together.

Terracotta pots filled with clipped shapes are popular courtyard features. Let your imagination determine the shapes you select.

Hedges

Traditionally hedges have been used to mark boundaries and provide privacy. They have also been used to conceal unsightly areas or highlight interesting aspects of the garden. While these uses are valid and will always remain popular, hedging plants have much more potential. They are now being used in new and interesting ways and have been moved from the perimeter to be placed in the centre of things.

Hedges can be used to accentuate particular garden features. A courtyard may be separated from the rest of the garden by a neatly clipped hedge, while a hedge around a birdbath, fountain, seat or statue will highlight both the feature and its

position. Low hedges placed around herb and vegetable gardens always look good. Feature trees surrounded by low-growing hedges will produce a vertical emphasis in landscape design.

Hedges give definition and permanence in cold climates during winter when the garden is at its barest. And in many small court-yards and balconies clipped hedges or potted topiary create essential form and definition. In some small courtyard gardens the only plantings are clipped plants that have become permanent foliage features. The owners like the fact that they are low-maintenance plants and even the occasional necessary clipping is regarded as fun.

An interesting approach is to divide areas on courtyards or balconies by using long, oblong pots planted with clipped hedging.

Planting hedges

Most hedging plants are easy to grow. When purchasing, determine the mature width of the plant. Placing plants slightly closer to

A clipped lonicera hedge provides a strong background for this interesting succulent bed.

This clipped cypress hedge divides the garden and makes a good background to the garden bed.

each other than their natural width will quickly produce 'the look' and make a thick, bushy hedge. Give each plant a good start by digging the hole for the shrub twice the width of the pot.

Mix compost or well-rotted manure into the removed soil before replacing it. Mulch with lucerne and feed with a complete plant food in spring. Water regularly while the hedge is becoming established. If you are planting hedging plants in pots for topiary, then it is essential to start with a good potting mix and ensure they are kept watered.

If you are planting a straight hedge, always use a stringline as a planting guide. For curved hedges, make the intended shape on the ground by sprinkling lime or flour as a guide. To make a dense, wide hedge, place the plants in a double, staggered row.

Maintaining hedges

Apply a slow-release plant food in spring or mulch with well-rotted compost or manure. Water regularly. Competing root systems and shade cast by nearby trees can cause uneven growth, as can poor drainage.

Pruning hedges

Correct pruning is a must. Pruning depends on the species, but the aim with hedges or topiary is to have compact, solid growth. Make sure you have a good pair of hedge clippers.

The general rule is to prune in late spring after new growth has appeared. The next new growth should be pruned in late summer. The main aim of pruning the new tips is to encourage the stem to branch two or three times in order to create denser growth.

The vegetable garden

As our awareness of environmental issues and concerns grows, there is an increasing desire by gardeners to grow their own produce. The good news is that you don't need a huge area if you want to grow your own fresh, chemical-free vegetables. You only need a small ground space or some large pots.

Cultivating vegetables

When you plan your garden, be daring and leave space for vegetables in garden beds. From a design point of view, the inclusion of vegetables in a decorative bed creates an element of surprise. Why not have a border of mignonette lettuces, beetroot or carrots? The colour and texture of many vegetable leaves create interest and lift the appearance of your garden as a whole.

You should also include some interesting vegetable cultivars in your garden. In addition to the well-known staple vegetables, think about growing some that have unusual and distinctive tastes and that are not easily obtainable from the greengrocer.

Creating a vegetable patch

The easiest way to grow vegetables is, of course, in a patch of their own. Make sure your vegie garden suits the style of your house and garden. A natural native garden could be surrounded with logs, for example, while a vegetable patch near a Federation style house might be enclosed by a small picket fence.

Don't be afraid to make the vegetable garden a feature in itself. You may choose an informal design with meandering pathways, or a formal design with structured lines.

Choosing the right site

You need to follow some basic rules if you are to gain the maximum yields from your vegetable garden. The amount of sun your plot receives, protection from the wind,

LEFT   The vegetable and herb garden is the star attraction of this backyard. Brick paths have been used to divide the garden beds.

BELOW   This vegetable patch has an adjoining chicken run. The manure is collected and used to feed the vegetables.

good soil and adequate drainage are the most important considerations.

- **Sun:** Vegetables generally require as much sun as possible. Plant them away from the shade of fences and trees. Some lettuce and beetroot prefer a little summer shade, but this can be obtained by planting them on the south side of a tall crop such as tomatoes or corn.
- **Wind:** Windy conditions can reduce the yield of a vegetable garden by half. If necessary, create a windbreak by planting small shrubs or a low hedge.
- **Soil:** Preparing the soil correctly will ensure that your vegetable plot will be a success. Before you plant, dig in a large amount of compost, mushroom compost or well-rotted cow or chicken manure.
- **Drainage:** Vegetables require good drainage. If your area is poorly drained, raise the garden beds. You can build a wall around the vegie patch, or around parts of the patch with lower paths between the sections. Logs, railway sleepers or bricks are suitable for this purpose. Build up the patch with compost, manure or topsoil (or a mixture of these) until it is level with the wall.

Getting the most from your vegetable patch

There are several techniques for gaining the largest yield from the space you have available. Some vegetables such as beetroot, carrots, Chinese cabbage, lettuce, radishes, shallots and spinach produce a high yield in a very small space.

Growing crops vertically is another way to maximise your crop yield. Sunny areas beside a house or against a fence are suitable. Beans, chokos, cucumbers and peas can be grown like this, as long as they have enough support to prevent their weight from pulling down the vines.

You can also save space by cultivating climbing beans or peas

RIGHT **You can grow vegetables in any space. A wandering pumpkin spreads out over the lawn.**

BELOW **Raised garden beds are good when drainage is poor. These beds have been raised by the use of railway sleepers.**

on tepees constructed from wooden stakes. Simply plant the seeds at the bottom of each stake.

Crop rotation

In earlier times, crop rotation was the main way of controlling pests and diseases. Crop rotation allows nutrients in the soil to be used in sequence for crops with different feeding requirements that are planted progressively. Leaf crops, for example, need a great deal of nitrogen, and should be followed by root crops, which do not.

Vegetables are either heavy feeders or light feeders. Heavy feeders include cabbage, cauliflower, cucumber, tomatoes, lettuce, endive, spinach, celery, leek and pumpkin. These vegetables should be planted initially in newly built-up and fertilised soil and should be followed by lighter feeding plants such as beans, beetroot, carrots, cress, mustard, peas, radishes, shallots or turnips.

You should rotate the crops every year so that plants from the one family are not placed in the same spot.

Succession planting

You should try to plant vegetables at fortnightly intervals so that one crop can be harvested as another finishes bearing. This will provide you with a continuous supply of vegetables, rather than having too much of the one crop.

You can also plant vegetables that have a variety of maturity dates. Some vegetables are classified as early, mid-season or late.

Growing vegetables in containers

If space is limited, grow your vegetables in containers. A head start can be gained on the season by placing vegetables outdoors during warm daylight hours. When cool evenings approach, the containers can be moved inside or to a sheltered area.

The main requirement for any container used for growing vegetables is that it must have good drainage. If the drainage hole is small make new holes around the perimeter at the bottom of the pot. A good quality potting mixture is also essential. The size of the container will determine what can be planted in it.

Smart tips

In small gardens:
- plant tomatoes, salad greens and herbs in containers
- grow plants together for a closer yield, providing they are fed and watered more regularly than those planted at conventional distances
- plant salad vegetables among flowers – they add interest, colour and different foliage textures
- use air space as much as possible by building tepees, trellis and wire supports for growing vine plants. Use existing fences.
- interplant in rows between other vegetables.

Container depths for potted vegetables

10–15 cm deep	Lettuce, radish, beetroot, chives, low-growing herbs, shallots.
15–20 cm deep	Kohlrabi, baby carrots, turnips, Chinese cabbage, spinach, silver beet.
20–25 cm deep	Beans, cabbage, capsicum, cucumber, zucchini, celery, peas.
25–30 cm deep	Broccoli, cauliflower, deep-rooted carrots, tomatoes, eggplant, chillies.

Use air space as much as possible by building tepees for climbing vegetables such as beans.

Vegetables – sowing times

VEGETABLE	TROPICAL	SUBTROPICAL	TEMPERATE	COLD
Artichokes, suckers	Spring	Spring	Spring	Spring
Asparagus, crowns	Not suitable	Not suitable	Winter	Winter
Beans, climbing	All seasons	All seasons	Spring, summer	Mid-spring, summer
Beans, dwarf	All seasons	All seasons	Spring, summer	Mid-spring, summer
Beetroot	Late summer, autumn, winter, spring	Late summer, autumn, winter, spring	Late winter, spring, summer, early autumn	Late winter, spring, summer, early autumn
Broad beans	Not suitable	Not suitable	Late autumn, early winter	Early autumn, late winter, early spring
Broccoli	Autumn, winter	Autumn, winter	Late summer, autumn	Late spring, summer, autumn
Brussels sprouts	Not suitable	Not suitable	Summer, early autumn	Late spring, summer, early autumn
Cabbage	Late summer, autumn, winter, spring	All seasons	All seasons	Spring, summer, early autumn
Capsicum	All seasons	Spring, summer, autumn, winter	Spring, early summer	Spring
Carrots	Autumn, winter, spring, mid-summer	Autumn, winter, spring, mid-summer	Mid-winter, spring, summer, early autumn	Spring, summer
Cauliflower	Late summer, early autumn	Late summer, early autumn	Summer, early autumn	Late spring, summer
Celery	Summer, early autumn	Late spring, summer, early autumn	Late winter, spring, summer	Spring, early summer
Chinese cabbage	All seasons	All seasons	Late winter, spring, summer, early winter	Spring, summer, autumn
Choko	Autumn, winter	Autumn, winter	Late winter, spring	Not suitable
Cress	All seasons	All seasons	All seasons	All seasons
Cucumber	All seasons	All seasons	Spring, early summer,	Late spring, early summer
Eggplant	All seasons	All seasons	Spring, early summer	Spring
Kohlrabi	Late summer, autumn	Mid-summer, autumn	Mid-winter, early spring, late summer, early autumn	Late winter, early spring, late summer, early autumn
Leeks	Autumn, early winter	Late summer, autumn, early winter	Spring, summer, mid-autumn	Spring, summer
Lettuce	All seasons	All seasons	All seasons	All seasons
Mustard	All seasons	All seasons	All seasons	All seasons
Okra	Late winter, spring, summer	All seasons	Spring, early summer	Late spring, early summer
Onions	Late summer, autumn	Late summer, autumn	Autumn, winter	Autumn, winter
Parsnip	Autumn, winter	Late summer, autumn, winter	Mid-winter, spring, summer, early autumn	Late winter, spring, summer
Peas, climbing	Autumn, early winter	Autumn, early winter	Late summer, autumn, winter	Winter, early spring
Peas, dwarf	Autumn, winter	Autumn, winter	Late summer, autumn, winter	Winter, early spring
Potatoes, tubers	Mid-summer, autumn, winter, early spring	Mid-summer, autumn, winter, early spring	Late winter, early spring, late summer	Late winter, early spring
Pumpkin	All seasons	All seasons	Spring, early summer	Spring, early summer
Radish	All seasons	All seasons	Spring, summer, autumn, early winter	Spring, summer, autumn
Shallots, bulbs	Late summer, autumn, early winter	Late summer, autumn, early winter	Late summer, autumn, early winter	Late summer, autumn
Silver beet	All seasons	All seasons	Late winter, spring, summer, early autumn	Late winter, spring, summer
Spinach	Not suitable	Winter	Autumn, early winter	Late summer, autumn, winter
Squash	All seasons	All seasons	Spring, early summer	Late spring, early summer
Swedes	Late summer, autumn	Late summer, autumn	Late summer, autumn	Late summer, spring
Sweet corn	All seasons	All seasons	Spring, early summer	Spring, early summer
Tomatoes	All seasons	All seasons	Spring, early summer	Spring
Turnips	Late summer, autumn	Late summer, autumn	Mid-summer, autumn	Mid-winter, early spring, late summer, early autumn

Fruit trees

Landscaping with fruit trees allows you to combine practicality and beauty. And a few fruit-bearing trees are sufficient to improve the atmosphere of your garden, especially if you select unusual varieties instead of the more common types. You should also include those which produce the fruit you like to eat and cook.

You don't have to plant fruit trees and berries by themselves. Feature them in perennial or shrub borders or drape them over a pergola to provide some summer shade.

Many of these delicious crops produce an abundance of fruit while taking up very little ground space. And many berries and vines begin to bear fruit in a short space of time – some during the first season after planting.

To grow these crops successfully, you need a good soil, plenty of sunshine and regular applications of compost, manure or a complete plant food.

The herb garden

Herbs are very obliging plants. They are easy to grow and are endowed with sumptuous leaves and flowers. Most of their foliage and flower forms are very ornamental and the leaves and flowers of many are essential in the kitchen. Herbs by their nature add charm and fragrance when grown with perennials, roses, annuals and shrubs. An important quality of herbs lies in their ability to attract a multitude of bees and insects to the garden. Their presence always makes a garden seem special.

What is a herb?

How does one define a herb? Most herbs grown in gardens are the culinary types, but in the broadest, non-botanical sense, a herb is any plant that has some useful part. Lilies, roses, catnip and columbines all have healing qualities but are generally valued for their ornamental qualities. In today's gardens, culinary herbs are grown alongside healing herbs and those used for beauty treatments. You can grow them in formal herb gardens, in containers or sprinkled among other plants in a garden bed.

Cultivating herbs

For herbs to grow successfully, they need friable, well-drained soil and plenty of sun. Some will, however, grow in partial shade (see chart on page 249). A mulch of cow manure during spring is beneficial or you can feed them with a complete plant food.

Smart tip

Grow lemon balm or lavender as a hedge around the orchard to attract bees for better pollination.

Smart tip

Create scented pathways by planting chamomile, thyme, pennyroyal or sweet violets between stepping stones or bricks.

A colourful lemon tree in a container adds charm to this area of the garden.

Smart tip

There is something satisfying about being able to go into the garden and pick some fresh herbs for a soothing tea to treat minor ailments. Herbal teas can be made simply by using 2 tablespoons of fresh leaves or flowers in a teapot and pouring 2 cups of boiling water over them. Allow the tea to brew for at least 5 minutes and sweeten it with honey, if desired. Drink one or two cups per day. You can use chamomile, lemon grass, lemon balm, parsley, thyme or sage.

RIGHT   A herb garden is a valuable culinary investment and a delightful addition to the garden as a whole.

BELOW   Variegated sage and chives make a delightful, eye-catching combination.

Harvesting herbs

Pick fresh herbs for culinary purposes as they are required. Herbs that can be dried well, such as sage, oregano, marjoram, thyme and rosemary, can have their stems cut when the plants are well grown, which can then be tied with string, bunched, and hung upside down in a dark spot until the leaves are crumbly. Alternatively, you can use the microwave. Fleshy leaves will take longer to dry than small, thin ones, so you may need to experiment. Try working in 30-second increments, turning the leaves as you check on them. Crush the fully dried leaves and store them in airtight containers.

Parsley, chives, basil, tarragon, chervil and dill will all freeze well. You can freeze them by conventional methods or by placing the chopped herbs in ice-cube trays, covering them with water and freezing them. When you require a particular herb, place the whole ice-cube in the pot.

Growing herbs in containers

A terracotta pot brimming with a variety of herbs looks fabulous. Lemon grass looks fantastic in a pot. Pots containing parsley, chives and marjoram also look attractive.

Container growing allows you to meet the cultivation needs of herbs throughout the year as the containers can be moved to catch the sun. Place the containers near your back or front door, so you have ready access to them.

Always use a good commercial potting mix and feed the plants at least once every 6 to 8 weeks with a soluble complete plant food.

Herbs – a selection

NAME	DESCRIPTION	SITUATION	USES
Angelica (*Angelica archangelica*)	Green leaves and heads of greenish white flowers. Height 1.5–3 m	Semi-shade	Culinary
Basil, sweet (*Ocimum basilicum*)	Apple-green leaves and white flowers. 'Dark Opal' and 'Purple Ruffles' have deep-purple foliage. Height 30–60 cm	Full sun	Culinary
Bay tree (*Laurus nobilis*)	Deep-green leaves and small, cream flowers. Slow growing. Height 10–20 m but 1.8 m in pots	Full sun to partial shade	Culinary
Borage (*Borago officinalis*)	Grey-green leaves and blue flowers. Height 90 cm	Full sun to partial shade	Culinary
Caraway (*Carum carvi*)	Finely divided leaves and white flowers. Height 30–60 cm	Full sun	Culinary
Chamomile, Roman (*Chamaemelum nobile*)	Aromatic, lacy leaves and white flowers. Height 25 cm	Sun to partial shade	Culinary, medicinal
Chervil (*Anthriscus cerefolium*)	Fern-like leaves and white flowers. Self-seeding. Height 60 cm	Sun to partial shade	Culinary
Chicory (*Cichorium intybus*)	Green leaves and blue flowers. Height 1 m	Sun	Culinary
Chives (*Allium schoenoprasum*)	Grass-like, tubular leaves and purple flowers. Height 30 cm	Sun	Culinary
Coriander (*Coriandrum sativum*)	Lace-like foliage and white flowers. Height 90 cm	Full sun to partial shade	Culinary (leaves/seeds), medicinal
Cumin (*Cuminum cyminum*)	Finely divided leaves and white flowers.	Sun	Culinary (seeds)
Curry plant (*Helichrysum italicum*)	Grey foliage and yellow flowers. Height 90 cm	Sun and good drainage	Culinary
Dill (*Anethum graveolens*)	Deeply dissected leaves and yellowish white flowers. Height 90 cm	Full sun	Culinary
Fennel (*Foeniculum vulgare*)	Feather-like leaves and strong odour. Yellow flowers. Invasive. Bronze fennel is not as invasive and makes an interesting feature plant. Height 1.2 m	Sun to partial shade	Culinary, medicinal
Fenugreek (*Trigonella foenum-graecum*)	Clover-like stems and leaves and white flowers. Height 30–60 cm	Full sun	Culinary, medicinal
Garlic (*Allium sativum*)	Foliage resembles onions. Pink flowers. Height 60 cm	Full sun to partial shade	Culinary, medicinal
Common ginger (*Zingiber officinale*)	A tender perennial with yellow-green flowers. Height 60–120 cm	Partial shade	Culinary, medicinal
Lavender (*Lavandula* species)	Grey-green perfumed leaves and purple flowers. Height varies with species and cultivars	Full sun, well-drained soil	Culinary, medicinal, dried flowers, attracts bees
Lemon grass (*Cymbopogon citratus*)	The grass-like foliage looks magnificent in ornamental garden beds. Height 1.5 m	Full sun to partial shade	Culinary, medicinal
Lemon verbena (*Aloysia triphylla*)	Deciduous, woody shrub with light-green, scented leaves and pale-mauve flowers. Height 1.5–3 m	Full sun	Culinary, medicinal
Lovage (*Levisticum officinale*)	Glossy, celery-like leaves and greenish yellow flowers. Height 1.8 m	Full sun to partial shade	Culinary, leaves taste like celery
Marjoram, sweet (*Origanum majorana*)	Grey-green leaves and white or pink flowers. Height 60 cm	Full sun	Culinary, medicinal, attracts bees
Mint (*Mentha* species)	Many different species of mint. Height depends on species.	Full sun to partial shade. Moist soil	Culinary
Oregano (*Origanum vulgare*)	Bluish green, strongly scented leaves and white- to rose-coloured flowers. Height 75 cm	Full sun to light shade	Culinary
Parsley (*Petroselinum crispum* var. *crispum*)	Bright-green leaves and greenish yellow flowers. Height 30 cm	Full sun	Culinary, medicinal
Rosemary (*Rosmarinus officinalis*)	Grey-green, scented, needle-like leaves and pale blue flowers. Height 60–150 cm	Full sun to partial shade	Culinary, medicinal, attracts bees
Sage (*Salvia officinalis*)	Grey-green leaves and purple flowers. Height 30–60 cm	Full sun to partial shade	Culinary, medicinal, attracts bees
Savory, summer (*Satureja hortensis*)	Downy leaves and pale-lavender or white flowers. Height 45 cm	Full sun	Culinary, medicinal
Savory, winter (*Satureja montana*)	Strongly scented leaves and white or pink flowers. Height 45 cm	Full sun	Culinary, medicinal
Tarragon, French (*Artemisia dracunculus* var. *sativa*)	Strongly flavoured leaves. Height 60 cm	Full sun to partial shade	Culinary
Thyme (*Thymus* species)	Many different species and cultivars. Height varies	Full sun to partial shade	Culinary

Your planting guide

Once you have designed and landscaped your backyard, built the features you have chosen and included any other elements, you will need to think about the plants you would like to include. The plants you choose and how you use them will determine the look of your backyard. This planting guide gives expert advice on selecting the right trees, shrubs, annuals, perennials, roses, groundcovers and other plants so that you can make the most of your backyard. It includes cultivation requirements and details on colour, shape and foliage to help you achieve the look you want.

Climatic regions

This map shows the various climatic regions found in Australia. You should use it as a guide for selecting suitable plants for your backyard.

Plants have a variety of requirements, but will grow best within their preferred range of temperature. The suitable range will depend on the species. Plants can be affected by variations in sun and shade and by their ability to withstand heat, cold and frosts.

While these considerations should be kept in mind, it is also true to say that some plants have the ability to survive in areas that are colder or warmer than their recommended conditions.

Many plants are also affected by the particular micro-climates that exist in your backyard. Some tropical plants will grow in temperate or warm temperate conditions if they are situated in a warm micro-climate.

Highland regions have shorter growing periods than cool temperate, temperate, warm temperate, subtropical and tropical regions. Frost-hardy plants should be chosen for highland areas.

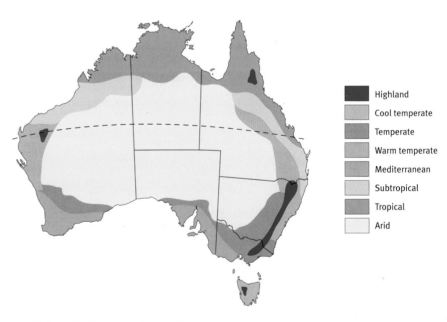

Highland
Cool temperate
Temperate
Warm temperate
Mediterranean
Subtropical
Tropical
Arid

OPPOSITE   A well-fed garden will be healthy and less prone to pests and diseases.

Annuals

Annuals offer the garden many exciting possibilities. They allow you to experiment with colour and plant combinations in a way that is not possible with structural plants. And you are not punished severely if the experiment fails, as annuals can be removed when the season is over and any errors quickly rectified. Annuals provide quick colour, which can be bold or subtle, depending on your backyard theme.

Using annuals

In new gardens, annuals may be used for filling bare spaces while more permanent plantings are growing. If annuals are planted thickly enough, they will cover bare earth and prevent weed growth. They can be planted *en masse* under trees to create a woodland effect or be used as trim around a garden bed while slower growing hedges or border plants mature.

Plant annuals in clumps and merge them in groups of not less than five. To achieve a continuity with annuals, you must keep purchasing them throughout the year or sow seed each season for the next one.

Annuals are also important to achieve a sense of change through the seasons. You can choose different-coloured annuals each season and those that have different heights, flower shapes and sizes.

In addition to the flowers of annuals, you should consider the leaf colour and texture of both the annuals themselves and the surrounding plants. Try to combine lacy and bold leaves, or jagged leaves with plain leaves. This creates interest even before the flowers have appeared.

Potted annuals

Mix and match is the go with annuals. You can create fantastic

ABOVE   Potted *Impatiens* will enliven shady corners.

RIGHT   Evocative Canterbury bells fill in a bare spot behind the perennial catmint.

colour schemes because annuals that look brash in other situations make lively pot plantings. Use a range of plant heights in the one pot to create an abundant, informal look. Potted annuals are ideal for small gardens where you do not want to take up ground space but want to have colour changes throughout the seasons.

Use trailing plants in window boxes, hanging baskets and containers attached to walls. Lobelias provide a mass of colour over a long period, as do verbenas and *Petunia* 'Million Bells'.

A good potting mix is the key to success with pot plants. For best results choose a premium mix that carries the Australian Standards logo. You can also buy mixes for specific purposes, such as those formulated especially for terracotta pots. Because of their porous nature, you should line the inside of terracotta or stone pots with black plastic. But be careful not to line the bottom or drainage will be impeded.

Checklist for growing annuals

- [ ] Don't plant seedlings too close together. Give plants enough room to reach their full size. You'll have more flowers.
- [ ] Plant sun-loving annuals in sun only and shade-lovers in shade only, otherwise the plants will not thrive.
- [ ] Make sure the soil is rich and healthy before planting. Compost or manure can be dug into the soil or used as a mulch.
- [ ] Don't sow seeds too early in spring as the soil is colder than the air temperature and the seeds won't germinate. In cold areas, wait until frost has finished.
- [ ] Avoid planting in straight rows. Instead, plant in drifts for a more informal look.
- [ ] Choose colours that suit your existing colour scheme and ensure that the colours of the annuals don't clash with each other.

Annuals for cutting

Annuals are ideal for cutting gardens. Allocate a special space in your garden for flowers suited for cutting. The effect can be stunning, and you don't have to worry about spoiling a favourite display in your garden.

LEFT Nasturtiums are fast-growing and attractive groundcovers.

BELOW Iceland poppies flower during winter and make good cut flowers.

Annuals – a selection

NAME	HEIGHT	SITUATION	FLOWER COLOUR	FLOWERING TIME	USES	ZONE
Ageratum houstonianum (floss flower)	15–30 cm	Sun or lightly dappled shade	Blue, pink or white	Spring, summer	Ideal for containers. Mixes well with petunias.	All zones
Agrostemma githago 'Milas' (corn cockle)	60–90 cm	Sun	Purplish pink	Spring, summer	Its fast-growing habit makes it ideal for filling bare spots.	All zones except tropical
Alcea rosea (hollyhock)	1–2 m	Sun and shelter from wind	Various depending on the cultivar	Summer	Plant at the rear of the bed. Ideal for hot, dry areas.	All zones except tropical
Ammi majus (Queen Anne's lace)	1–1.5 m	Sun	White	Spring, summer	Fast growing. Suited to cottage gardens.	All zones except tropical
Antirrhinum majus (snapdragon)	20–100 cm	Sun	Various	Spring, summer, autumn, winter	Will supply colour throughout the year in frost-free climates.	All zones except tropical
Bellis perennis (English daisy)	10 cm	Sun or semi-shade	White and pink	Spring	Cultivars include shades of red, pink and white.	All zones except tropical
Bracteantha bracteata (native everlasting daisy)	1 m	Sun	Yellow, pink, bronze red, cream and purple	Summer, autumn	Ideal for native and natural gardens.	All zones
Calendula officinalis (pot marigold)	30–60 cm	Sun	Orange, yellow	Winter, spring	Good with blue ageratum in a container.	All zones except tropical
Campanula medium (Canterbury bells)	1 m	Sun or semi-shade	White, blue, lavender pink or violet	Spring, early summer	Pretty biennial – ideal for cottage gardens.	All zones except subtropical and tropical
Centaurea cyanus (cornflower)	75–100 cm	Sun	Blue, white, pink, maroon or violet	Spring, summer	Remove dead flowers to to induce more flowering.	All zones except tropical
Cleome hassleriana (spider flower)	1.5–2 m	Sun	Rose-pink	Summer	Gives height quickly to new garden beds.	All zones
Cosmos bipinnatus (common cosmos)	1 m	Sun	Red, white, yellow or pink	Spring, summer, autumn	Ideal for providing height in cottage gardens.	All zones
Digitalis purpurea (foxglove)	1–1.5 m	Sun or semi-shade	White, pink, cream or purple	Spring	Tall flowers make a dramatic statement.	All zones except tropical
Eschscholzia californica (California poppy)	30 cm	Sun	Yellow, orange, scarlet or white	Spring, summer	Remove flowers before they go to seed to prevent prolific self-seeding.	All zones except tropical
Gypsophila elegans	60 cm	Sun	White, pink or carmine	Summer, autumn	The dainty flowers look good next to bolder flowers like those of cosmos.	All zones except tropical
Gypsophila paniculata (baby's breath)	90 cm	Sun or semi-shade	White	Spring	Flowers are ideal for picking.	All zones except tropical
Helianthus annuus (annual sunflower)	1–3 m	Sun	Yellow	Summer	Brightly coloured flowers add height and colour to the garden.	All zones
Iberis umbellata (globe candytuft)	15–30 cm	Sun	Mauve, lilac, pink, purple, carmine or white	Spring, summer	Grow in containers or garden beds.	All zones
Impatiens balsamina (balsam)	30–65 cm	Sun or semi-shade	Various	Summer, autumn	Ideal for brightening up semi-shaded areas of the garden.	All zones except highland and cool temperate
Lathyrus odoratus (sweet pea)	Varies	Sun	Various	Late winter, spring, early summer	Climbing and groundcover varieties are available.	All zones except subtropical and tropical
Lobelia erinus (edging lobelia)	10–20 cm	Sun	Blue-violet, blue or white	Spring, summer, autumn	Ideal for hanging baskets and containers.	All zones
Lobularia maritima (sweet alyssum)	20 cm	Sun	White. Lilac, pink and violet shades are also available.	Spring, summer, autumn	Lightly perfumed flowers. Grow along the edges of pathways.	All zones except tropical
Lunaria annua (honesty)	75 cm	Sun or semi-shade	Violet-purple or white	Spring	The seed heads are used in dried flower arrangements.	All zones except subtropical and tropical

NAME	HEIGHT	SITUATION	FLOWER COLOUR	FLOWERING TIME	USES	ZONE
Malcolmia maritima (Virginia stock)	20 cm	Sun or semi-shade	Mauve, pink, white or cream	Spring, summer, autumn	Grow the perfumed flowers near a seat or window.	All zones
Moluccella laevis (bells of Ireland)	60 cm	Sun	Green and white	Summer	Tall flower spikes are ideal for picking.	All zones except tropical
Myosotis sylvatica (garden forget-me-not)	30 cm	Sun or semi-shade	Blue, pink or white	Late winter, spring	They have a prolific self-seeding habit.	Cool temperate
Nemesia strumosa (annual nemesia)	20–50 cm	Sun	Various	Spring	Bright colours make pretty pot plantings.	Temperate, warm temperate, subtropical and tropical
Nemophila menziesii (baby blue-eyes)	20–30 cm	Sun or semi-shade	Blue	Spring	Ideal for containers.	Temperate, warm temperate, subtropical and tropical
Nicotiana alata (flowering tobacco)	1 m	Sun or semi-shade	White, red or shades of pink	Summer, autumn	The flowers open in the evening and release a sweet perfume.	All zones
Nigella damascena (love-in-a-mist)	60 cm	Sun or semi-shade	Blue, pink or white	Spring	Self-seeds readily throughout the garden.	All zones except tropical
Oenothera speciosa (white evening primrose)	50 cm	Sun	Pink-tinted white	Summer	Remove flowers before they go to seed to prevent self-seeding.	All zones except tropical
Papaver nudicaule (Iceland poppy)	30–60 cm	Sun	Red, orange, yellow pink or white	Winter, spring	Pretty poppies that are ideal for picking.	All zones except tropical
Papaver rhoeas (Flanders poppy)	60 cm	Sun	Scarlet. The cultivated Shirley Series is available in pinks, reds, whites and bi-colours.	Spring	Ideal for natural gardens.	All zones except subtropical and tropical
Phlox drummondii (annual phlox)	10–40 cm	Sun or semi-shade	Various	Summer, autumn	Fast-growing, long-lasting flowers.	All zones except tropical
Primula malacoides (fairy primrose)	30 cm	Sun or semi-shade	Mauve, purple, pink, red, white or carmine	Winter, spring	Ideal for brightening up semi-shaded areas.	All zones
Reseda odorata (common mignonette)	30–60 cm	Sun	Shades of red and yellow	Spring, summer, autumn	Fast growing with perfumed flowers.	All zones except tropical
Rudbeckia hirta 'Becky Mixed' (coneflower)	1–1.5 m	Sun	Yellow and brown, lemon or red	Summer, autumn	Brightly coloured flowers last through autumn.	All zones except tropical
Torenia fournieri (wishbone flower)	30 cm	Semi-shade	Deep blue	Late spring, summer, autumn	Great for hanging baskets and containers.	All zones
Tropaeolum majus (garden nasturtium)	30 cm	Sun or semi-shade	Orange, scarlet, red, mahogany or yellow	Late spring, summer, autumn	Large, edible leaves. Provides quick cover.	All zones
Viola tricolor (heartsease)	10–30 cm	Sun or semi-shade	White, yellow, blue and shades of purple	Late winter, spring	Pretty, self-seeding flowers.	All zones
Viola × wittrockiana (pansy)	30 cm	Sun or semi-shade	Various	Late winter, spring and summer in cooler climates	Ideal for supplying late winter colour in containers.	All zones

Perennials

With their wonderful colours, textures and spreading habits, perennials are undoubtedly the backbone of a garden. They create the framework in which annuals and biennials are used. You can have interesting groups of perennials flowering from spring to autumn, and a few will flower even in winter. Perennials are ideal for creating an established look while the framework of trees and shrubs is growing.

There is a huge variety of perennials. Perennials range from tall background plants to groundcovers that can be used between paving. You can think of them as the lower storey underneath trees and shrubs. Unlike annuals, which need constant replanting, perennials will perform for many years. And there is a perennial for every position in the garden, whether it is in full sun or shade.

What is a perennial?

The simplest definition of a perennial is 'a plant that lives for more than two years'. While many plants fit this category, including trees, shrubs and bulbs, the word commonly refers to perennial flowering plants that are herbaceous. This means that their stems are soft and fleshy, not woody like those of shrubs and trees.

These herbaceous perennials survive the winter because their roots are stronger and more vigorous than those of annuals and biennials. With the onset of cold the tops die down, but the roots remain alive in a dormant state, sending forth new foliage and flowers each year when the weather warms up.

Some perennials are evergreen, so their foliage performs throughout the year.

Smart tip

The most common mistake when using perennials is to overplant. The majority of perennials spread every year and this should be taken into consideration from the outset. Although the garden bed may look bare initially, it will be full before long. If you don't like the appearance of bare earth, you can always grow some annuals around the perennial while you are waiting for it to spread.

Annuals and perennials provide attractive groundcovers in an informal garden setting.

Planting perennials

A perennial will grow in the same
spot for many years, so its initial
planting is important. As with all
plants, it is important to choose
the right perennial for a particular
situation. If you have a dry area,
for example, choose a perennial
that does not require a great deal
of water. Among the perennials,
you will find one to suit most
situations.

If you are starting a new garden
bed, it is advisable to incorporate
organic matter such as cow manure
or compost into the soil before
planting. Water the perennial in its
container about an hour before
transplanting. Dig the hole for the
perennial deeper than required,
add manure or compost to the
bottom of the hole, then cover it
with a little soil.

The hole should always be
several centimetres larger in
diameter than the spread of the
roots, as this will give the roots
space to become established
quickly. Fill in around the plant
with a mixture of soil and compost
or manure.

Water thoroughly after planting
and keep the perennial watered
until it has established.

Maintaining perennials

The essential maintenance of
perennials usually includes staking
the taller varieties and giving them
a supply of food when the new
growth appears. Staking should
always be done subtly, using
wooden or bamboo stakes.

When flowerbuds appear, feed
the plant with an application of
soluble plant food.

Perennials checklist

- [ ] Consider the height and width of each plant, allowing room for it to spread.
- [ ] Check flower colour and flowering times for colour harmony.
- [ ] Only plant perennials that will grow in your climate.
- [ ] Plant more than one of each type for a massed effect.
- [ ] Consider foliage colour and texture and the structure of the plant – they add strength to the border.

Perennials – a selection

NAME	HEIGHT	SITUATION	FLOWER COLOUR	FLOWERING TIME	USES	ZONE
Acanthus mollis (bear's breeches)	100 cm	Sun or shade	Purple and white	Late spring, early summer	Make use of the large architectural foliage.	All zones except tropical
Achillea species (yarrow)	75–100 cm	Sun	Yellow, pink, white or red	Late spring, summer, autumn	Ideal for dry or natural gardens.	All zones except tropical
Agapanthus praecox	100 cm	Sun or semi-shade	Blue or white	Summer	Very hardy, ideal for natural and gravel gardens.	All zones
Alstroemeria hybrids (Peruvian lily)	60–90 cm	Sun or semi-shade	Various	Spring, summer	Free-flowering.	All zones except subtropical and tropical
Anemone × hybrida (Japanese windflower)	90 cm	Sun or shade	White, pink or mauve	Autumn	Hardy plants that will brighten up a shady spot.	All zones except tropical
Aquilegia vulgaris (columbine)	90 cm	Sun or shade	Various	Spring	Ideal for the cottage garden.	All zones except subtropical and tropical
Argyranthemum frutescens (Marguerite daisy)	90 cm	Sun	White, pink or yellow	Spring, summer, autumn	Fast growing. Ideal for new gardens to provide quick colour.	All zones
Armeria maritima (thrift or sea pink)	10–12 cm	Sun	White to pink	Spring, summer	Ideal for dry or rock gardens.	All zones except subtropical and tropical
Artemisia absinthium (common wormwood)	100–120 cm	Sun	Creamy yellow	Summer	Make use of its pretty silver foliage.	All zones except tropical
Aster novi-belgii (New York aster)	60–120 cm	Sun	Various	Autumn	There are many different cultivars in a variety of colours.	All zones except subtropical and tropical
Astilbe species (false spirea)	60–90 cm	Semi-shade	Pink, red, white	Summer	Ideal for damp areas.	All zones except subtropical and tropical
Bergenia × schmidtii (Norwegian snow)	35 cm	Sun or shade	Rose-pink	Winter, spring	Take advantage of its large leaves in shady positions.	All zones except tropical
Callistephus chinensis (China aster)	60 cm	Sun	Pink, white, red, blue or purple	Summer	Fast growing with an attractive daisy-like flower.	All zones except subtropical and tropical
Campanula species	Varies	Sun or semi-shade	Shades of blue	Spring, early summer	Some of the species make attractive ground-covers.	All zones except subtropical and tropical

Campanula persicifolia always adds interest to a shady corner.

Japanese windflowers will brighten up a shady area during autumn.

Hardy penstemons are available in a range of colours.

NAME	HEIGHT	SITUATION	FLOWER COLOUR	FLOWERING TIME	USES	ZONE
Centranthus ruber (red valerian)	45–90 cm	Sun or semi-shade	Rose-red	Spring, summer, autumn	Hardy plant that will grow in dry conditions.	All zones except tropical
Cerastium tomentosum (snow-in-summer)	10–15 cm	Sun	White	Late spring, summer	A good groundcover that can trail over walls or onto pathways.	All zones except subtropical and tropical
Dahlia cultivars	Varies	Sun	Various	Summer, autumn	Brightly coloured flowers add interest to garden beds.	All zones
Delphinium elatum 'Pacific Giant'	1–2 m	Sun	Various	Spring, summer, autumn	Cut back spent flowerheads to induce another flush.	All zones except subtropical and tropical
Dianthus plumarius (cottage pink)	20–30 cm	Sun	Red, pink, white or mauve	Spring, summer	Sweetly scented flowers.	All zones except subtropical and tropical
Dicentra spectabilis (bleeding heart)	60 cm	Shade or semi-shade	Pink and white	Spring, summer	Delightful heart-shaped flowers. Ideal for cottage gardens.	All zones except arid, subtropical and tropical
Dictamnus albus (burning bush)	60 cm	Sun	White, pink or lilac	Early summer	Bears spikes of fragrant flowers.	All zones except subtropical and tropical
Dierama pulcherrimum (angel's fishing rod)	1 m	Sun	Pink	Summer	Grass-like foliage and arching stems of bell-shaped flowers.	All zones except subtropical and tropical
Echinacea purpurea (purple coneflower)	1 m	Sun	Reddish purple	Summer	Tall, daisy-like flowers. Ideal for cottage gardens.	All zones except tropical
Erysimum cheiri (English wallflower)	60 cm	Sun	Orange, yellow, red, brown, crimson or white	Late winter, spring	Fragrant flowers. There are many different cultivars.	All zones except tropical
Euphorbia characias subsp. *wulfenii*	1–1.2 m	Sun	Yellow-green	Winter	Colourful bracts last for months.	All zones except tropical
Felicia amelloides (blue marguerite)	50 cm	Sun	Blue and yellow	Late spring, summer, autumn	Ideal for seaside gardens.	All zones except highland, where it may be grown as an annual

Plant blue marguerite in seaside gardens.

Chocolate-leafed heuchera contrasts well with hostas and orange dahlias.

Perennials – a selection (cont'd)

NAME	HEIGHT	SITUATION	FLOWER COLOUR	FLOWERING TIME	USES	ZONE
Geranium species	Various	Sun or shade	Blue, pink or white	Spring, summer, autumn	Ideal for woodland gardens. There are many different species.	All zones except subtropical and tropical
Helianthemum nummularium (sun rose)	25–30 cm	Sun	Yellow, pink or orange depending on the cultivar	Spring, summer	Low-growing plant makes a pretty groundcover.	All zones except tropical
Helleborus foetidus (stinking hellebore)	80 cm	Semi-shade	Green	Winter, early spring	Flowers last for months.	All zones except subtropical and tropical
Helleborus × hybridus (Lenten rose)	45 cm	Semi-shade	Purple, pink, cream or white	Winter, early spring	Plants readily self-seed in the garden. Ideal for woodland gardens.	All zones except subtropical and tropical
Helleborus lividus	60 cm	Semi-shade	Pinkish green	Winter, early spring	Pretty woodland plant.	All zones except subtropical and tropical
Helleborus niger (Christmas rose)	40 cm	Semi-shade	White ageing to pink	Winter	Likes moist but well-drained soil.	All zones except subtropical and tropical
Hemerocallis hybrids (daylily)	Depends on the hybrid	Sun or semi-shade	Various	Spring, summer	Free-flowering plants with strap-like leaves.	All zones
Heuchera sanguinea (coral bells)	50 cm	Sun	Red	Spring, summer	Attractive leaves and a long flowering period. Some cultivars have chocolate-coloured leaves.	All zones except tropical
Hosta species	Various	Shade	Various	Summer	Grown for their ornamental leaves.	All zones except tropical
Kniphofia hybrids (red-hot pokers)	50–100 cm	Sun	Various	Summer	Tall flower spikes add interest to garden beds.	All zones except tropical
Leucanthemum × superbum (shasta daisy)	60–90 cm	Sun	White	Summer	Ideal for cottage gardens.	All zones except tropical
Liatris spicata (gay feather)	1 m	Sun	Pinkish purple	Summer	Will grow in damp soil. Flowers attract bees.	All zones except tropical
Limonium latifolium (perennial statice)	50 cm	Sun	Lavender-blue	Summer	Dried flowers are ideal for indoor decoration.	All zones except tropical
Lychnis coronaria (rose campion)	50–60 cm	Sun	Bright magenta	Late spring, summer	Has pretty silver foliage. Self-seeds.	All zones except subtropical and tropical
Nepeta × faassenii (catmint)	40 cm	Sun or semi-shade	Mauve	Late spring, summer	Cut finished flowers to induce another flush. Ideal for dry gardens.	All zones except subtropical and tropical
Ophiopogon japonicus (mondo grass)	30 cm	Shade	Violet-pink	Summer	Grown for its grass-like leaves. Ideal for edges.	All zones
Penstemon hybrids	60–90 cm	Sun	Various	Late spring, summer	Remove spent flowers to induce another flush.	All zones except tropical
Phlox paniculata (perennial phlox)	70–100 cm	Sun	Various	Summer	Ideal for cottage gardens.	All zones except subtropical and tropical
Platycodon grandiflorus (balloon flower)	50–60 cm	Sun	Blue	Late spring, summer	Pretty cottage-garden plant.	All zones except tropical
Primula (Polyanthus Group)	25 cm	Semi-shade	Various	Late winter, spring	Ideal for containers or garden beds.	All zones except subtropical and tropical

NAME	HEIGHT	SITUATION	FLOWER COLOUR	FLOWERING TIME	USES	ZONE
Pulmonaria officinalis (medicinal lungwort)	30 cm	Shade	Pinkish purple	Spring	Pretty, spotted white leaves.	All zones except warm temperate, subtropical and tropical
Rudbeckia fulgida (orange coneflower)	1–1.5 m	Sun	Yellow and brown	Summer, autumn	Ideal for cottage gardens.	All zones except tropical
Salvia species (sage)	70 cm	Sun	Depends on the species	Spring, summer, autumn	Most of the sage species are hardy and free-flowering.	All zones
Santolina chamaecyparissus (cotton lavender)	60 cm	Sun	Yellow	Summer	Attractive silver foliage. Ideal for low hedges.	All zones except subtropical and tropical
Stachys byzantina (lamb's ears)	50 cm	Sun	Rosy-purple	Spring	Beautiful silver foliage. Ideal for dry gardens.	All zones except subtropical and tropical
Stokesia laevis (Stokes' aster)	60 cm	Sun	Blue-mauve	Spring, summer, autumn	Free-flowering.	All zones
Verbena × *hybrida* (garden verbena)	40–50 cm	Sun	Various	Late spring, summer	Ideal for containers or garden beds.	All zones
Veronica spicata (digger's speedwell)	40 cm	Sun	Blue	Late spring, summer	Flower spikes appear freely.	All zones except warm temperate, subtropical and tropical
Viola odorata (sweet violet)	5–10 cm	Sun or semi-shade	Violet, white, red, pink or blue	Late winter, spring	Perfumed flowers are ideal for picking.	All zones except subtropical and tropical

Purple-leafed salvia and other perennials combine happily with roses.

Bulbs

The change that bulbs undergo is amazing. It's extraordinary that those dull brown bulbs you bring home from the nursery contain the promise of a beautiful flower. A bulb actually contains the embryo of the entire plant. Roots, stems, leaves and flowers are stored in this form until conditions are right for growth. While most people associate them with spring, it's possible to have different bulbs flowering throughout the year.

Cultivating bulbs

Hardy and relatively pest-free, bulbous plants are among the easiest plants to grow. Their first requirement is good drainage. They should be fed with a complete plant food in early spring and again after the flowers have finished, as bulbs start to store food for the following year at this time.

Planting depth

The general rule is to plant bulbs at a depth equal to about twice the width of the bulb.

Growing bulbs in containers

Pots of varying sizes and shapes are ideal for creating delightful bulb displays and look good on patios, courtyards and situated throughout the garden. One of the main advantages of growing bulbs in pots is the possibility of bringing them indoors to be enjoyed at the peak of their flowering period. When the bulbs have died down, plant flowering annuals over them.

Daffodils and jonquils herald the beginning of spring.

Why bulbs don't flower

'Why don't my bulbs always flower?' people often ask. It's because the embryo flower and foliage have already been produced within the bulb during the previous season. Hence, the treatment given to bulbs during the previous season will often determine their performance. The main reasons for bulbs not flowering are:

- **overcrowding:** most bulbs can be left in the ground for years, but sometimes the clumps become so congested they can't produce bulbs of flowering size.
- **excessive dryness:** lack of water during the flowering season and while the leaves are still green.
- **a position that is too shady:** if the bulb is not shade-tolerant, it will not be able to make enough food to store for the following year.
- **foliage removed prematurely:** the foliage of bulbs should be allowed to die down naturally.
- **temperature:** tulips, and to a lesser extent daffodils and hyacinths, require a cold winter to flower. In warm temperate climates, store tulip bulbs in the vegetable compartment of the refrigerator for 8 to10 weeks before planting in late April or May.

Ixias creates a delightful meadow effect.

Bulbs – a selection

NAME	SITUATION	FLOWERS	PLANTING SEASON	USES	ZONE
Amaryllis belladonna (belladonna lily or naked ladies)	Sun or semi-shade	Pink summer flowers	Late autumn to early winter	Garden beds in positions where they will not be disturbed as they dislike root disturbance.	All zones
Babiana stricta (baboon flower)	Sun	The freesia-like blue or mauve flowers appear in spring.	Late summer, autumn	Ideal for naturalising with freesias, ixias and sparaxis.	Warm temperate, Mediterranean, subtropical, and tropical
Clivia miniata (fire lily)	Shade or semi-shade	Late winter and spring orange to scarlet flowers.	Any season	Its attractive evergreen leaves are ideal for shady spots. Good container plant.	Mediterranean, arid, temperate and warm temperate
Colchicum autumnale (autumn crocus)	Sun or semi-shade	Late summer and autumn lilac-pink or white flowers.	Summer	Ideal for bordering a garden bed or for containers.	All zones except subtropical and tropical
Crinum species	Sun, semi-shade or shade depending on the species	Flowers in summer in white and shades of pink depending on the species.	Autumn to spring	Use as feature plants. *C. moorei* will grow in deep shade.	All zones depending on the species
Crocus species	Semi-shade	Late winter and early spring in shades of purple, lavender and white.	Autumn	Ideal for rockeries or naturalising under trees.	All zones except subtropical and tropical
Freesia hybrids	Sun	Wide range of colours. Some are perfumed. Flower in spring.	Autumn	Good for containers or naturalising on dry, sunny banks.	All zones except tropical
Galanthus nivalis (common snowdrop)	Semi-shade	Fragrant, white, bell-shaped late-winter flowers	Autumn	Naturalise under deciduous trees.	All zones except subtropical and tropical
Gladiolus species	Sun	Wide range of colours depending on the variety. Flower in summer.	Spring	The tall flower stems add height to garden beds. Good cut flower.	All zones depending on the species
Hippeastrum hybrids (amaryllis)	Sun or semi-shade	Magnificent trumpet-shaped flowers during late spring and summer. Colours include salmon, deep pink, red and variegated red and white.	Winter – plant with the neck of the bulb at the soil surface.	Good container plants. Plant in clumps in garden beds.	Warm temperate, Mediterranean, arid, subtropical and tropical
Hyacinthoides hispanica (Spanish bluebell)	Sun or semi-shade	Bell-shaped, lilac-blue spring flowers	Autumn	Can be grown in containers. Ideal for naturalising.	All zones except subtropical and tropical
Hyacinthus orientalis (hyacinth)	Sun or semi-shade	Fragrant spring flower spikes are available in shades of blue, white, cream, pink or purple.	Autumn	Grow in containers and bring indoors when in bloom to enjoy the perfume. Also suited to garden beds.	All zones except subtropical and tropical
Iris species	Sun	Wide range of colours depending on the variety or species.	Autumn	Valued for their strap-like foliage and flower stems. Cottage gardens or flowerbeds.	All zones except subtropical and tropical
Ixia species	Sun	Shades of white, yellow, pink, orange, red or green spring flowers.	Autumn	Ideal for naturalising on dry sunny banks. Good cut flowers.	All zones except tropical
Lachenalia aloides (cape cowslip)	Sun or semi-shade	The yellow, late winter and spring flowers have a green base and red tips.	Autumn	Good for rockeries, naturalising or cottage gardens.	All zones except tropical
Leucojum vernum (spring snowflake)	Sun or semi-shade	The pretty, white, bell-shaped, late winter to spring flowers have green tips on the petals.	Autumn	Ideal for naturalising under deciduous trees.	All zones except tropical
Lilium species	Sun	There are many different species and varieties in a wide range of colours. Mostly summer flowering.	Late autumn, winter	Ideal cut flowers. Plant in clumps in garden beds.	All zones except tropical

NAME	SITUATION	FLOWERS	PLANTING SEASON	USES	ZONE
Lycoris radiata (red spider lily)	Sun	The red, late summer or autumn flowers have curled petals and long stamens.	Winter, early spring	Plant so the neck of the bulb is above the soil. Grow in garden beds or on dry banks. The bulbs like to be left undisturbed.	All zones except tropical
Muscari species (grape hyacinth)	Sun or semi-shade	Blue or white, small, bell-shaped flowers.	Autumn	Naturalise under deciduous trees or rockeries.	All zones except tropical
Narcissus species (daffodil, jonquil)	Sun or semi-shade	There is a huge range of flower shapes and colours ranging from creamy-whites to yellows, pinks and deep, rich oranges. Flower late winter to spring.	Autumn	Ideal for naturalising in lawns. Grow in clumps in garden beds. Good cut flowers.	All zones except tropical
Nerine bowdenii (pink spider lily)	Sun	Pink autumn flowers appear before the foliage appears.	Winter, early spring	Plant so the neck of the bulb is above the soil surface. Grow in garden beds or on dry banks. The bulbs like to be left undisturbed.	All zones except subtropical and tropical
Polianthes tuberosa (tuberose)	Sun	The fragrant, creamy-white flowers are borne on tall flower spikes in summer or early autumn.	Winter, early spring	Good cut flowers. Plant in groups. Ideal for cottage gardens.	All zones
Sparaxis tricolor (velvet flower)	Sun	Multi-coloured spring flowers in shades of red, yellow and orange with black markings. Spring and summer flowering.	Autumn	Ideal for naturalising or rock gardens. Can be grown in containers.	All zones except tropical
Tulipa species (tulips)	Sun or semi-shade	Beautifully formed, large spring flowers in a variety of colours.	Autumn	Plant in containers and bring indoors while in flower. Plant in clumps in garden beds.	All zones except subtropical and tropical
Zephyranthes grandiflora (storm lily, autumn crocus)	Sun or semi-shade	Dusky-pink, late summer and autumn flowers with white throats.	Late autumn, winter, early spring	Plant as a pretty border for pathways. Good for rock gardens.	All zones. Protect from frost

Tulips and hyacinths create a colourful display.

The beautiful belladonna lily.

The dainty flowers of spring snowflakes.

The brightly coloured flowers of sparaxis.

Climbers

What would gardeners do without climbing plants? They are versatile, useful and visually impressive. Climbers are often the mainstays of small gardens that have limited ground space. And fragrant climbers draped over pergolas or around windows present their perfumes at nose level. Tepees and other structures made from lattice, wire, stakes or branches clothed in climbers give height to garden beds and can be features in themselves. And there's nothing more appealing than a shady arbour covered in climbing plants.

Selecting climbers

It's important when selecting a climber to ensure that the growth habit is equal to its intended task and that it suits its support. Climbers with hanging flowers should be displayed over an arch or pergola where the flowers will be fully appreciated. Climbers on a wall should be able to cling without support.

Climbing plants have various aids that enable them to climb. Understanding these aids will enable you to choose the right climber for the right support:

- **Sucker discs:** Some climbers have discs that develop from their long stems for support. The discs find their way into small cracks and joints of masonry or rough timber and hold on with great tenacity. Ivy and Virginia creeper are good examples of climbers that employ sucker discs.
- **Scramblers:** The climbing rose is perhaps the most common example of this type of climber. Scramblers bear hooks or prickles that curve downwards, enabling the plant to attach to another plant or object.
- **Twiners:** The support for this type of climber is given by the stem that coils around itself for support. Wisteria and honeysuckle are good examples.

Wisteria makes a pretty backdrop to this garden bed.

- **Tendril climbers:** This type of climber spreads by means of thread-like tendrils. Tendrils are usually modified stems, leaves, leaflets or, as in the case of nasturtiums, modified petioles. The entire tendril usually winds itself around the support by developing a spring-like coil.

Planting climbers

Proper planting will determine the health of the climber for many years and encourage prolific growth.

Water the climber in its container at least an hour before transplanting. Dig a hole slightly deeper than the container and approximately twice as wide. Water the hole before planting and allow it to drain. Add some compost to the bottom of the hole. Check to see if the roots are root bound. If they are running around the root ball, try to straighten them out as much as possible. Prune away any broken or damaged sections. Place the plant on top of the compost mix, spreading the roots evenly. Fill in the hole with the remaining soil and water thoroughly. All newly planted climbers require regular watering to help them become established.

Feeding climbers

Mulch young climbers with compost or manure. This will keep the soil moist and supply essential plant food. In spring and again in early summer, apply a complete soluble fertiliser around the base of the climber. Alternatively, apply a six-month, slow-release plant food in spring. Always water the soil well before and after applying fertiliser.

Climbers in trees

In their natural habitat, climbers growing through trees and shrubs form an integral part of the ecology. Despite this fact, many people wrongly believe that any climber weaving its way through a tree or shrub will eventually strangle it. While this may be true of a wisteria or large ivy, softer climbers like clematis and most climbing roses imbue a garden with charm as they harmlessly wind through the lower branches of trees.

Plant climbers that flower at different times from the host tree or shrub. This will help provide a long period of colour, often encompassing several seasons. The same effect can be achieved on pergolas and arches by planting more than one type of climber to lengthen the flowering period.

LEFT   The edible grape has been used to create shade during summer.

BELOW   Clematis is ideal for growing over trellis.

Climbers – a selection

NAME	DECIDUOUS OR EVERGREEN	SITUATION	FLOWERS	USES	ZONE
Actinidia kolomikta (kolomikta)	Deciduous	Sun	White flowers in late spring and summer	Grown for its beautiful leaves, which are reddish green when young, maturing to bright green with the outer half of each leaf white or deep rose-pink.	All zones except subtropical and tropical
Akebia quinata (five-leaf akebia)	Deciduous or semi-deciduous in warm climates	Sun or semi-shade	Lime to slatey-purple spring flowers	A vigorous vine that needs a strong support.	All zones
Allamanda cathartica (golden trumpet vine)	Evergreen	Sun	Yellow, trumpet-shaped, spring to autumn flowers	row on fences or pergolas.	Warm temperate, subtropical and tropical
Antigonon leptopus (coral vine)	Deciduous	Sun	Bright, rose-pink summer flowers	Suited to light structures, such as trellis, and arbours.	Temperate, warm temperate, subtropical and tropical
Beaumontia grandiflora (herald's trumpet)	Evergreen	Sun or semi-shade	Fragrant, white, trumpet-shaped, spring and summer flowers	Needs a strong support, such as a pergola.	Warm temperate, subtropical and tropical
Bougainvillea species	Evergreen in tropical areas but can be deciduous in cooler areas	Sun	Showy spring and summer flower bracts make colourful displays.	Grow on pergolas. Suited to Mediterranean-style gardens.	Mediterranean, arid, warm temperate, subtropical and tropical
Campsis grandiflora (Chinese trumpet vine)	Deciduous	Sun	Terracotta-coloured summer and autumn flowers	Needs a strong support, such as a pergola.	Temperate, Mediterranean, warm temperate, subtropical and tropical
Clematis species (virgin's bower)	Deciduous or evergreen depending on the species	Grow clematis so their roots are in the shade. They grow up to the sun.	There is a wide variety of cultivars and species in a range of flower colours. Depending on the species, you can have a clematis flowering all year round.	Grow on tripods, teepees, arches, up trees or on trellis.	All zones depending on the species
Clerodendrum splendens (glory bower)	Evergreen	Sun or semi-shade	Scarlet summer flowers and glossy foliage	Grow on a pergola or on trellis as a screen.	Warm temperate, subtropical and tropical
Clytostoma callistegioides (violet trumpet vine)	Evergreen	Sun or semi-shade	Trumpet-shaped lavender flowers are streaked with purple and appear from late spring and into summer.	Grow over fences, up dead tree stumps or over pergolas.	Warm temperate, subtropical and tropical
Ficus pumila (creeping fig)	Evergreen	Sun or shade	Grown for its attractive foliage, which clings to walls by its aerial roots.	Grow on walls, brick fences.	Mediterranean, temperate, warm temperate, subtropical and tropical
Hardenbergia violacea (purple coral pea)	Evergreen	Sun or semi-shade	Purple, pea-like winter and spring flowers	Grow on trellis, arches, fences or let it scramble along the ground as a groundcover.	All zones
Hedera species (ivy)	Evergreen	Sun, semi-shade or shade	Grown for its glossy-green or variegated leaves.	Ideal for walls, old tree stumps and pillars.	All zones
Hibbertia scandens (Guinea gold vine)	Evergreen	Sun or semi-shade	Valued for its yellow, buttercup-like flowers.	Ideal for sandy, seaside gardens or low-water-use gardens. Also suited to native gardens.	Mediterranean, arid, warm temperate, subtropical and tropical
Hoya carnosa (wax plant)	Evergreen	Semi-shade	Pinkish white, star-shaped summer flowers. Do not cut the flowers as the same flower spurs continue to flower for several years.	Use on trellis or grow as a container plant with wall support.	Warm temperate, subtropical and tropical
Jasminum species	Evergreen	Sun or semi-shade	Valued for their perfumed flowers.	Grow over arches, trellis or pergolas where you can appreciate the perfume.	All zones

NAME	DECIDUOUS OR EVERGREEN	SITUATION	FLOWERS	USES	ZONE
Lathyrus odoratus (sweet pea)	Evergreen	Sun	Perfumed spring flowers in a variety of shades	Annual climbers valued for cut flowers. Grow on trellis, tepees, arches and wire fences.	All zones except tropical
Mandevilla × amoena 'Alice du Pont'	Evergreen	Sun or semi-shade	Deep-pink, bell-shaped, summer flowers are produced among handsome glossy leaves.	Fences, old tree stumps, pergolas or on screens.	Warm temperate, subtropical and tropical
Mandevilla laxa (Chilean jasmine)	Semi-deciduous	Sun or semi-shade	Produces very fragrant, white summer and autumn flowers.	Ideal for pergolas, fences, walkways or old tree stumps.	Warm temperate, subtropical and tropical
Mandevilla sanderi (Brazilian jasmine)	Evergreen	Sun or semi-shade	Large, deep-pink flowers are produced for months (early summer to late autumn). 'My Fair Lady' has pink buds that open to white.	Ideal for pergolas, fences, walkways or old tree stumps.	Warm temperate, subtropical and tropical
Pandorea jasminoides (bower vine)	Evergreen	Sun or semi-shade	The pale-pink, trumpet-shaped flowers have deep-carmine throats. Flowers from spring to autumn. 'Lady Di' has white flowers.	Ideal for native gardens, pergolas, old tree stumps or walkways.	Warm temperate, subtropical and tropical
Pandorea pandorana (wonga-wonga vine)	Evergreen	Sun or semi-shade	Spring and summer, creamy-white flowers have reddish throats.	Grow over arches, pergolas, wire fences or up old tree stumps. Ideal for native gardens.	Warm temperate, subtropical and tropical
Parthenocissus species	Deciduous	Sun or semi-shade	Grown for their attractive leaves that colour in autumn.	Ideal for walls or building facades.	All zones except tropical
Passiflora species (passion flower)	Evergreen	Sun	Grown for their beautiful flowers or edible fruit.	Grow on trellis, wire fences, pergolas or archways.	All zones
Podranea ricasoliana (pink trumpet vine)	Evergreen	Semi-shade	Valued for its pink, funnel-shaped, spring to autumn flowers. Attractive foliage.	Grow on trellis, wire fences, pergolas or archways.	Mediterranean, warm temperate, subtropical and tropical
Pyrostegia venusta (orange trumpet creeper or flame vine)	Evergreen	Sun	Bright-orange flowers appear during late winter and spring.	Grow on trellis, fences, arbours or pergolas.	Temperate (tolerates light frosts), warm temperate, subtropical and tropical
Quisqualis indica (Rangoon creeper)	Evergreen	Sun or semi-shade	The perfumed flowers open white and age to pink and red during summer.	Suited to fences, pergolas or on trellis for screening.	Subtropical and tropical
Rosa species (climbing roses)	Deciduous or evergreen	Sun	There is a huge choice of climbing roses in a wide range of colours. Many are perfumed.	Ideal for trellis, arches, fences, arbours and pergolas.	All zones except tropical
Solandra maxima (golden chalice vine)	Evergreen	Sun	Very large, creamy-yellow, spring flowers	A rampant vine that is ideal for covering large areas.	Warm temperate, subtropical and tropical
Solanum jasminoides 'Album' (potato vine)	Evergreen	Sun	Clusters of white flowers appear throughout summer and autumn.	Fast-growing vine ideal for quick screening.	All zones (needs protection from frost in highland zones)
Stephanotis floribunda (Madagascar jasmine)	Evergreen	Filtered sunlight	Fragrant white flowers appear among attractive shiny leaves.	Ideal for trellis, arches or arbours.	Warm temperate, subtropical and tropical
Tecomaria capensis (cape honeysuckle)	Evergreen	Sun	Orange-red to scarlet spring and summer flowers.	Use for covering old tree stumps, outbuildings or wire fences.	Subtropical and tropical
Trachelospermum jasminoides (Chinese star jasmine)	Evergreen	Sun or semi-shade	Grown for its perfumed white flowers, which sit among deep-green foliage.	Ideal for courtyards, walls, arches, pergolas and arbours.	All zones except highland and cool temperate
Vitis vinifera (wine grape)	Deciduous	Sun	Grown for its attractive leaves and edible fruit.	Grow on pergolas, wire fences or trellis.	All zones except tropical
Wisteria species	Deciduous	Sun	Beautiful racemes of perfumed purple, pink, white or mauve flowers in spring.	Grow on arches, pergolas or walkways. Need a strong support.	All zones except tropical

Shrubs

Shrubs are team players. They have a cohesive quality that can pull the garden together. In fact, shrubs are the skeletal structure of a garden design. They provide a permanent framework of wonderful hedges, sight and sound barriers, and interesting leaf and flower forms. They fill the spaces between trees and lower growing annuals and perennials. Shrubs perform a background role that unifies the overall design throughout the year.

Choosing shrubs

Variety is a key aspect of shrub use. You should try to select shrubs with different bases, branch forms and leaf textures. Small-leafed shrubs make the garden seem larger, while big leaves attract attention and reduce the sense of distance. Light-coloured foliage looks good when placed in front of dark foliage. Sun shining on lighter leaves has a particularly intense and striking appearance when placed against a dark backdrop. Different shades of green provide necessary contrast in the garden. And one should not overlook seasonal colour changes that come with the exposed bark and bare branches of winter, the bright new growth and flowers of spring, the muted tones of summer, and the fruit and changing foliage of autumn.

Planting shrubs

Proper planting will determine the health of the shrub for many years and encourage prolific growth. All newly planted shrubs require regular watering to help them become established.

Water the shrub in its container about an hour before transplanting. Dig a hole slightly deeper than the height of the container and approximately twice as wide. Water the hole before planting and allow it to drain. Add some compost to the bottom of the hole. Check to see if the roots are root bound. If they are running around the root ball, try to straighten them out as much as

RIGHT   A variety of differently shaped and coloured shrubs have been used to create interest in this garden.

BELOW   Hydrangeas are hardy shrubs and produce their flowers during summer.

possible. Prune away any broken or damaged sections. Place the plant on top of the compost mix, spreading the roots evenly. Fill in the hole with the remaining soil and water thoroughly.

Feeding shrubs

Mulch young shrubs with compost or manure. This will keep the soil moist and supply essential plant food. Apply a complete soluble fertiliser around the base of the shrub in spring and again in early summer. Alternatively, apply a six-month, slow-release plant food in spring. Always water the soil well before and after applying fertiliser.

Growing roses

If you have a position with well-drained soil that receives full sun – or at least six hours of sun per day – you will be able to grow roses. Clay soils can be improved with gypsum or organic matter and beds can be raised. Ideally, the garden bed should be prepared some weeks in advance by digging it over and incorporating compost and old manure. But few of us live in an ideal world, and if you have good friable soil this is not necessary.

Planting bare-rooted roses

Dig the hole so that it's large enough to take the plant and have loosened soil around it in which the fine roots can grow easily. It should be deep enough for the bud union (a knot on the stem) to be about 2.5 cm above ground level. Mound the centre of the hole and spread the roots over it. Backfill with the loosened soil, firmly tamping it down as you go, and water the plant to remove any air pockets.

You can add a slow-release fertiliser to the soil surface at the rate of approximately one dessertspoon per plant, but don't add other fertiliser as you may burn the roots. Alternatively, wait until late winter/early spring and feed with a complete rose food. Repeat after the first flush of flowers. You can also mulch with old manure or compost. Roses love a mulch of lucerne, which is high in nitrogen and potassium.

> ### Smart tip
>
> Consider the eventual height and spread of shrubs and leave enough room between them to avoid cluttering. You can always plant 'filler' plants to cover any bare spaces while the shrubs are maturing.

LEFT *Weigela florida* is covered in pink flowers during spring.

BELOW The pretty pink and white flower of *Camellia* 'Gillian'.

Shrubs – a selection

NAME	HEIGHT	EVERGREEN OR DECIDUOUS	SITUATION	FLOWERS	USES	ZONE
Abelia × *grandiflora*	2 m	Evergreen	Sun or semi-shade	Pale pink	Can be clipped to form a hedge.	All zones except tropical
Abutilon × *hybridum* (Chinese lantern)	2 m	Evergreen	Sun or semi-shade	Various – some flower during winter.	Long-flowering plants that can be used at the rear of garden beds.	All zones
Acacia species (wattle)	Varies	Evergreen	Sun	Pale-lemon to yellow depending on the species.	Wattles make fast-growing screening shrubs.	All zones
Acalypha wilkesiana (Fijian fire plant)	3 m	Evergreen	Sun or semi-shade	Grown for its pretty bronze leaves. There are various cultivars with different leaf colours.	Ideal for tropical-looking gardens.	Warm temperate, subtropical and tropical
Acer palmatum 'Dissectum Atropurpureum'	Varies	Deciduous	Semi-shade	Delicate purple leaves. There are other cultivars that are also appreciated for their foliage.	Use in Japanese gardens or as foliage statements in garden beds or among shrubs.	All zones except tropical
Alyogyne huegelii (native hibiscus)	2.4 m	Evergreen	Sun	Pretty hibiscus-like lilac flowers open from spring to late summer.	Pretty background shrub. Tip-prune after flowering for a bushier habit.	Temperate, warm temperate, subtropical and tropical
Artemisia species	Varies	Evergreen	Sun	Valued for their beautiful silver and grey foliage.	Ideal feature shrubs.	All zones except subtropical and tropical
Aucuba japonica (Japanese aucuba)	1.5 m	Evergreen	Shade or semi-shade	Large, glossy leaves. The cultivar 'Variegata' has spotted, yellow leaves. 'Crotonifolia' has green leaves heavily splashed with yellow.	Very hardy shrubs tolerant of neglect and pollution. Ideal for shady spots where nothing else will grow.	All zones
Banksia species (banksia)	Varies	Evergreen	Sun	Valued for their beautiful flowers and interesting foliage.	Birds are attracted to the pretty flower spikes. 'Birthday Candles' makes a good groundcover.	All zones
Bauera rubioides (river rose)	1.5 m	Evergreen	Semi-shade	A variable plant that can be pruned to keep at a lower height. Pretty pink flowers cover the plant from late winter to mid-summer.	Ideal for cottage gardens. Likes a moist, well-drained soil but is adaptable.	All zones except tropical
Brunfelsia australis (yesterday-today-and-tomorrow)	2 m	Evergreen	Sun with afternoon shade	The spring and summer flowers open violet and fade to blue, then white.	Suited to cottage gardens or for use as a feature shrub.	All zones except cool temperate
Buddleia davidii cultivars (butterfly bush)	2.5 m	Deciduous or semi-evergreen	Sun	Purple, white or pink flowers depending on the cultivar.	Good cottage garden shrub. Attracts butterflies.	All zones except tropical
Buxus microphylla var. *japonica* (box)	2.5 m if unclipped	Evergreen	Sun or shade	The glossy-green leaves are the main feature.	Makes an ideal low hedge or topiary shape.	All zones except tropical
Callistemon species	Varies	Evergreen	Sun	Available in a variety of heights and colours in shades of red, pink or white. Buy one locally that is suited to your climate.	Suited to native or cottage gardens. Good feature shrubs. Bird attracting.	All zones
Camellia species	Depends on the cultivar.	Evergreen	Sun or semi-shade	Hundreds of cultivars in a variety of flower shapes and colours in shades of white, pink or red.	Can be used for edging, screening or as feature shrubs. May be grown in containers.	All zones
Cestrum nocturnum (night-scented jessamine)	3 m	Evergreen	Full sun	The pale-green summer and autumn flowers are strongly scented at night.	A straggly shrub that can be made more compact with pruning. Plant where the evening perfume can be appreciated.	Warm temperate, subtropical and tropical

NAME	HEIGHT	EVERGREEN OR DECIDUOUS	SITUATION	FLOWERS	USES	ZONE
Chaenomeles speciosa (Chinese flowering quince)	2.5 m	Deciduous	Sun	The pink, white or red flowers start appearing before the leaves in late winter.	Ideal for cottage gardens.	All zones except subtropical and tropical
Chamelaucium uncinatum (Geraldton waxflower)	3 m	Evergreen	Sun	Fine, needle-like foliage and mauve, pink or white late winter and spring flowers.	Ideal for native, foliage, cottage, seaside or gravel gardens.	All zones except tropical
Choisya ternata (Mexican orange blossom)	2 m	Evergreen	Sun or semi-shade	Fragrant, white spring flowers and glossy leaves.	Can be clipped to a hedge.	All zones
Cistus × purpureus (orchid rock rose)	1.5 m	Evergreen	Sun	Rose-red flowers with chocolate blotches.	Ideal for gravel or low-water-use gardens.	All zones except subtropical and tropical
Coleonema pulchellum (diosma)	1.5 m	Evergreen	Sun	Fine, needle-like foliage and pink star-like winter and spring flowers. The cultivar 'Sunset Gold' is more compact and has yellow foliage and pink flowers.	Can be trimmed to shape after flowering. Pretty cottage-garden plant.	All zones except subtropical and tropical
Cordyline australis (New Zealand cabbage tree)	2.4 m	Evergreen	Sun	Grown for its architectural shape and long, strap-like leaves. The cultivar 'Purpurea' has purplish leaves.	Can be grown in a container in courtyards. Ideal for seaside gardens.	Temperate, warm temperate, subtropical and tropical
Correa reflexa (common correa)	Variable 0.6–2 m	Evergreen	Sun or semi-shade	Flower colours vary depending on the form but are usually red and green or red and yellow.	Ideal for native gardens. Will grow near the coast.	All zones except tropical
Cotinus coggygria (smoke tree)	3.5 m	Deciduous	Sun	New leaves are a pinkish bronze and age to a greyish purple. The cultivar 'Royal Purple' has deep-purple foliage.	Ideal accent or specimen shrub.	All zones except tropical
Dais cotinifolia (pompom bush)	3.5 m	Evergreen but semi-deciduous in cooler climates	Sun	Fragrant clusters of pink flowers appear in spring among blue-green leaves.	An attractive background shrub.	Temperate, warm temperate, subtropical and tropical
Daphne odora (winter daphne)	1.2 m	Evergreen	Semi-shade. The ideal position for daphne is facing east with shelter from the afternoon sun.	The rose-purple buds open to reveal pinkish white flowers. Very fragrant. The cultivar 'Alba' has white flowers.	Grow near a window so you can appreciate the perfume.	All zones except tropical

Clipped box makes an attractive border for this garden bed.

Shrubs – a selection (cont'd)

NAME	HEIGHT	EVERGREEN OR DECIDUOUS	SITUATION	FLOWERS	USES	ZONE
Deutzia scabra	3 m	Deciduous	Semi-shade	White, bell-shaped flowers in mid-spring.	Pretty feature shrub with a graceful habit.	Highland and cool temperate
Erysimum bicolor 'Bowles' Mauve' (wallflower)	1 m	Evergreen	Sun	Rosy-purple flowers appear for months even during winter.	Continual flowering makes it a good feature shrub. Prune back lightly when flowering slows.	All except tropical
Euonymus fortunei cultivars (winter creeper euonymus)	Depends on the cultivar	Evergreen	Sun	Grown for its attractive leaves. 'Emerald Gaiety' (1 m high) has dark-green leaves margined with white. 'Silver Queen' (1.8 m high) has white margins and pink-tinged winter leaves.	Screening or feature shrubs.	All zones except subtropical and tropical
Eupatorium megalophyllum (mist flower)	1.8 m	Evergreen	Sun or semi-shade	Dramatic heads of lilac flowers and large leaves.	An outstanding feature shrub.	Warm temperate, subtropical and tropical
× *Fatshedera lizei* (tree ivy)	1.8 m	Evergreen	Sun or semi-shade	Valued for its large, glossy leaves.	An attractive spreading shrub that can be used as a groundcover or trained against a wall.	Temperate, warm temperate, subtropical and tropical
Fatsia japonica (Japanese aralia)	1.5–3.5m	Evergreen	Shade	Large, glossy leaves and creamy-white flowers that are followed by black berries.	Good screening shrub or courtyard feature shrub.	Temperate, warm temperate, subtropical and tropical
Forsythia × intermedia (border forsythia)	3 m	Deciduous	Sun	Yellow spring flowers.	Makes a good feature shrub.	Temperate, cool temperate and highland
Fuchsia species (fuchsia)	Varies	Deciduous or evergreen	Sun or semi-shade	There are thousands of cultivars in a variety of colours.	Good container or garden subjects.	All zones
Gardenia augusta 'Florida' (common gardenia)	1 m	Evergreen	Semi-shade	Strongly perfumed white flowers and dark-green glossy leaves. 'Radicans' is almost prostrate and has smaller leaves and flowers.	Grow in courtyards or alongside pathways where its perfume can be appreciated. Makes a good low, informal hedge.	Temperate, warm temperate subtropical and tropical
Grevillea species	Varies	Evergreen	Sun	There are many different species and cultivars suited to every zone.	Suited to hedging, as groundcovers or feature shrubs. Bird attracting.	All zones
Hakea laurina (pincushion bush)	6 m	Evergreen	Sun	Pretty, ball-shaped crimson flowers and narrow, grey-green leaves.	Ideal for screening or as a tall hedge. Bird attracting.	All zones except cool temperate and highland
Hebe species (veronica)	Varies	Evergreen	Sun or semi-shade	Hardy shrubs with mainly white flowers. Also shades of blue, purple or reddish purple.	Ideal for low hedging (can be clipped) or as feature shrubs. Good for containers.	All zones
Hibiscus rosa-sinensis cultivars (Chinese hibiscus)	1–3 m	Evergreen	Sun	Large flowers in a variety of colours.	Good feature shrubs.	Temperate, warm temperate, Mediterranean subtropical and tropical
Hydrangea macrophylla (garden hydrangea)	1–1.5 m	Deciduous	Shade or semi-shade	Large flowerheads in shades of white, pink or blue.	Attractive feature shrub.	All zones except tropical
Justicia carnea (Brazilian plume)	1.5 m	Evergreen	Sun	Beautiful spikes of white, pink or purplish flowers. Attractive deep-green leaves.	Use as a feature shrub. Ideal for tropical gardens.	Subtropical and tropical
Kolkwitzia amabilis (beauty bush)	3 m	Deciduous	Sun or semi-shade	Pale-pink flowers cover the shrub in spring.	Use as a feature or background shrub.	All zones except warm temperate, subtropical and tropical

NAME	HEIGHT	EVERGREEN OR DECIDUOUS	SITUATION	FLOWERS	USES	ZONE
Lavandula species (lavender)	1–1.2 m	Evergreen	Sun	Grown for their fragrant flowers and foliage. Colours include white, mauve, purple, crimson and pink.	Ideal for cottage gardens, herb gardens or as hedges lining a pathway. Must have well-drained soil.	All zones except subtropical and tropical
Leptospermum petersonii (lemon-scented tea-tree)	7.5 m	Evergreen	Sun	A large shrub or small tree. The narrow leaves smell of lemon. White spring flowers. There are also other species suited to a variety of climates.	Good, tall screening or feature shrub. Native gardens. Bird attracting.	Warm temperate, subtropical and tropical
Leucadendron species	Varies depending on the species	Evergreen	Sun	Grown for their beautiful bracts that surround the flowers.	Ideal shrubs for sandy, well-drained soil. Can be grown in tubs.	All zones
Lonicera nitida (box honeysuckle)	2–3 m	Evergreen	Sun or semi-shade	Bears small, creamy-white flowers but is grown for its foliage.	A faster growing alternative to box. It can be clipped to shape.	All zones except tropical
Luculia gratissima (luculia)	2.4 m	Semi-evergreen	Sun	Fragrant pink flowers appear during winter. Its large leaves are also attractive.	Cottage gardens. Grow near a window where you can appreciate the perfume.	Temperate, warm temperate and subtropical. Give protection from frosts.
Luma apiculata	12 m but can be kept lower by pruning	Evergreen	Sun or semi-shade	Creamy-white flowers are followed by deep-purple berries. Aromatic leaves and attractive bark.	Makes a good screen or tall, clipped hedge.	Temperate, warm temperate and subtropical
Mackaya bella (forest bell bush)	2.4 m	Evergreen	Semi-shade	Pink, funnel-shaped flowers appear from spring to autumn among lustrous dark-green leaves.	Pretty feature shrub for tropical gardens.	Warm temperate, subtropical and tropical
Magnolia stellata (star magnolia)	3–4 m	Deciduous	Sun or semi-shade	Perfumed, star-like white flowers appear in late winter before the leaves.	Feature shrub – ideal for cottage gardens.	All zones except tropical
Mahonia lomariifolia	3–4 m	Evergreen	Sun in cool climates. Shade or semi-shade in warmer climates.	Long, dark-green leaves and bright-yellow, fragrant autumn and winter flowers followed by purple berries.	Make use of its architectural shape.	All zones except tropical

The drooping flowerheads of *Pieris japonica*.

Colourful hibiscus brighten up the backyard.

Shrubs – a selection (cont'd)

NAME	HEIGHT	EVERGREEN OR DECIDUOUS	SITUATION	FLOWERS	USES	ZONE
Melaleuca species (paperbark)	Varies	Evergreen	Sun	Grown for their pretty bottle-brush-like flowers.	Ideal for seaside and native gardens. Bird attracting.	All zones
Michelia figo (Port wine magnolia)	3 m	Evergreen	Sun or semi-shade	Its small, cream flowers are streaked with purple and are heavily perfumed. Attractive, shiny leaves.	Grow near a window or doorway where you can appreciate the perfume. Good screening plant.	Temperate, warm temperate and subtropical
Murraya paniculata (orange jessamine)	3 m	Evergreen	Sun or semi-shade	Perfumed, creamy-white flowers sit among shiny, dark-green leaves.	Makes a good clipped hedge.	Warm temperate, subtropical and tropical
Nandina domestica (sacred bamboo)	1.8 m	Evergreen	Semi-shade or shade	The evergreen foliage is red while young, turns green and colours again in cool weather.	Ideal for Japanese gardens, courtyards and containers. The cultivar 'Nana' reaches a height of only 45 cm.	All zones
Osmanthus fragrans (sweet osmanthus)	3 m	Evergreen	Sun or semi-shade	Very small, white, fragrant flowers appear among deep-green leaves.	Can be trained as a small tree for courtyards or small gardens.	All zones
Pelargonium species	Varies	Evergreen	Sun	There is a good choice of species and cultivars available. Some have perfumed leaves and others have colourful flowers.	Ideal for Mediterranean gardens, courtyards and containers.	All zones. In cool climates grow in containers to protect from frosts.
Philadelphus coronarius (mock orange)	1.8 m	Deciduous	Sun or semi-shade	The white flowers smell like orange blossom and open in late spring or early summer among bright-green leaves.	Pretty cottage-garden plant or background shrub.	All zones except subtropical and tropical
Philodendron bipinnatifidum (tree philodendron)	3 m	Evergreen	Shade	Grown for its very large (60 cm or larger), shiny, green leaves.	Its dramatic leaves look spectacular in tropical gardens.	Warm temperate, subtropical and tropical
Phlomis fruticosa (Jerusalem sage)	75 cm	Evergreen	Sun	Pretty yellow flowers appear in whorls among felty green leaves.	Cottage-garden or low-growing feature shrub.	All zones except subtropical and tropical
Photinia × fraseri (photinia)	3–3.5 m	Evergreen	Sun or semi-shade	Grown for the colourful new leaves. White flowers. 'Robusta' has coppery-red leaves and 'Red Robin' has bright-red leaves.	Ideal hedging plant. Regular clipping encourages colourful new growth.	All zones except tropical
Pieris japonica (lily-of-the-valley shrub)	1.8 m	Evergreen	Semi-shade	Coppery-red new growth and panicles of small, white, bell-shaped spring flowers.	Pretty feature shrub.	All zones except subtropical and tropical
Pimelea ferruginea (rice flower)	1 m	Evergreen	Sun	Rose-pink spring flowerheads sit above small leaves.	Pretty, small feature shrub. Suited to seaside, cottage and native gardens.	Temperate, warm temperate, subtropical and tropical
Pittosporum species	Varies	Evergreen	Sun or semi-shade	Grown for their foliage. Some cultivars have variegated leaves.	Ideal hedge planting, screens and specimen shrubs.	All zones
Plectranthus argentatus	1 m	Evergreen	Sun or semi-shade	Valued for its beautiful grey, velvety, large leaves. Pale-blue flower spikes.	Pretty feature shrub. Native and low-maintenance gardens.	Temperate, warm temperate, subtropical and Mediterranean
Plumbago auriculata (Cape plumbago)	1.8 m	Evergreen	Sun	Produces its pale-blue flowers prolifically through late spring and summer.	Makes a delightful formal or informal hedge. Feature shrub. 'Alba' has white flowers. 'Royal Cape' is more tolerant of frost.	Warm temperate, subtropical and Mediterranean
Prostanthera rotundifolia (round-leafed mint bush)	1.8 m	Evergreen	Sun	Produces lilac or mauve spring flowers. Aromatic, deep-green leaves.	As a feature shrub or for native gardens.	All zones except arid, subtropical and tropical

NAME	HEIGHT	EVERGREEN OR DECIDUOUS	SITUATION	FLOWERS	USES	ZONE
Protea species	Varies	Evergreen	Sun	Valued for their interesting flowerheads and colourful bracts.	Feature shrubs. Grow well in native gardens.	Cool temperate (some species require frost protection), temperate and warm temperate
Prunus glandulosa (dwarf flowering almond)	1.5 m	Deciduous	Sun	Produces a thicket of vertical shoots that bear pink or white spring flowers.	Suited to cottage gardens. Pretty feature shrub.	All zones except subtropical and tropical
Reinwardtia indica (yellow flax)	1 m	Evergreen	Sun	Bears golden-yellow winter flowers amid bright-green, oval leaves.	Feature shrub, tropical gardens.	Warm temperate, subtropical and tropical
Rhododendron species	Varies	Evergreen or deciduous	Sun or semi-shade	Azaleas and rhododendrons are in this genus. There are hundreds of cultivars and flower forms. Beautiful feature shrubs. Can be grown in containers.	Vireya rhododendrons are suited to tropical and warm zones.	All zones
Rhodotypos scandens	4 m	Deciduous	Sun or semi-shade	Simple, 5 cm wide, white spring flowers that are followed by glossy, black berries. Attractive, mid-green leaves.	A tall shrub with a graceful habit.	All zones except subtropical and tropical
Rosa species	Varies	Evergreen or deciduous	Sun	There are many different roses in a variety of colours. Some are perfumed, especially the old-fashioned roses and English or David Austin roses.	Roses may be used in a variety of ways. Tea and shrub roses add height to garden beds. Standard roses look good in containers and as focal points in the garden.	All zones except tropical
Russelia equisetiformis (coral plant)	1 m	Evergreen	Sun	Slender branches hold clusters of red flowers virtually throughout the year.	Suited to seaside gardens and for trailing over walls. Also as a feature shrub.	Warm temperate, subtropical and tropical
Salvia leucantha (Mexican bush sage)	1 m	Evergreen	Sun	The spikes of purple and white flowers appear above grey-green foliage.	Good for dry gardens as a feature shrub or low hedge. Other species are equally attractive.	Temperate, warm temperate, subtropical and Mediterranean
Santolina chamaecyparissus (cotton lavender)	45 cm	Evergreen	Sun	Valued for its attractive, silver leaves. Yellow flowers.	Makes a good garden border or low hedge. Mediterranean gardens.	All zones except subtropical and tropical

The fragrant flowers of lavender 'Swan River Pink'.

Make a statement using the pretty silver foliage of *Plectranthus argentatus*.

Shrubs – a selection (cont'd)

NAME	HEIGHT	EVERGREEN OR DECIDUOUS	SITUATION	FLOWERS	USES	ZONE
Solanum rantonnetii (blue potato bush)	1.8–2.4 m	Evergreen	Sun	Produces masses of violet-blue flowers during summer. 'Royal Robe' flowers virtually throughout the year.	Large feature shrub or can be trained as a climber for an arbour or trellis.	Warm temperate, subtropical and tropical
Spirea cantoniensis (Reeves' spirea)	1.8 m	Deciduous or semi-deciduous	Sun or semi-shade in warm areas	White flowers cover the arching branches during spring.	Pretty feature shrub or can be used as a hedge.	All except tropical
Syringia vulgaris (common lilac)	Varies	Deciduous	Sun or semi-shade	Grown for their heads of fragrant white, purple, mauve or purplish pink flowers.	Pretty feature shrub. Cottage gardens.	Suited to cool temperate and highland zones
Telopea speciosissima (New South Wales waratah)	3 m	Evergreen	Sun or semi-shade	Grown for its magnificent large, scarlet flowers.	Ideal for native gardens.	Highland, temperate and warm temperate
Tibouchina 'Jules'	1 m	Evergreen	Sun	Large, purple, late-summer and autumn flowers. Attractive, velvety leaves.	Pretty, small feature shrub. Cottage gardens. Can be grown in a tub.	Warm temperate, temperate (needs frost protection), subtropical and tropical
Viburnum species	Varies	Evergreen or deciduous	Sun or semi-shade	Grown for their flowers, berries and leaves depending on the species.	Good screening shrubs, hedges or feature shrubs.	All zones except subtropical and tropical
Weigela florida	3 m	Deciduous	Sun or semi-shade	Pink, trumpet-shaped flowers cover the arching branches in spring.	Suited to cottage gardens. Feature shrub.	All zones except subtropical and tropical
Westringia fruticosa (coast rosemary)	1.8 m	Evergreen	Sun	Grown for its grey-green foliage and white and purple flowers.	Can be clipped as a hedge. Good container plant.	Temperate, warm temperate, Mediterranean and subtropical
Xanthorrhoea australis (grass tree)	1 m (takes many years to form a trunk)	Evergreen	Sun	Grown for its beautiful, grass-like leaves.	Great architectural value. Native gardens. Container subject.	Temperate, warm temperate, Mediterranean and subtropical
Yucca species	Varies	Evergreen	Sun	Attractive, strap-like leaves.	Excellent architectural value. Can be grown in containers.	All zones

The purple leaves of *Cotinus* 'Grace' make a statement.

White and pink weigelas flank the pathway.

Trees

Trees determine the nature and quality of our environment more than any other plants. Because they live for many decades, they give the landscape a sense of stability. Trees are an exciting reminder of the changing seasons: the brilliant colours of autumn, the strong silhouettes of winter, the flowers and soft green tones of spring and summer. Trees are barriers against wind, they provide shade and they add structure to the garden. In addition, they provide fruit, nuts and berries.

Using trees in the landscape

Trees for ornamental effect should be chosen for their form and foliage as well as their flowers. Do not plant too many large trees or over-plant the garden with trees. The overplanting of trees is a common and very costly mistake, especially if large trees have to be removed at a later date.

You can always buy annuals and perennials on impulse, but you should avoid taking the same approach with trees. Think carefully about where you will place them, taking into account their mature height and spread in relation to the size of your garden. You should also consider which areas will be shaded as the tree grows. Choose at least one tree with a spreading habit for a new garden as it will eventually provide a shaded sitting area for hot days.

Planting trees

Correct planting will determine the health of the tree for many years and encourage prolific growth. All newly planted trees require regular watering to help them become established. Trees planted in windy areas should be staked so their growth will remain upright.

Water the tree in its container one hour before planting. Dig a hole slightly deeper than the container's height and approximately twice as wide. Water the hole before planting and allow it to drain. Add some compost to the bottom of the hole. Check to see if the roots are root bound. If they are running around the root ball, try to straighten them out as much as possible. Prune away any broken or damaged sections. Place the plant on top of the compost mix, spreading the roots evenly. Fill in the hole with the remaining soil and water thoroughly.

Feeding trees

Mulch young trees with compost or manure. This will keep the soil moist and supply essential plant food. In spring and again in early summer apply a complete soluble fertiliser around the base of the tree. Always water the soil well before and after applying fertiliser.

Smart tip

It's often better to plant two or three small trees rather than a large one that dominates the garden. Fruit trees are ideal – they provide visual interest when they are in flower and as the fruit is ripening. There is also the satisfaction gained from the harvested fruit.

The colour of Japanese maples is quite stunning during autumn.

Trees – a selection

NAME	HEIGHT	DECIDUOUS OR EVERGREEN	SITUATION	DESCRIPTION	USES	ZONE
Acacia fimbriata	7 m high and 6 m wide	Evergreen	Sun	Yellow, ball-shaped spring flowers and narrow leaves.	Makes a good screen.	All zones
Acacia pendula (weeping myall)	10 m	Evergreen	Sun. Ideal for arid areas.	Pale-yellow spring flowers. Has a pretty, weeping habit.	Makes a good shade or ornamental tree.	Warm temperate, arid, subtropical and tropical
Acacia species	Varies	Evergreen	Sun	Lemon to yellow flowers.	There is a wattle for every position in the garden.	There are many different species of wattles suited to all zones.
Acer buergerianum (trident maple)	6 m	Deciduous	Sun	Tolerates poor soil and exposed conditions.	Insignificant flowers. Grown for its beautiful autumn foliage. Makes a good small shade tree.	All except subtropical and tropical
Acer palmatum (Japanese maple)	4.5 m	Deciduous	Needs shade from the hot afternoon sun to prevent its leaves from burning.	Insignificant flowers. Grown for its ornamental foliage.	A pretty feature tree. Will colour in warm climates. There are many different cultivars with a variety of leaf colours and shapes.	All except tropical
Albizia julibrissin (silk tree)	8 m	Deciduous	Sun	A deciduous tree with beautiful feathery fern-like foliage and creamy-white to pink flowers.	A pretty shade or feature tree but not very long-lived (approx. 30 years).	Suited to warm temperate, Mediterranean, subtropical and tropical zones
Allocasuarina littoralis (black she-oak)	9 m	Evergreen	Sun. Tolerant of poor soils and salt spray.	Fine, dark-green foliage. Male flower spikes tint trees brown during winter.	Ideal tree for seaside gardens. Fast growing.	Grow in temperate, warm temperate, subtropical and tropical zones
Allocasuarina verticillata (drooping she-oak)	9 m	Evergreen	Sun. Tolerant of poor soils and salt spray.	An attractive tree with pendulous branches.	Perfect for seaside gardens.	All zones
Arbutus unedo (strawberry tree)	5 m	Evergreen	Sun	Has attractive, grey-brown bark. Clusters of white flowers are followed by orange berries.	A hardy tree. Dislikes damp soil.	All zones except subtropical and tropical
Banksia integrifolia (coast banksia)	15 m	Evergreen	Sun	Attractive green leaves with silver undersides. Arresting yellow flower spikes.	Bird attracting. Ideal for coastal plantings.	All zones
Bauhinia variegata (orchid tree)	8 m	Semi-evergreen in moist tropical climates, deciduous in drier climates	Sun	Fragrant, rose-pink or white flowers appear in spring followed by large seed pods.	Pretty feature tree. Ideal for cottage gardens.	All zones except cool temperate
Betula pendula (silver birch)	9–15 m	Deciduous	Sun	Grown for its silver bark and shimmering leaves.	Ideal for planting as a copse. Good feature tree.	All zones except subtropical and tropical
Callistemon species (bottlebrush)	Varies	Evergreen	Sun	Grown for their pretty bottle-brush flowers. *C. salignus* will tolerate damp soil.	Make good screens or small feature trees. Bird attracting.	All zones
Callitris rhomboidea (Port Jackson pine)	9 m	Evergreen	Sun or light shade	A columnar tree with fine foliage.	Ideal for screening. Can be clipped to form a tall hedge.	All areas
Ceratopetalum gummiferum (NSW Christmas bush)	4 m	Evergreen	Sun or semi-shade	Grown for its colourful red calyces, which last after the small, insignificant white flowers have disappeared. 'White Christmas' has white calyces.	Can be used for screening or as a feature tree. Seaside gardens. Bird attracting.	All zones except tropical

NAME	HEIGHT	DECIDUOUS OR EVERGREEN	SITUATION	DESCRIPTION	USES	ZONE
Cercis siliquastrum (Judas tree)	6–8 m	Deciduous	Sun	Pretty, bluish green foliage and deep-pink flowers.	Makes a pretty feature tree.	All zones except tropical
× *Cupressocyparis leylandii* (Leyland cypress)	30 m but is kept clipped	Evergreen	Sun	Deep-green foliage that responds to clipping.	The cultivar 'Leighton Green' can be kept clipped to make a tall screen.	All zones except arid, subtropical and tropical
Elaeocarpus reticulatus (blueberry ash)	5 m	Evergreen	Semi-shade or shade	Attractive toothed leaves and white or pink-fringed, bell-shaped flowers.	Makes a pretty feature tree. Suited to coastal plantings.	All zones except highland
Eucalyptus species	Varies	Evergreen	Sun	Choose a species that is indigenous to your area.	Depending on the species they make good feature trees or screens. Bird attracting.	All zones
Gordonia axillaris	8 m	Evergreen	Sun or dappled shade	Grown as a large shrub or small tree. Large white flowers sit among its deep-green foliage.	Attractive small feature tree. Tip-prune while young to make it bushier.	Temperate, warm temperate, Mediterranean, subtropical and tropical
Hakea salicifolia (willow hakea)	8 m	Evergreen	Sun or shade	Attractive lanceolate leaves and white flowers followed by hard, warty fruits.	Ideal fast-growing and hardy screen tree.	All zones
Hoheria populnea (New Zealand lacebark)	6 m	Evergreen	Sun or semi-shade	Glossy foliage is highlighted by white flowers.	Fast-growing feature tree.	Temperate, warm temperate, Mediterranean and subtropical
Hymenosporum flavum (Australian frangipani)	9 m	Evergreen	Sun or dappled shade	Dark-green, glossy leaves and fragrant cream flowers that age to yellow.	A narrow tree that is ideal for small spaces.	Temperate, warm temperate, subtropical and tropical

A copse of silver birch is an arresting sight on this lawn.

Robinia pseudoacacia 'Frisia' is valued for its yellow-green foliage.

Apple trees are very attractive when in flower.

Trees – a selection (cont'd)

NAME	HEIGHT	DECIDUOUS OR EVERGREEN	SITUATION	DESCRIPTION	USES	ZONE
Jacaranda mimosifolia (jacaranda)	15 m	Deciduous	Sun	Attractive, fern-like foliage and mauve-blue flowers.	Makes a pretty shade or feature tree.	Temperate, warm temperate, subtropical and tropical
Koelreuteria paniculata (golden rain tree)	9–12 m	Deciduous	Sun	Colourful autumn foliage and yellow summer flowers.	Ideal shade or feature tree in arid zones.	All zones except subtropical and tropical
Laburnum × watereri 'Vossii' (Voss laburnum)	8 m	Deciduous	Sun	Pretty foliage and fragrant, long racemes of yellow, late spring flowers.	Ideal feature tree. Often used to create 'laburnum arches'.	Suited to temperate zones
Lagerstroemia indica (crepe myrtle)	8 m	Deciduous	Sun	There are many different cultivars in a variety of flower colours.	Pretty flowering feature tree for small gardens.	All zones
Litchi chinensis (lychee)	9 m	Evergreen	Sun	Insignificant, greenish yellow flowers are followed by delicious edible fruit.	Pretty feature tree, especially while the fruit is ripening.	Tropical and subtropical
Macadamia tetraphylla (rough shell macadamia nut)	12 m	Evergreen	Sun	Pink or white pendulous flower spikes are followed by edible nuts.	Makes a good feature tree but requires fertile, moist soil.	Tropical and subtropical
Magnolia × soulangeana (saucer magnolia)	8 m	Deciduous	Sun or dappled shade	Large white, pink or purple-pink flowers appear before the new spring leaves.	There are many different cultivars in a variety of flower colours. A pretty feature tree.	All zones except subtropical and tropical
Malus ioensis (Iowa crab)	8 m	Deciduous	Sun	Fragrant, pale-pink flowers followed by small crab-apples. The cultivar 'Plena' has double flowers.	Makes a pretty feature or shade tree.	All zones except subtropical and tropical
Malus sieboldii 'Gorgeous'	8 m	Deciduous	Sun	White blossoms appear from pink buds. The fruit is used for jams and jellies.	Pretty feature tree.	All zones except tropical
Melaleuca armillaris (bracelet honey myrtle)	9 m	Evergreen	Sun	Spikes of white flowers appear during spring and summer.	Fast-growing screen or feature tree. Bird attracting.	All zones

These magnificent flowers belong to *Magnolia × soulangeana*.

The pretty flowers of crepe myrtle appear during summer and autumn.

NAME	HEIGHT	DECIDUOUS OR EVERGREEN	SITUATION	DESCRIPTION	USES	ZONE
Metrosideros excelsus (pohutukawa)	12 m	Evergreen	Sun	Deep-green, glossy leaves with a felty underside. Red flowers appear in summer.	Ideal for exposed seaside conditions.	Warm temperate and subtropical
Michelia doltsopa	9 m	Evergreen	Sun or semi-shade	Large, fragrant, white late winter and spring flowers.	Pretty feature tree.	All zones except tropical and arid
Michelia yunnanensis	4.5 m	Evergreen	Sun or semi-shade	Perfumed, cream spring flowers sit among deep-green foliage.	Good feature tree for small gardens.	All zones except tropical and arid
Olea europaea (olive)	9 m	Evergreen	Sun	Pretty, grey-green leaves with silver undersides. Fruit is valued for its oil.	Good shade tree or feature tree. Can be planted in groves if you have the space.	All zones except tropical
Parrotia persica (Persian witch-hazel)	8 m	Deciduous	Sun	Valued for its richly coloured autumn leaves.	Its spreading habit makes it a good shade tree.	All zones except subtropical and tropical
Pistacia chinensis (Chinese pistachio)	8 m	Deciduous	Sun	Inconspicuous flowers are followed by blue autumn fruits. Leaves colour in autumn.	An ideal shade or feature tree. Bird attracting.	All zones except tropical
Plumeria rubra (frangipani)	8 m	Deciduous	Sun	Pretty, pale-pink to crimson perfumed flowers. There are many cultivars with different flower colours.	Ideal for small gardens. Feature tree.	Warm temperate, subtropical and tropical
Prunus cerasifera (cherry plum)	9 m	Deciduous	Sun	White spring flowers and bronze leaves. The cultivar 'Nigra' has deep-purple leaves.	Very tolerant of dry conditions.	All zones except subtropical and tropical
Prunus serrulata hybrids (Japanese cherry)	Varies	Deciduous	Sun	There are many different cultivars in double and semi-double form and a variety of colours.	Pretty feature or shade trees.	All zones except subtropical and tropical
Prunus × *subhirtella* (flowering cherry)	9 m	Deciduous	Sun	Pretty, pale-pink spring flowers. Hybrids include double and semi-double flowers.	Feature or shade tree.	All zones except subtropical and tropical
Pyrus salicifolia 'Pendula' (weeping silver pear)	8 m	Deciduous	Sun	A graceful tree with arching branches and silver-grey leaves.	Ideal feature tree. Good for small gardens.	All zones except subtropical and tropical
Robinia pseudoacacia 'Frisia' (black locust)	15 m	Deciduous	Sun	Scented, white spring flowers. The golden-yellow foliage deepens in autumn. The cultivar 'Tortuosa' has twisted branches.	Pretty feature tree.	All zones except tropical
Schinus molle var. *areira* (pepper tree)	15 m	Evergreen	Sun	Dark-green leaves, pendulous cluster of cream flowers followed by pink berries.	Excellent shade tree. Ideal for dry areas.	All zones except highland
Sorbus americana (American mountain ash)	9 m	Deciduous	Sun or semi-shade	The attractive, bright-green leaves turn yellow in autumn and are followed by clusters of red berries.	Feature tree.	All zones except subtropical and tropical
Syzygium luehmannii (small-leafed lillypilly)	6–8 m	Evergreen	Sun or semi-shade	Shiny leaves with pink new growth. White flowers are followed by reddish fruits.	Good shade or screening tree.	Temperate, warm temperate, subtropical and tropical

Garden maintenance

Once your backyard has been established, you will need to maintain it. Fortunately this is straight-forward and easy when you understand what is required. This chapter shows you how to select the essential tools for the job, make compost and use worm bins, and regenerate the soil to keep it healthy. Then it's simply a matter of mulching, feeding and watering your plants, weeding and pruning. This chapter also shows you how easy it is to save money by propagating your own plants and there are some hints on controlling pests and diseases to help you keep your backyard healthy.

Tools

There are some tools that are absolutely essential for making and maintaining a garden. These tools can be classified as digging and cultivation tools, pruning tools and maintenance tools.

Digging tools

Most of these tools have been in existence for many years but have been modified as technologies have improved. Spades, forks, rakes, hoes and trowels are included in this group of necessary digging and cultivation tools.

Spades are essential for digging planting holes and for lifting and moving soil. The standard type of spade has a rectangular blade 28 × 18 cm. Blades are metal and are often coated for ease of cleaning, and some are even made of stainless steel. Shafts are commonly made from timber, but some spades feature metal shafts. Lighter, smaller spades for particular purposes, such as edging and digging in garden beds, are also available.

Forks are generally used for preparing and breaking up soil. Forks are also commonly employed for moving bulky material and turning compost. Garden forks are useful to avoid damage when digging up root vegetables. A standard garden fork has a head 30 × 20 cm and four prongs. The head and neck of the fork should be made of forged steel for durability. Smaller, lighter forks are also available.

Rakes have a variety of uses in the garden. General garden rakes have steel heads and are used for breaking up the soil surface and levelling it before planting. Ensure that the handle is long enough for comfortable use.

There are other rakes for specific purposes, the most useful and inexpensive of which is the plastic

OPPOSITE   **Choose a wheelbarrow with an inflatable tyre for ease and comfort of use.**

leaf rake. This rake should only be used for leaves and light material, as the plastic teeth are easily broken during heavy use.

Hoes are very handy for turning over soil and weeding. Swan neck and Dutch hoes are the most popular and versatile. The swan neck hoe is very useful for moving soil up around plants and for chipping weeds. Its curved neck allows access between plants without causing damage. The Dutch hoe is used parallel to the soil's surface to remove annual weeds between plants.

Mattocks have one or two chisel-like blades. Their heavy weight makes them ideal for breaking up small areas of hard ground. They are used with a swinging action.

Hand forks are used for weeding and loosening soil in garden beds and containers.

Trowels are used for planting small plants. There is a narrow-bladed trowel designed for working in confined spaces.

Pruning tools

Secateurs are invaluable for pruning and cutting everything from woody stems to flowers. It is worth buying good secateurs with comfortable handles and replaceable blades. Check the grip and pressure before purchasing.

Long-handled loppers are used for pruning small branches from tall shrubs and small trees. Make sure the lopper is not too heavy, as you will often be holding it above head height. You can also buy short-handled loppers.

Standard **pruning saws** have small, sharp blades and are designed for use in confined spaces. There are also curved pruning saws that are designed to cut when pulling towards you.

Garden shears are mainly used to trim hedges and shrubs. The blades are adjustable and should be sharpened regularly.

Powered hedge trimmers are handy if you have large hedges that require regular trimming. There are both petrol and electric hedge trimmers available. Home gardeners will generally find electric trimmers to be adequate, as they are easier to handle than the heavier petrol models.

Maintenance tools

Nylon-line trimmers have a nylon cutting line that spins at high speed to trim grass and weeds. There are petrol and electric models available. Petrol models are heavier, but have the great advantage of being much more portable and versatile. Goggles to prevent injury from flying debris and stones should be worn at all times while using these trimmers.

Rotary mowers have revolutionised the care and maintenance of lawns and have become icons of suburbia. These petrol-driven mowers are popular because of their capacity to handle rough and overgrown grassed

BELOW LEFT   Rakes can be used for breaking up the soil surface and levelling it before planting.

BELOW CENTRE   Mattocks are useful tools for breaking up hard ground.

BELOW RIGHT   Loppers are ideal for cutting larger branches.

areas. Blades should be checked regularly and replaced if blunt.

Electric mowers are suitable for relatively small and level areas of lawn. They are not as powerful as petrol mowers and are not designed for rough conditions or tough or wet grass.

Hand mowers should not be overlooked, especially for small or medium-sized lawns. They are not, however, very effective on coarse grass or uneven surfaces.

Ride-on mowers are essential for large or country gardens. There are many different types to choose from – some have a small turning circle making them ideal for average-sized gardens.

Blowers, which are commonly called blower vacs, are designed to blow leaves into a heap and then vacuum them up. Their use can only really be justified in very large gardens. Otherwise keep it simple and use a rake.

Mulchers, or chipper shredders, have become popular with recycling-aware home gardeners.

They are designed to handle leaves, small branches, prunings and even kitchen scraps. These items are fed into the top of the mulcher through a chute and are then shredded. The resulting mulch can be spread on the garden to improve water retention and provide nutrients. When purchasing a mulcher, check that it doesn't clog easily and that it can be unblocked easily. Make sure you wear safety glasses and gloves when using these machines.

Wheelbarrows are essential for all but the smallest gardens. You can carry just about everything for the garden in a wheelbarrow, including plants, soil, manure and compost. The best type is one that has a steel bin, wooden handles and an inflatable tyre. The steel will eventually rust, but its life can be prolonged by storing it in a shed or, if that is not possible, turning the wheelbarrow upside down or leaning it against a wall at an angle that will prevent water accumulating in the bin.

Dos and don'ts of mowing

- Don't cut your lawn too low or you will weaken the grass and encourage weeds.
- Set the blades high for the first cut of a new lawn.
- Set blades high in summer as a longer lawn keeps roots cool and healthy.
- Mowing wet grass leads to a poor cut and the creation of tracks in the lawn.
- Add lawn clippings to your compost heap.

This small and confined area of lawn makes mowing by hand the most sensible option.

Simple rules for making compost

While composting is easy, it's not just a matter of throwing waste vegetable matter into a heap and waiting for it to change into rich humus. These guidelines will help you produce great compost.

- Make sure your compost heap is in the right place. A semi-shaded location is best, as direct sun will dry out your heap too frequently. Don't place your heap in a depression, as it will become waterlogged during heavy rain. The decomposition process is much slower in a waterlogged heap.
- Turn your compost heap regularly. Many kinds of bacteria and fungi go to work inside a compost heap to decompose materials in the pile. Aerobic bacteria (those requiring oxygen to live and work) are the most desirable because they are more effective than anaerobic bacteria. Turning the heap regularly makes it more attractive for aerobic bacteria, and this in turn hastens the decomposition process.

A rotating compost bin produces compost within three weeks if rotated daily.

Compost

The statement that 'there's nothing new under the sun' is certainly true of making compost. Indian and Chinese gardeners, for example, have used compost for centuries. But it has only been in the last fifty or sixty years that the science of composting has been studied in the West.

Making compost seems simple, but many gardeners have problems doing it. It's too smelly, it won't decay or it takes too long are the usual complaints. But there are ways around these difficulties, and the benefits of compost to the soil are well known.

The compost heap is the site of a remarkable transformation. A cycle of regeneration takes place, involving the change from life to death and back again when the stalks and leaves of dying and dead plants give life to the growth of the coming season.

A natural process

Composting takes place all the time in nature. Leaves fall to the ground and slowly decay, producing fresh food for plants. In gardens, this process has been interrupted by the process of cultivation, so compost has to be created by the gardener. Composting is actually an intensified version of what happens in nature.

Compost is nothing more than well-rotted organic matter. Organic matter is good for the soil only when it is decaying. Even so-called 'finished compost' is only partially decayed. While it is breaking down it creates food for growing populations of micro-organisms. Compost is also a good breeding ground for beneficial bacteria and moulds that attack many of the fungi that produce plant diseases.

What to use

Compost will improve the structure, water retention and aeration of soils that have too much clay or sand. And there is a wide range of suitable materials for making compost. You can use all sorts of leaves, hay, vegetable matter, vegetable garden refuse, sawdust, paper, grass clippings and any animal manures, except those made from cat and dog excrement. Torn or shredded paper makes an excellent compost extender (bulk). Nitrogen-rich lucerne and clover hays can also be added.

Building your heap

While it is not absolutely necessary to have an enclosure around the compost heap, an enclosure will make the pile a lot easier to build and maintain. The type of bin you choose to build can be simple or elaborate, depending on the type of materials you have to hand. Bricks and concrete blocks can be used as long as you leave spaces between them to allow air in and water to escape. Ideally, there should always be two piles of compost going at once: the completed pile that is decomposing and one in the process of being built. For small gardens, however, it may be preferable to buy a plastic compost bin.

Size counts

The ideal size for your compost heap is 1.25 m square and 1.5 m high. The easiest way to build a compost container is to use metal fencing posts and chicken wire. Use four stakes for a single heap and six for a double structure. You only need to enclose three sides of the structure with chicken wire. The great advantage of this design is that it allows air to circulate freely around it.

Creating the right balance

For the heap to work properly it must contain the right balance of nitrogen and carbon. Micro-organisms use up large amounts of nitrogen as they break down material high in carbon. Ingredients high in nitrogen include green weeds (no seeds), vegetable scraps, manure and grass clippings. Ingredients high in carbon include leaves, straw, sawdust and paper.

Getting started

Layering your materials so that decomposition will take place more rapidly is the best way to get started. You should start by spreading a 20 cm layer of waste material over the bottom of the pit. Add a layer of manure or fertiliser, then add about 3 cm of topsoil and moisten thoroughly. Add some lime if you require an alkaline compost.

Repeat the layering process until you reach the desired height. For an organic heap, use manure or blood and bone rather than fertiliser. Keep in mind, however, that adding a fertiliser high in nitrogen to each layer will feed bacteria in the heap so that they can do their work more efficiently.

Mixing your materials

Try to use different types of materials for each layer of your compost heap. Layers of one material, such as leaves, will not decompose rapidly. Add layers of soil throughout the heap to encourage microbes, absorb odours and retain the structure of the heap.

Maintaining your compost heap

Three weeks after establishing your heap, turn it over with a garden fork. Turn your compost every three to four weeks and it will be ready for the garden in two to three months.

The bacteria that are essential for transforming waste material into compost need a certain amount of moisture. Composting material should be spongy rather than soggy. Too much water will block out oxygen and stop aerobic bacteria from working properly. But some water is required because of the high temperatures inside the heap, and these temperatures can dry out your compost. If the compost dries out, it will burn and thus be of little value to your soil.

The finished product

You know that your compost is ready when it is dark brown in colour with an earthy smell. Dig it into the soil prior to planting or use it as a mulch in the garden around flowers, shrubs and vegetables. Compost is an excellent way to add structure to the soil.

You can apply compost liberally to the garden at any time of the year at the rate of 5–10 cm.

There is no danger from burning caused by overuse. Apply it as a mulch or dig it in to new garden beds.

If your compost is ready to use and you don't need it yet, cover it with plastic so that the nutrients it contains won't leach away.

Quick and easy compost

To save time when making compost, shred the materials you are going to use in your heap. You can buy compost shredders that will process all the ingredients, including small branches and hedge clippings. Because shredded material is less likely to pack down, the aeration of the heap is improved.

Don't layer a shredded heap, but simply pile on the ingredients and add manure or fertiliser. Turn the heap after three days and twice weekly thereafter. This is easy as the material is light. Your compost will be ready to use in as little as four weeks.

ABOVE Finished compost is dark brown in colour and has an earthy smell.

LEFT A double compost heap built with fencing posts and chicken wire.

ABOVE   The large leaves of comfrey are an excellent compost accelerator and rich in certain vitamins.

RIGHT   Borage is a useful addition to the compost heap and looks pretty in the garden.

Making better compost

- Compost activators or accelerators speed up the microbiological activity in a heap, and this in turn speeds up the decomposition process. There are commercial compost activators available, but adding manure produces equally good results. Other compost activators include commercial seaweed plant food and herbs such as yarrow, borage, comfrey, dandelion, stinging nettle and valerian.

- Grass clippings added to a heap heat up rapidly and produce carbon dioxide, which in turn activates the process of nitrogen-fixation by bacteria.

- Liquid compost may be made by placing finished compost in a bucket and filling it with water. Use a ratio of one part compost to three parts water. Leave it for three days, stir it occasionally and use it as a liquid fertiliser. This can be repeated several times with the same compost. The remaining compost can be returned to the heap or added to the garden as a mulch.

- Tea leaves should be added to the heap as they have a high nitrogen content and also contain phosphorus and potash.

- A smell like rotten eggs indicates that there is insufficient air (anaerobic) in the heap. Alternate flourishing of anaerobic and aerobic bacteria is encouraged by frequent turning of the heap.

- Seaweed contains the bacteria stimulator alginic acid and is thus an excellent compost accelerator. Dry seaweed in the sun so that it becomes brittle and easy to shred. Then add the pieces into the layers of your compost heap.

- Paper makes an excellent compost extender. Tear or shred it and add it to the heap.

- Lucerne and clover hays can be added to the compost heap. They have a higher nitrogen content than wheaten or oaten hays.

Regenerating the soil

Your soil needs to be regenerated on a yearly basis to keep it healthy. Composting regularly is an ideal regeneration method as it adds organic matter to the soil that in turn encourages earthworms to flourish.

Adding manure as a mulch around your plants in spring will add nutrients and organic matter to the soil.

If you don't have enough compost and you are starting a new garden, you will need to buy an organic garden mix from a local landscaper. This should be added to the top of existing soil at a depth of at least 10 cm.

Mulching with lucerne or other organic materials will also add structure and organic matter to your soil.

Worms and soil

A soil without earthworms is not alive. A soil with earthworms hosts a large population of bacteria, fungi, viruses, insects and spiders and is rich in humus. The burrowing earthworm breaks down root mats and opens up tunnels for oxygen and water to penetrate the soil. These tunnels are coated with nitrate-rich mucus. The roots of plants quickly take advantage of the tunnels and take nutrition from the mucus.

Worms can eat their own weight every day and produce the same amount of vermicast or castings. These castings are far richer in minerals than the soil the worms ingest, and when added to the soil they act as an enhancer. Although worms have a very simple digestive system, a proportion of insoluble minerals passing through them is converted into a plant-available, soluble form. This digestive process is carried out by enzyme-producing bacteria and, when the castings are excreted, the bacteria and enzymes are excreted with them. These beneficial bacteria continue in the soil the work they carried out in the worm's gut.

Recycling the natural way

Worms are particularly effective at recycling your household organic waste. Worm bins are ideal for small gardens because they take up little space and the waste is confined to a box. It's relatively easy to make your own worm bin after studying some designs, but the easiest way is to purchase a worm farm kit comprised of worms, worm bin and instructions.

How a worm bin works

The majority of worm bins are divided into two or three shelves separated by a screen that enables the worm castings to be collected separately. Bins are available in wood or plastic. Around 2000 worms are required initially for a bin that will be kept full of material. Red or tiger worms are the most commonly used and, when given optimum conditions, worms will double their number in 10–12 weeks. All that is needed to keep them alive and healthy is a constant supply of organic matter and sufficient aeration. Simply place all your organic waste in the bin and the worms will do the rest.

Reaping the rewards

The worm's deposit is your reward. Two to three millimetres of worm castings sprinkled onto the soil, worked in to a depth of 25–50 mm and watered well will produce amazing results in one season. Castings will aerate the soil, loosen up clay soils to improve both structure and drainage, and improve the water-holding capacity of sandy soils.

Each year will bring better results with regular applications.

Worm bins are ideal for small gardens because they take up little space.

What is mulch?

There are two types of mulches –
organic and inorganic.
• Organic mulches consist of materials
  such as straw, leaf mould, lawn
  clippings, bark, sugar cane mulch and
  tea tree mulch.
• Inorganic mulches include gravel,
  pebbles or rock. These mulches are
  not beneficial to the soil, but are used
  to keep down weed growth.

How mulching helps

Fertiliser: Organic mulches release
nutrients into the soil as they break down.
Insulation: Mulching keeps the soil
warm during winter and cool in summer.
Moisture retention: A layer of mulch
will prevent evaporation. This means the
garden has to be watered less frequently,
and because of this the nutrients are
not washed out of the soil too rapidly.
Weed suppression: We all hate weeding,
and a mulched garden needs to be
weeded less often.
Plant protection: Ground-hugging
vegetables such as cucumbers,
strawberries and zucchinis don't rot
when they are grown on a layer of mulch.
They tend to spoil more quickly when
they are touching the bare soil.

Mulching

In a natural environment leaves
and other plant material are
constantly falling to the ground to
produce a mulch. This mulch helps
to keep the soil moist during the
summer months as well as providing
nutrients to growing plants.

This natural process is now
being widely copied in home
gardens and is proving to be among
the most popular developments in
garden maintenance.

The mulch test

If you are unsure about the
benefits of mulching, try this test.
Mulch around half a row of
vegetables, leaving the other half
mulch free. The difference in the
growth rate of the mulched
vegetables will soon convince you
of the value of mulching.

Three functions of mulching

Mulch performs three important
functions:
• it conserves moisture by
  reducing evaporation;
• it prevents weed growth by
  restricting light at the soil surface;
• it modifies soil temperatures by
  cooling or warming the soil.

Benefits of organic mulch

Organic mulches are
biodegradable, and this means
that they eventually break down
and add their matter to the soil.
This leads to an improvement in
soil structure, which increases
the water and nutrient-holding
capacity of the soil.

Earthworms thrive in the layer
of soil just below the mulch where
they carry on their work of
aerating and enriching the soil.
Worms carry broken-down bits of
mulch below the surface, which
increase the amount of humus
around the roots.

The best way to mulch

The best time to mulch is when
your soil is completely free of
weeds and is well watered. How
thickly you apply the mulch
depends on the type of mulch used.
To prevent weed growth you will
need to apply at least 5 cm of
mulch. Most mulches will last two
or three months and they can be
added to as they decompose.

With a vegetable patch, the
mulch can be dug into the soil after
harvest to provide structure to the
soil and a new mulch can be
applied with the next planting.

A mulched vegetable garden will give better
yields than an unmulched one.

Feeding

Feed plants regularly if you want them to grow steadily and remain free from pests and diseases.

Elements plants need

Plants require fifteen elements to grow satisfactorily. Three of these are carbon, hydrogen and oxygen, which are found in both air and water. The other twelve elements are divided into two groups – major elements and minor or trace elements. The major elements are nitrogen, phosphorus, sulphur, potassium, magnesium and calcium. The trace elements are iron, manganese, boron, molybdenum, copper and zinc. Most of these elements are ever-present in the soil, but the demands on nitrogen, phosphorus and potassium are such that they need to be replenished regularly.

Nitrogen is the element necessary for the growth of new tissue. If the soil in your garden has been properly prepared with organic manures and compost, it is unlikely that there will be a shortage of nitrogen.

Apply organic fertilisers while the plants are growing. The most commonly used nitrogen-rich fertilisers are animal manure (poultry, horse, cow, sheep or rabbit) and seaweed for those who live near the beach.

An overdose of nitrogen in the soil will cause soft, sappy growth with a lot of foliage but few flowers.

Phosphorus is essential for strong roots and healthy growth. Phosphorus also helps plants to resist disease. Plants that are deficient in phosphorus will appear to be stunted and will have poor root growth. Leaves will turn purple, red or bluish green.

Organic sources of phosphorus are animal manures and wood ash. The inorganic source is superphosphate, which should always be used sparingly, as it leaches out of the soil slowly and can build up over years.

Potassium is required for the development of strong plants. It builds up the firm outer tissues. A soil deficient in potassium will result in plants having little resistance to heat, cold or disease and the process of photosynthesis will be slowed considerably. Organic sources of potassium include wood ash, straw and all animal and poultry manures.

Smart tip

Australian plants belonging to the *Proteaceae* family do not like fertilisers that contain phosphorus. Buy a proprietary native plant food or use cow manure.

Pebbles are a decorative form of inorganic mulch.

Smart tip

Only use fertiliser according to directions on the packet. Over-fertilising can kill plants. Do not think that more is better. Always water the soil before and after applying fertiliser.

Liquid manure

You can make a very effective liquid manure easily by combining one-third manure with two-thirds water in a plastic bucket and letting it steep for about two weeks.

Any type of animal manure can be used. Chicken manure works wonders when used on nitrogen-loving vegetables such as spinach, lettuce, cabbage, endive, sorrel, mustard and cress.

Compost and straw have been added to this bed. They are being dug into the soil to add organic matter before the bed is planted.

Seaweed

Seaweed is a very valuable source of plant food. It contains as much nitrogen, half the phosphorus and twice as much potassium as manure. It also contains an enormous variety of trace elements and powerful antibiotics. Between 20 per cent and 50 per cent of some seaweeds are minerals.

You should hose the seaweed down before use to get rid of the salt. Seaweed can be dug into the ground when the garden bed is being prepared or it can be used as a mulch around plants. Because seaweed is so low in phosphorus, add some rock minerals or blood and bone.

Commercial fertilisers

You can buy commercial fertilisers that have all the ingredients necessary to keep your garden healthy. But it is still important to continually add organic matter to your soil in the form of compost or mulch to keep the soil healthy.

There are many different types of fertiliser available on the market. Soluble fertilisers are usually the cheapest source of fertiliser per unit of nutrient. Because they are soluble, the plant can absorb the nutrients quickly. You can buy sprayers that hold the fertiliser and fit onto the end of your hose. The fertiliser is automatically mixed with water. Otherwise you must mix the fertiliser in a watering can and apply it to the garden. Soluble fertilisers are ideal for flowers, vegetables, trees and shrubs.

Concentrated organic fertilisers are usually mixtures of fishmeal and blood and bone. They will supply the major nutrients and elements required by plants. The fertiliser is applied to the soil surface directly around the plants.

Pellets, tablets and granules are applied directly to the soil or placed just below the root depth and are available in organic and inorganic mixes. These are suited to flowers, vegetables, roses, bulbs, trees and shrubs.

Controlled-release fertilisers are not cheap but they release nutrients to plants over a long period. This can be three, six or nine months or in some cases over a period of a year. They are applied directly to the soil and there are formulations for flowers, pot plants, vegetables, trees and shrubs.

When to fertilise

Most trees and shrubs like to be fertilised at least twice a year. This should preferably be undertaken in early spring and again in summer. Perennials like to be fed in spring and again when flower-heads start to appear. Annuals and vegetables need more frequent feeding and respond well to regular applications of soluble fertiliser.

How to fertilise

Before applying any type of fertiliser to your garden, especially a common fertiliser, it's important that you water the soil thoroughly. Simply sprinkle the fertiliser onto the soil and water it in.

Weeding

Most of us regard weeding as very boring, but it's an essential chore and should be approached in a routine way. Weeds compete with plants for soil nutrition and harbour pests and diseases.

Controlling weeds

You can control weeds by hand weeding, hoeing or forking. Herbicides can be used on areas such as driveways or pathways where there is no risk of harming ornamentals or vegetables.

Hand weeding is best carried out after wet weather as the weeds are easily loosened from the damp soil. If you are using a hoe, always use it lightly around cultivated plants so that you do not disturb their surface roots.

Always make sure that you remove the whole root of the plant when weeding, especially in the case of perennial weeds such as oxalis or couch grass. Many rhizomes and bulbils will grow again if they are left in the soil.

Mulching your soil with an organic mulch such as lucerne, or whatever is available in your area, will help to control weeds. Mulch in late winter before weeds start to grow and top up the mulch again in summer.

Watering

The main rule for watering is to give a thorough soaking every few days rather than a light watering every day. Light watering encourages the plants' roots to rise in search of water, making them shallow rooted and not as hardy.

Overwatering can also be detrimental because the soil does not get an opportunity to become aerated when air is taken into the soil as it dries out. Air in the soil is necessary for healthy plants.

If you have a vegetable patch, you should water it regularly. This is especially true if you are growing salad vegetables, which are almost 90 per cent water. Lack of water will slow growth and lead to a lack of nutrients. Leaf crops require more watering than root crops.

Always water in the early morning or early evening to prevent evaporation.

The best ways to water

Hand watering: Hand watering is certainly time consuming. Nevertheless, it has the advantage of being a relaxing thing to do at the end of a busy day.

Trickle irrigation: This is good for gardens that are well planned out. Trickle irrigation makes a little water go a long way. Water is delivered in small quantities under low pressure directly to where it does the most good – the root zones of the plants. Because the soil is not too flooded, most of the air passages remain open. Oxygen is thus always available to the roots and the stresses caused by overwatering are removed.

Sprinkler system: A sprinkler system can irrigate the whole garden at once and it's ideal for those with little time. It can be turned on when required to give plants a thorough soaking.

A thorough watering every few days is more beneficial than a light watering every day.

Growing from seed

The process of a seed sprouting roots and leaves is one of the miracles of nature. Three conditions must be met before germination takes place: the presence of air, adequate moisture and a suitable temperature. Moisture is necessary to soften the seed coat and allow the embryo (the undeveloped plant) to expand and grow. A suitable temperature is needed to break dormancy.

The importance of drainage

Air is an essential requirement for seeds to survive. If the soil is waterlogged for an extended period or if the seeds are started in a heavy potting mix, they will die. This is one of the reasons it is essential to have a potting mix that drains well, so that air can enter the soil.

Seed-raising mixtures

The mixture in which seeds are sown is very important. Ordinary garden soil used in containers will pack too tightly once it has been watered and will not allow enough air into the soil. Seed-raising mixtures can be obtained from nurseries. Choose one that contains vermiculite, so the mix will be open enough for the roots to penetrate easily and for air to circulate. It will hold water without becoming soggy.

Seeds or seedlings?

Many people choose to buy seedlings from a nursery rather than start their own plants. The main advantage of starting your own seeds is that there is a larger choice of varieties. Selection of ready-grown seedlings is always restricted to a few popular varieties. There is also great satisfaction knowing that you are fully responsible for a crop from seed to harvest.

Fresh seeds are best

It's a good idea to start each season with fresh seeds. Some seeds are long-lived under ideal conditions, but high humidity and other factors can cause rapid deterioration. A packet of seeds will more than pay for itself in one season.

Storing seeds

After planting, you may find that you have many left-over seeds in the packet. To maintain viability, seeds must be kept cool and dry. Incorrect

---

What is a seed?

A seed is the product of a fertilised ovule and consists of an embryo enclosed by a protective seed coat. It is a young, undeveloped plant with a food source.

How to sow seeds

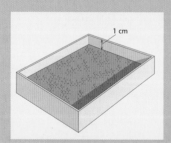

1   Press the seed-raising mixture firmly down to about 1 cm from the top of the tray.

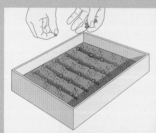

2   Make rows in the mixture and place the seeds into the rows individually.

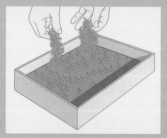

3   Cover the seeds with seed-raising mixture. Larger seeds usually need a soil covering of twice their thickness. The depth is usually indicated on the seed packet.

4   Tamp the seeds in with a wooden block or your hand. Water with a fine spray.

storage conditions may affect the length of seed life. Keep the seed in its original packet and store it in either a paper bag or a loosely sealed jar. Don't store seeds in plastic containers as they tend to sweat.

Seed-sowing containers

The main requirement for any container that is to be used for sowing seed is that it has efficient drainage.

All containers should be thoroughly washed with warm, soapy water before use. This will eliminate any residual diseases from previous plants.

The size of the container depends, of course, on the quantity of seeds to be germinated, but the depth of the container should be no more than 5–10 cm.

One type of commercially available seed tray consists of a number of small pots joined together. A couple of seeds are sown in each little pot and can later be thinned to the strongest seed. These containers are available in plastic or compressed peat.

Peat pellets

Peat pellets are made of compressed peat that expands to seven times its volume when moisture is added. Netting holds the peat together, and there is a depression in the top of each pellet for seeds. At transplanting time, the entire pellet can be planted into the garden without shock to the seedlings.

It's a good idea to remove the netting before planting in case it restricts growth.

Direct sowing

Large seeds that are easy to manage can be planted directly into the ground where they are to grow. This saves transplanting and stops any setbacks that can occur when young plants are moved.

Always follow the directions on the packet for the planting depth and distance apart. The soil that covers the seeds should be fine and not lumpy. A seed-raising mixture will give best results. Keep the ground moist after planting until the young seedlings emerge from the ground.

Smart tip

Different seeds germinate at different temperatures. Spinach, for example, can germinate at a temperature of 2 degrees Celsius, but tomatoes need at least 15 degrees Celsius and higher before germination occurs. Make sure you check the individual temperature requirements of the particular seeds you are using.

Time to transplant

After the seedlings have made their second or third leaves, they need to be transplanted. Always water the seedlings prior to transplanting and make sure that the ground into which they are to be transplanted is also damp.

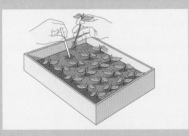

1 Transplant by removing all but the most promising seedlings. Lever the seedling out of the container with a small, pointed tool.

2 When removing a seedling from its container take care not to damage its roots.

3 When placing the seedling in a container or the ground, make sure that the roots are not cramped, then replace the soil gently around it. Do not replant at more than the previous depth.

During the first week or so after transplanting, keep the plants well watered to encourage steady growth.

Cuttings

In propagation by cuttings, a new independent plant is produced from a piece of stem, root or leaf cut from the parent plant. The new plant is identical to the parent plant. Stem cuttings are the most common types of cutting and these can be divided into four groups according to the nature of the wood used in making the cuttings: hardwood, semi-hardwood, soft-wood and herbaceous.

Hardwood cuttings
This is an easy method of propagating deciduous trees and shrubs. Hardwood cuttings are taken in winter, once plants are dormant (see diagrams below).

Semi-hardwood cuttings
Semi-hardwood cuttings are generally used for propagating evergreen plants and are taken just after a flush of growth when the stems have become partially mature.

Make the cuttings 8–15 cm long, retaining a couple of leaves at the top of the cutting. If the leaves are very large, they should be reduced in size to prevent excessive loss of water. This can be done easily by cutting them in half with a sharp pair of scissors. The basal cut should be made just below a pair of nodes where a hormone for root production accumulates naturally.

It's necessary that leafy cuttings be rooted under conditions that will keep water loss from the leaves to a minimum. The pot of cuttings can be placed either in a propagating case or enclosed in a plastic bag propped up by a couple of sticks. The plastic bag is not removed, except when watering is necessary, until the cuttings have taken root. Keep the cuttings in a warm, sheltered and shaded position.

Softwood and herbaceous cuttings
This type of cutting is taken from either deciduous or evergreen plants. Take it during early spring when the growth is rapid and the stems are quite flexible. Softwood cuttings generally root more easily and more quickly than the other types but require more attention.

How to propagate by hardwood stem cuttings

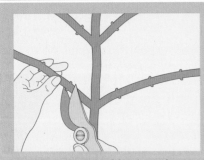

1   Select strong, healthy, ripened stems that are about 20 cm long. Avoid old wood and stems that are weak and spindly.

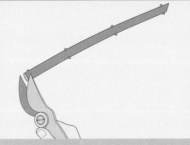

2   Trim the stems to a length of about 8–15 cm. Make an angled top cut just above a node and a horizontal cut below a pair of nodes at the bottom of the stem.

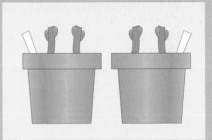

3   Place the cuttings into pots containing commercial cutting mix, leaving about 5 cm of the cutting above the mix. Label and place in a warm, shaded position. Cuttings will have taken root by the end of next spring, when they can be repotted until the following spring or placed directly into garden beds.

The best softwood cutting material has some degree of flexibility, but is mature enough to break when bent sharply. Superior cutting materials are the lateral or side branches of the stock plant.

Cuttings should be 8–15 cm long, with two or more nodes and the basal cut made just below a node. The leaves on the lower portion of the cutting are removed, and those on the upper part are retained. Large leaves can be cut in half. Keep the cuttings pot in a propagating case or seal it in a plastic bag until it has rooted. Check after six weeks.

The correct propagating medium

The correct propagating medium will influence the number of cuttings that will root and the quality of the root system formed. You can buy mixtures specially prepared for cuttings or you can make your own. A mixture of two parts river sand and one part compost is most effective.

Plant division

Plants such as perennials that have multiple stems arising from the base of the plant are usually propagated by division. Dividing perennials keeps them vigorous and enables you to increase your stocks. You can lift your perennials and divide them every three or four years. Plants that have become congested, are flowering less freely or are dying back in the centre benefit from division. Late winter and early spring are good times to undertake this task.

Smart tip

Plant hormones (ask at your local plant nursery) can be applied to cuttings to encourage the production and even distribution of roots. Hormones also shorten the time taken by the plant to root. The end of the cutting is dipped into the powder before it is placed in the propagating medium.

Division in 6 easy steps

1 Carefully remove the plant from the ground by digging it out with a fork. (The plant pictured is *Phlomis russeliana*.)

2 Shake away some of the soil so the roots are easily seen.

3 The root ball can now be divided by either pulling it apart with your hands or cutting it with a pair of secateurs or a sharp knife.

4 Cut off old top growth leaving some young shoots.

5 Make a new hole and place some well-rotted compost in the base.

6 Replant the divided section to the same depth as before. Firm down around it and water thoroughly until it is established.

Shrubs that benefit from pruning

***Abelia* species** Cut out old canes in winter. Tip-prune for a compact form.

***Acacia* species** Cut back flowering stems by half after flowers have finished.

***Buddleia* cultivars** Prune back heavily during winter.

***Callistemon* species** Prune back as flowers fade. Picking the flowers is a good method of pruning.

Crowea exalata Prune back by about one-third when flowers finish.

***Eupatorium* species** Cut back to half or lower as flowerheads finish.

***Fuchsia* species** Cold climates: prune in late winter or early spring. Frost-free climates: prune in autumn.

***Gardenia* species** Straggly plants can be cut back in spring.

***Grevillea* species** Prune after flowering, but not into old wood.

***Hydrangea* species** Prune in winter by cutting back stems bearing dead heads and removing any weak or unwanted shoots. Cut back to the first or second pair of buds, as cutting any lower than this can prevent flowers appearing in the following season. *H. arborescens* and *H. paniculata*, however, flower at the tips of the current season's growth and can thus be cut back to any pair of buds.

Hibiscus rosa-sinensis Prune in spring by cutting back by two-thirds. In frost-free areas, prune again in January.

***Lavandula* species** Prune after flowering but not into old wood.

***Philadelphus* species** Old canes may be cut back if necessary to the point at which a new cane has begun to emerge near the base after flowering.

Pruning

Skilful pruning shapes and guides plants and, in some cases, produces more flowers. The best pruning results are achieved when the habit of the particular plant and the general guidelines for pruning are understood.

When to prune

- Plants that flower on the previous year's wood are pruned straight after flowering. This allows enough time to produce new flowering wood for the next year.
- Plants that flower on new wood and produce blooms in late summer and autumn are pruned during winter.
- Deciduous shrubs that are grown for foliage may be pruned in mid-winter.

Pruning tips

- Always use sharp, clean tools.
- Make the cut just above an outward-facing bud. Cut at an angle, not straight across.
- Prune stems with opposite buds to just above a pair of buds.

Pruning roses

Pruning roses keeps them healthy and encourages new, vigorous growth, which in turn produces numerous flowers. But too many people agonise about the correct way to prune their roses. Take comfort from the fact that if you do make a mistake, the worst outcome will be a reduction in flower numbers. Roses are hardy and not killed easily.

When to prune roses

Repeat-flowering shrub roses such as the Hybrid Teas, Floribundas, Hybrid Musks, Bourbons and David Austins should be given their main pruning in early winter in temperate climates and during August in cold climates. Lighter prunings may be undertaken during late spring and summer as flowers finish by removing the dead flowers about three nodes down the stem. Species roses that bloom only in spring and once-flowering climbers such as the Banksias are pruned after flowering, not during winter.

How to prune roses

The rose pruning process is relatively simple. Start by removing all dead, dying and unproductive wood. Unproductive wood has rough bark, while younger, productive wood has smooth bark. Cut the wood you wish to prune back to a strong young branch or right to the base. Next, cut out any branches that are crowding near, or crossing over, good branches. Remove or shorten any thin, twiggy shoots that are less than the thickness of a pencil. (The pencil rule does not apply to small roses with naturally thin wood, such as some of the David Austins.) Shorten the retained branches to an outward-facing bud. Very hard pruning used to be the fashion, but the current practice is to shorten your retained branches by a third to encourage a larger number of blooms and a more decorative display.

Rose-pruning tips

The first pre-pruning step is to invest in a good pair of secateurs. Modern secateurs are well-made precision instruments. For more mature roses you can use a pair of long-handled pruners.

Sterilising your secateurs and pruning saw will prevent the spread of disease. Use household bleach or disinfectant, and keep a container of either next to you to sterilise your tools before moving from one bush to another.

To prevent the spread of disease, it's important to collect all rose clippings and leaves and place them in the dustbin.

Pests and diseases

The best way to prevent pests and diseases is to have correct garden planning and management. This is because a plant is subject to a number of problems when it is weakened by lack of care. If you organise your garden so that it is healthy and strong enough to withstand pests and diseases, you will reduce the need to resort to chemical cures. Even if a cure becomes necessary, there are many organic methods available.

Chemical free?

Where possible, it is best to have a chemical-free, natural pest control system in your garden. These days many people are aware of the dangers of using chemicals that affect both humans and animals. Chemicals can have long-lasting effects on the entire natural food chain. Many of the inorganic substances found in pesticides can remain in a physical state in the environment for years, stored in the tissue of both plants and animals.

Some pesticides are very stable and will accumulate in the food chain at much higher levels than those found naturally in the environment. And some pesticides destroy insects, animals and plants apart from those for which they are intended. Because of this, natural predators that live in the garden are killed unintentionally.

When you start using pesticides on a regular basis, you quickly get onto a chemical treadmill, as most pests reproduce more prolifically than their natural enemies. Once this happens, it is difficult to re-establish an effective natural control system.

The bio-diverse garden

An attitude based on the principles of bio-diversity is ecologically sound and often produces more beautiful results than those achieved using conventional chemical methods. A bio-diverse garden is one that contains a wide variety of plants. In fact, growing large numbers of the same plant is inefficient because it is an open invitation to pests attracted to that plant.

Companion planting and the use of nursery crops to attract birds and beneficial insects integrate plants for specific purposes. And the fact that you have a bio-diverse garden will integrate it with the neighbourhood because the beneficial insects it attracts will find their way into other gardens.

Smart tip

Most 'safe' sprays are made from pyrethrum, eucalyptus or garlic. Unfortunately these sprays kill beneficial insects as well as pests. To avoid this outcome, spray or dust on dry days, either early in the morning or late in the afternoon when beneficials are relatively inactive.

A bio-diverse garden containing a wide variety of plants.

Garden beds that contain a diverse collection of plants will attract beneficial insects to the garden.

Although your garden is only a small part of the environment, it is nevertheless significant. A group of small, bio-diverse gardens will contribute greatly to the environment as a whole.

Nursery crops

Nursery crops are those that provide food and shelter for beneficial pest-eating insects. Mix the attractant plants among those you want to protect (especially vegetables) so that the predators will always be close to your flowers and crops. Many plants are capable of sheltering beneficial insects, but some plants are particularly attractive to them.

Many beneficial insects like flowers that are small and abundant, such as those of yarrow or Queen Anne's lace. These flowers supply the nectar required by the beneficials to supplement their diets when pests are scarce. The adult lacewing, for example, will feed on nectar but its larvae are voracious aphid predators.

Birds are the natural predators of many insects. Lure them to your garden with bird-attracting native plants that are indigenous to your area and place perches throughout the garden.

Attracting beneficial insects

All plants belonging to the daisy family (*Asteraceae*) are excellent sources of both pollen and nectar and will attract a wide variety of beneficial insects including assassin bugs, ladybirds, green lacewings and parasitic wasps. Use annual daisies such as cosmos, sunflowers, calliopsis (*Coreopsis tinctoria*), marigolds, *Rhodanthe* species, native everlasting daisies (*Bracteantha* species), China asters (*Callistephus chinensis*) and dahlias.

Perennials that attract beneficial insects include coreopsis, tansy, golden marguerite (*Anthemis tinctoria*), perennial sunflowers, golden rod, coneflowers, asters and gayfeathers.

Plants in the mint family (*Lamiaceae*) tend to have aromatic foliage and clusters of numerous small, two-lipped flowers that attract bees and other beneficial insects. The mint family includes

basil, sweet marjoram, thyme, mint, garden sage, lavender, lemon balm, hyssop, oregano, catmint, Russian sage and bergamot.

The carrot family (*Apiaceae*) bears flowers grouped in large, umbrella-shaped clusters that attract ladybirds, hover flies, parasitic wasps, spiders, lacewings and other beneficial insects. Insect-attracting plants in this family include dill, caraway, bronze fennel and Queen Anne's lace.

Biological control

Biological control – in which one organism is used against another – is becoming an increasingly popular method of insect management. Dipel is the most commonly known product and is based on the bacterium *Bacillus thuringiensis*.

Dipel is safe for use on fruit and vegetables, and although used mainly on vegetables of the cabbage family, it will kill any type of caterpillar. It is essential to spray the plants thoroughly. Repeated applications may be necessary as the bacteria remain viable on the foliage for short periods only

and are easily killed by hot temperatures.

You can also buy beneficial insects. Predatory mites can be obtained to control two types of spotted mite. Also available are ladybirds that target mealy bugs and lacewings that will eat caterpillars, aphids, thrips, mealy bugs, various moth eggs and whitefly.

Fresh produce

When it comes to the vegetable patch, using chemicals of any kind will defeat the purpose of trying to cultivate fresh, healthy vegetables. But finding viable alternatives to the use of chemical sprays is simply a matter of changing attitudes. It's worth remembering that sprays and poisons were not used in vegetable cultivation until quite recently. We have been conditioned to believe that sprays are necessary and convenient, without looking into the possibility of growing plants organically. This is especially true of commercial vegetable growing, which has been dependent on chemicals for many years.

ABOVE   Lavender attracts bees and other beneficial insects.

LEFT   Plant natives such as grevillea to attract birds to the garden.

Smart tip

You can deter snails and white butterflies by placing a barrier around small seedlings. Surround the seedlings with several rounds of mosquito wire about 7.5 cm in height. When the plants are large enough to recover from the occasional chomp, the rounds of wire may be removed for use on the next crop.

Fungicides

Fungicides are sometimes required for vegetables, especially the *Cucurbitaceae* family, which includes zucchini, cucumbers, gourds and pumpkins. A spray made from 5 g of baking soda (sodium bicarbonate) mixed with 1 L of water will help prevent fungal spores from germinating. Some rose growers say this spray is helpful in keeping black spot at bay. Do not use it in very hot conditions and spray early in the morning. Lime sulphur and Neem oil also work as preventatives against fungal diseases.

Seaweed spray makes a good fungicide because it feeds the plants at the same time. Make it by mixing liquid seaweed fertiliser with water or by using fresh seaweed.

You can make seaweed fungicide by placing some large bunches of seaweed in a sack and immersing the sack in a plastic garbage bin full of water and leaving it for at least two weeks. Remove the seaweed and use it as a mulch, then use the liquid as a foliar spray.

Pest Oil and insecticidal soaps

Pest Oil has a low impact on beneficial insects. It may be used on aphids, mealy bugs, scale insects, two-spotted spider mite and whitefly. Insecticidal soaps such as Natrasoap are more effective than home-made sprays and work well against aphids, whiteflies, thrips, mealy bugs and two-spotted mites.

Common pests and diseases

INSECT	DAMAGE	ORGANIC CONTROL	CHEMICAL CONTROL
Aphid	Attacks buds, roots and new growth of many plants; spreads viral diseases.	Birds are natural predators. Hose off plant. Squash manually.	Spray with Pest Oil. A short, hard spray of the hose will help to dislodge aphids.
Azalea lacebug	Damages leaves of azaleas and rhododendrons.	Shake branches; use a soapy spray or sticky yellow traps.	Spray with Confidor.
Bean fly	Attacks leaves and young stems.	Keep beans well fed and watered.	Spray plants with Baythroid according to directions.
Borer	Grubs tunnel into trunk or branches of fruit trees, ornamental trees and shrubs.	Probe the hole with a piece of wire to try to kill the grub.	Inject Carbaryl into the hole.
Bronze orange bug	Attacks citrus stalks causing flowers to fall.	Spray with soapy water in winter.	Spray foliage with Folimat.
Cabbage white butterfly	Larvae attack broccoli, cabbages, cauliflower, radishes and turnips.	Apply Dipel, particularly to lower leaf surface. Dust with Derris Dust.	n/a
Christmas beetle	Makes saw-tooth holes in eucalypt leaves.	Hose off and destroy.	n/a
Citrus leafminer	Larvae tunnel through leaves and distort them.	Don't overfeed and overwater plants as citrus leafminer attacks new growth.	Use white oil on new growth only.
Codling moth	Larvae burrow into the core of the fruit.	Tree banding will trap larvae; destroy infected fruit.	Spray with Lebaycid.
Fruit fly	Attacks citrus and stone fruit, avocados, bananas and tomatoes.	Remove and burn infected fruit. Use Dak-pots.	Spray with Lebaycid following instructions carefully.
Harlequin bug	This brightly coloured beetle sucks sap from a range of trees and smaller plants.	Shake beetles into soapy water or spray them with pyrethrins.	Spray with Folimat.
Leafminer	Different species attack a range of plants leaving distinctive markings on the leaves.	Remove leaves and destroy larvae.	Spray with Lebaycid.
Leaf spots	Black spots are found on roses, tomatoes, capsicums, carrot and silver beet.	Usually more serious in wet weather. Remove infected leaves and burn. Spray with a baking soda or seaweed spray.	Black Spot and Insect Killer. Mancozeb Plus Garden Fungicide Spray.
Looper	Caterpillar of moth family that moves with a looping action and attacks undersurfaces of broad-leafed vegetables and soft-leafed indoor plants.	Remove by hand.	Use Carbaryl but only if necessary.
Mealy bug	Sucks sap from a variety of plants including indoor plants.	Dab with cotton bud dipped in methylated spirits; prune badly affected parts of plant.	Spray with Confidor.
Mildew, powdery	A fungus that leaves a whitish film over the leaves of plants. Attacks roses, dahlias, calendulas, zinnias, vine crops and sweet peas.	Regularly spray with a seaweed mix as a preventative measure. Spray with lime sulphur or Neem oil.	Mancozeb Plus Garden Fungicide Spray.
Mildew, downy	Whitish, downy spores on underside of leaves. Attacks vine crops, plants from the cabbage family, lettuce and stocks.	Regularly spray with a seaweed mix or baking soda mix as a preventative measure. Spray with lime sulphur or Neem oil.	Mancozeb Plus Garden Fungicide Spray.
Rust	Orange or red markings on leaves or stems. Found on gerberas, beans, snapdragons, calendulas and poplars.	Spray with lime sulphur.	Mancozeb Plus Garden Fungicide Spray.
Scale	Attacks leaves and fruit on a wide range of plants and can ultimately cause the death of a plant.	Spray with white oil or Pest Oil.	Spray with white oil.
Snails and slugs	Eat leaves and new shoots.	Place slug and snail barrier tapes around plants. Sink beer-filled margarine containers into the soil.	Use snail baits that contain pet deterrents.
Thrip	Attacks leaves and flowers of a range of plants.	Hose thrips or spray with pyrethrum.	Spray with Pest Oil.
Two-spotted mite (red spider mite)	Attacks a range of plants including azaleas, ornamentals, fruit trees and vegetables.	Prune and destroy affected foliage; use predatory mites, encourage ladybirds.	Spray with Confidor.
Vegetable weevil	Can damage a wide range of vegetables and annuals.	Crop rotation helps with weevil control; remove any weeds.	Spray with Carbaryl.
Whitefly	Sucks sap from leaves; attacks vegetables and annuals.	Overlook small numbers; use of parasitic wasps can reduce numbers.	Spray with Confidor.

Acknowledgements

Additional writing
Evan McHugh (for preparation and writing of material for projects)

Project editor
Wendy Skilbeck

Editors
Judy Brookes
Nan McNab

Text and cover design
Judith Summerfeldt Grace
Deborah Brash

Page layout and file management
P.A.G.E. Pty Ltd

Photography stylist
Julie Bilby

Illustrations
Shelley Communications (Alan Laver), technical illustrations
Green Room (Nicole Markby), garden plans

Technical consultants for projects
Kevin Drinkwell
Ian Winstone

Designs for garden plans
Janice Thorpe and Cheryl Maddocks

Indexer
Fay Donlevy

Proofreader
Liz McCormack

Photo credits

The publisher would like to thank the following businesses and organisations who kindly supplied photographs and props for photographs:

Aloha Pools, p. 17; Bunnings Warehouse; Catnip Australia Pty Ltd (Ph: 1800 369 998), p. 208; Freedom Furniture; Reln Plastics Pty Ltd, p. 292.

The publisher would like to thank the following designers and owners of private gardens photographed in the book:

Hal Walter, p. 2; Rock 'n' Root, pp. 4, 78, 80; Peter Stubbs, p. 7; J. Thorpe (design), pp. 8, 70, 95 (right); K. Ram, p. 8; Faulkner & Chapman (design), pp. 9, 42, 90 (right); A. Bettesworth, H. Searle, pp. 11, 113 (right); K. Kilsby, p. 12; G. McDonald, p. 14 (right); Mark Vowles (design), pp. 16, 116; The Garden of St Erth, pp. 18, 23; T. and I. Morphett, p. 22 (top); A. Anetts (design), p. 24; Secret Gardens of Sydney, pp. 27, 126; Imperial Gardens, pp. 28, 33 (left), 235 (left); Flowerpower, p. 32 (right); Betty Maloney, pp. 34, 38, 39; Fiona Brockoff (design), p. 36; D. and I. Norton, p. 38 (right); Polly Park, p. 40; Peter Fudge (design), pp. 44 (right), 92, 173; S. Riley, p. 45; Tuckeroo, pp. 46, 146; M. Davis, pp. 50, 108; Robert Boyle (design), p. 53 (right); Barbara Clare, p. 53 (left); Heronswood, p. 55; Reverie, p. 56; D. Weeks, p. 69; Michael Cooke, pp. 72, 226; Hillcrest Park, p. 74; Red Cow Farm, pp. 77, 98; D'Ortenzio garden, p. 82; C. McDonald, p. 84; Jill Morrow, p. 90 (left), Deauville gardens, p. 93; H. Baikitis, pp. 94, 267 (left); M. Pohl, p. 102 (left and right); J. Cameron, p. 103 (right); R. Sang, p. 111; Collector's Corner, p. 112; Amanda Oliver (design), pp. 115, 215; The Secret Garden, p. 119 (left); George and Wilma Chamberlain, pp. 122 (left and right), 123 (left and right); Jacob's garden, p. 138; Katisma Landscaping, p. 147; Darryl Mappin (design), p. 175; Karlenya, pp. 177, 225; J. Cameron, p. 136; J. Arnold, p. 212; Francis Minson, p. 220; Busker's End, pp. 262, 263, 270 (right); Cherry Cottage, p. 266; Venetiaville garden (front cover, top); Neil and Denise Shields; Michael and Fiona Brookes;

Leonie and Sean Keillor; Steve, Katrina, Samantha, Ashleigh and Benjamin White; Anne Shoebridge; Kate and Bill Robinson; Lynne Twelftree; Poyntons of Essendon.

The publisher would like to thank the following photographers for permission to reproduce the photographs on the pages listed:

Cheryl Maddocks pp. 7, 8, 10, 11, 12, 14 (right and left), 20, 22 (top), 30 (left), 32 (right), 49 (top), 50, 55, 59, 70, 76 (left and right), 81 (bottom left, top right, bottom right), 84, 86 (left), 88, 94, 95 (left and right), 96, 101, 102 (left and right), 103 (left and right), 108, 110, 111, 112, 113 (left and right), 114 (left and right), 118, 130, 134, 136, 139, 150 (bottom), 151 (bottom right), 176 (top), 209, 212, 222, 224, 227, 228, 229 (left and right), 230, 231 (left and right), 232 (left and right), 233, 234, 235 (right), 236–86, 289 (left and right), 290 (left and right), 292, 293, 294, 299–302, 303 (right), 304 (left and right).

Leigh Clapp pp. 4, 7, 9, 16, 18, 23, 27, 39, 40, 42, 44 (right), 46, 53 (left and right), 60, 72, 74, 77, 78, 80, 82, 92, 93, 98, 115, 116, 119 (left), 126, 138, 146, 147, 173, 175, 177, 215, 225, 226, 235 (left and right).

Lorna Rose pp. 24, 28, 30 (right), 31, 32 (left), 33 (left and right), 34, 38, 45, 50, 54, 56, 63 (left and right), 64 (left and right), 69, 71 (right), 86 (right), 90 (left), 217.

Ivy Hansen pp. 22 (bottom), 44 (left), 49 (bottom), 66, 194, 303 (left).

Andrew Chapman pp. 180, 295.
Lorrie Lawrence p. 289 (left).
Simon Griffiths p. 36.

Additional photography
Robert Ashton
Matt Harvey
Bill Thomas – Imagen

Cover photographs
Leigh Clapp (front top), Cheryl Maddocks (front bottom left and right; back left) and Matt Harvey (back right).

Index

VIKING

Published by the Penguin Group
Penguin Group (Australia)
250 Camberwell Road, Camberwell, Victoria 3124, Australia
(a division of Pearson Australia Group Pty Ltd)
Penguin Group (USA) Inc.
375 Hudson Street, New York, New York 10014, USA
Penguin Group (Canada)
90 Eglinton Avenue East, Suite 700, Toronto ON M4P 2Y3, Canada
(a division of Pearson Penguin Canada Inc.)
Penguin Books Ltd
80 Strand, London WC2R 0RL, England
Penguin Ireland
25 St Stephen's Green, Dublin 2, Ireland
(a division of Penguin Books Ltd)
Penguin Books India Pvt Ltd
11 Community Centre, Panchsheel Park, New Delhi – 110 017, India
Penguin Group (NZ)
Cnr Airborne and Rosedale Roads, Albany, Auckland, New Zealand
(a division of Pearson New Zealand Ltd)
Penguin Books (South Africa) (Pty) Ltd
24 Sturdee Avenue, Rosebank, Johannesburg 2196, South Africa

Penguin Books Ltd, Registered Offices: 80 Strand, London, WC2R 0RL, England

First published by Penguin Books Australia Ltd, 2002
This edition published by Penguin Group (Australia), a division of
Pearson Australia Group Pty Ltd, 2006

3 5 7 9 10 8 6 4 2

Colour separations by Splitting Image Colour Studio, Victoria
Printed in China by 1010 Printing International Ltd
Cover photography by Leigh Clapp (front top), Cheryl Maddocks
(front bottom left and right; back left) and Matt Harvey (back right).

National Library of Australia
Cataloguing-in-Publication data:

Maddocks, Cheryl.
The Australian backyard: how to create your ideal backyard.
Includes index.
ISBN-13: 978 0 670 91194 3
ISBN-10: 0 670 91194 1

635.90994

www.penguin.com.au